DATE DUE

FEB 1 7 1997

D0810723

HUDDLE FEVER

HUDDLE
FEVER

Alfred A. Knopf NEW YORK 1995

PEMBERTON

Living in the Immigrant City

JEANNE SCHINTO

306.09
S 336 h

Library of Congress Cataloging-in-Publication Data
Schinto, Jeanne, [date]
    Huddle fever : living in the immigrant city / Jeanne Schinto. — 1st ed.
      p.   cm.
    ISBN 0-679-42121-1
    1. Lawrence (Mass.)—Social conditions. 2. Social classes—Massachusetts—Lawrence. 3. Lawrence (Mass.)—Economic conditions. 4. Lawrence (Mass.)—Emigration and immigration—Social aspects. 5. Immigrants—Massachusetts—Lawrence—Social conditions.
    I. Title.
HN80.L32S35 1995
306'.09744'5—dc20   95-3041
                                                          CIP

The title-page illustration is a stereoview of Pemberton Mills, Lawrence, Massachusetts. From the collection of Bob Frishman.

You know what work is—if you're
old enough to read this you know what
work is, although you may not do it.

—PHILIP LEVINE,
What Work Is

Contents

PART III · TOMORROW LAND

Acknowledgments

My thanks to all those who took the time to speak with me about Lawrence, especially Jay and Susan Dowd, Kathy and David Rodger, Jane and David Sigillo, Tom Leavitt, Marion Dawson Barker, Terri Kelley, Tom and Margaret Troy, former mayor John Joseph Buckley, and Marguerite Kane. I am also grateful to Lawrence High School students Tracy Moran, Christian Rached, and Jenny Santos, who wrote letters to me about Lawrence and permitted me to quote from them in my final chapter; and to those important people whose words and stories are part of this book but whose names and certain minor identifying details I have changed or omitted to protect their privacy.

Thanks, too, to Eartha Dengler and her staff at the Immigrant City Archives, in Lawrence, for use of printed materials and tape-recorded oral histories. For access to their fine collection, including the oral-history project of Julie Christ, I am indebted to the Museum of American Textile History, formerly of North Andover. (In October 1994, the museum packed up its collection for relocation to Lowell, where it will reopen in 1996.)

Two books were particularly helpful among the many dozens I consulted to write this work, and both were published by the textile museum. As I think will be obvious from the text, I found indispensable the late Edward G. Roddy's biography of textile magnate William Madison Wood. Not apparent is my far larger debt to *Greater Lawrence: A Bibliography, An Annotated Guide to the History of Andover, Methuen, Lawrence, and North Andover*, compiled by Juliet Haines Mofford.

I'd also like to credit the librarians at the Lawrence Public Library; the Stevens Memorial Library, in North Andover; and the Memorial Hall Library, in Andover—both those in Reference and those in the Interlibrary Loan Department.

Special thanks to my parents, Josephine and Henry Schinto; to my friend and reader Wayne Koestenbaum; to my agent, Faith Hornby Hamlin; and to Corona Machemer, my editor extraordinaire.

Above all, here's to my partner in life and work, Bob Frishman. He's the man of the hour, every hour, and I dedicate this book to him.

PART I

AT THE VIOLET HOUR

CHAPTER 1

Neighbors

I DECIDED to write this book shortly after I learned that my next-door neighbor had committed suicide. I consider myself a perceptive person, but the news came as a complete surprise. People like my neighbor are supposed to be rocks. They are the ones who build America's bridges, paint its houses, assemble its cars and computers. In retirement, as my neighbor was, they tend their gardens, play bingo, and drive too slowly in the left lane. What they don't do is leave despairing messages by slashing open their wrists.

My neighbor was a resident of Lawrence, Massachusetts. Fate had landed this son of Italian immigrants there, just as it had landed my own Italian forebears in Connecticut. Lawrencians used to be famous for weaving woolen cloth, and for years John Piacenzo labored in Lawrence's textile mills; but he could just as easily have been making the clocks or hats or shoes that factory hands once made in any of a number of other mill cities along the rivers of New England—or tending the vast grounds of estates in the town where my grandparents ended up.

The odd thing about my own destiny is that it led me to Lawrence, and to the house next door to John, who is—or was—a blue-collar American. As a writer, I am considered white-collar, and it's just not all that common anymore for people like me to have as neighbors people like John. Actually, I suppose it never was customary for us to live right next door. But not so long ago, when I was a child, and John's son was young, too, we lived in the same towns and went to the same public schools, and our fathers and brothers used to meet each other in the army. Now when "people like me" cross paths with "Lawrencians," we feel increasingly uncomfortable, not (we insist) because anybody's better than anybody else (no, certainly not because people who work with their hands don't have enough money, status, or finesse to suit us) but simply because we have never learned to speak each other's language. Sometimes literally.

Did I say "simply"? It becomes quite complicated when the rough-palmed ones we occasionally encounter are the "same sort" as the parents and grandparents who made it possible for us to become our bookish selves in the first place.

When I began telling friends I was writing about Lawrence, they'd say, "Oh. A *history* of Lawrence?" As if anything of importance that was going to happen had already happened long ago in that city, which was known as the "cradle" of the Industrial Revolution in America. "Not exactly a history," I'd say, "though the past has to be taken into account. I guess you'd call it a contemporary history. But mostly it's a personal book. Think of it as a book I might write about a place I've traveled to," I'd suggest. "I've been 'traveling' in Lawrence, but the subject might just as easily have been Paris, if I'd spent the last ten years there instead."

That comparison always brought laughs (or were they sneers?) from those who know both places. For there are lots of good reasons to live in Paris and few to live in Lawrence. As I myself used to quip, Lawrence offers all the disadvantages of city living and none of the advantages. On the other hand, do we really need another book about Paris or any of the other cities—Rome, Venice, London—that require no last names?

"Somebody's already written a book about Lawrence, you know." I also heard this fairly often, and it was true enough, though the book to which my informants referred, *Immigrant City*, by Donald B. Cole, is a scholarly work—it originated as a Ph.D. thesis—and covers only Lawrence's first seventy-six years, from 1845 to 1921.

Not everybody agrees that Cole's is such a valuable work. "Did you ever read that? Well, there's a lot of stuff that's not right with it," an aged former mill worker told an oral-history student who recorded her words for a Boston University master's thesis in 1980. "He was a professor over at Andover. . . . What did he know?"

Actually, Cole taught at Phillips *Exeter* Academy for forty years, but the woman's point is made. Cole hadn't lived through what she had, so where did he come off writing about her life? I mention this to say that, though writers often show deference to those who have plowed the literary ground before them, I myself am more anxious about erstwhile mill hands. I have tried to write a book of which they might not entirely disapprove.

Other readers of mine, I'm afraid, while disputing neither the facts nor the interpretations that I've set forth, may find themselves disappointed, anyway. I refer to those who often expressed to me the hope that my book would offer solutions to Lawrence's pressing problems. "So hurry and finish," they'd implore. But I don't have answers. And when those same folks learn that I have put my house on the market and left Lawrence, they may cast me in the role of miscreant—another white middle-class deserter whom they'll find it easy to blame.

That I've flown in fear and bitterness is a charge I must protest, however. When my husband, Bob Frishman, and I moved to the city in 1984, we were being practical, not idealistic; a little unconventional, yes, but not pioneerish. Bob's

work was in Lawrence; house prices were reasonable; and anyway, the city didn't seem to require the pioneer spirit at the
time. When we decided to leave in 1994, we were being practical once again. It is true there had been some changes for
the worse in our neighborhood, but there were signs of hope,
too; and we would probably have stayed if Bob hadn't decided
to leave his job and start a home business—restoring and selling antique clocks—which we felt required a different setting
if it was to succeed (even in its heyday, Lawrence did not
abound in high-priced antiques shops).

So, no, I do not offer solutions. But in telling Lawrence's
story, I have come to believe one thing: that the real trouble
with Lawrence—with Lawrences everywhere—is not that the
middle class has moved out but that the *working* class is becoming extinct in those places. And if this is true, if the story
of Lawrence may serve as a paradigm for the rise and fall of
industrial cities all over America, then I will have done more
than I set out to do when I first began to put into words some
random thoughts about my neighbor's suicide. I might even
hope for this much more: that such a despair-filled death, far
from meaningless, offers a message for us all.

SPRING 1985. My next-door neighbor, Lucille Piacenzo, is
cooking, shuffling in her faded housedress and her bedroom
scuffs from stove to sink. Once, she tells me, she was big-eyed,
skinny, a looker, a turner of heads; now she's so fat that her
dimpled arm flab jiggles, hangs from the bone. Her flesh is the
color of paste, or dough worked too long, not a muscle apparent. But she is strong. She has to be, to stand and stir her huge
pots of tomato sauce, to carry caldrons of boiling macaroni to
the colander to drain. Sometimes she pretends to be helpless,
but she is only keeping her strength in reserve, to surprise
someone—her husband?—if necessary. John gives her no re-

spect, she says. He treats her like an idiot, when she, *she* is the one who has the style, the flare.

"Sit, siddown," Lucille says to me, sitting heavily herself, as if I might not know how. "Honey, don't be like that," she adds, angry now, because instead of taking a seat, I go out the door of her first-floor apartment to help John roll the unwieldy (fifty-five-gallon) metal trash barrels, his and mine, back into our adjacent yards.

After all, he is the man, isn't he? Why should a skinny girl go help him? (That's how she sees me; I'm thirty-two.) "Sit, sit," she entreats me again when John and I have finished our task. "Have a cup of coffee." A cup of tea, my preference, is not offered. Tea is not drunk in this household unless someone is ill. It's coffee, or wine, or a hit from the whiskey bottle—last year's Christmas gift, nearly empty now. Time for a new one. But I don't want to eat or drink anything in this kitchen. I'm nervous. Afraid they'll find me out? Discern that I'm an imposter, not using my full vocabulary (sometimes even pretending to fumble for words)? That I'm not entirely sincere? Though they seem genuinely to like me, and I do genuinely like them, the truth is that we share the unfenced side yard between our two houses, and a clothesline, and nothing else. At least outwardly. They are retired mill hands and I am someone who got to choose what I would do with my life.

I can imagine what John looked like years ago: a handsome man, not soft and slow as he is now, and knowing it. He remains attractive in an ineradicable way, even though at the moment he has a bad haircut, given to him by his landlord—a barber by part-time trade, but old now, too, like his tenants. "I got scalped," says John as his hands try to smooth the chopped white bristles.

He must be losing his touch—Freddy Colvito, who was christened Alfio back in Sicily. Or did he cut John's hair that way so he won't have to come back and cut it again for a while? It hardly matters. Freddy stops by every week to collect the rent the old-fashioned way—in cash: forty-five dollars. Prices from another era still in effect. But the bargain keeps John and Lucille uncomfortably beholden to Freddy.

At least, Freddy doesn't live upstairs anymore. When he was nearly ninety, he moved in with one of his daughters, who lives in the town next door—Andover—and rather pridefully so, with her attached greenhouse and doily under the cookie plate for even as casual a visitor as I. Andover, home of Phillips Academy, former president George Bush's prep school, is one of those old New England communities that look just like the postcards—so unlike down-and-dirty Lawrence. John puts on his thick, black-framed, owlish eyeglasses and drives over to Andover himself every Sunday to visit relatives who have done much better in life than he has. At any rate, that is his assessment of the situation, with two branches of the same family living in such very different places. Whose fault is it? I do not ask. I do not ask because I know Lucille would be quick to tell me that it is her hapless husband's.

As I'm leaving, Lucille asks me to grind some spices for her in my electric coffee grinder at home. She is making sausage and needs anise and fennel seeds ground together into a pungent powder. I have about a cup and a half of the mixture when I finish. She gives me a huge platter of spaghetti and meatballs in return. Lucille often makes me food: fried cauliflower, fried zucchini, *pasta e fagioli* ("pasta fazool"), pizza, beef bracciole. It's understood to be payment for favors—favors I haven't done for her yet. She is looking to the future.

Once, I tried to give her a little of my homemade bread. It was whole wheat, probably too coarse for her tastes, I suddenly realized, watching her cautiously break off a corner of a slice and chew without comment. (I later learned that she has a secret passion for white-bread sandwiches of peanut butter and Marshmallow Fluff.)

Seeing what I had brought over, John stepped up to me and said with angry pride, "My mother made the best bread in the world, and you know what? She made it in the morning *before* she went to work in the mills all day."

JOHN AND LUCILLE Piacenzo were the first Lawrencians I met. It was in late October 1984, shortly after Bob and I moved there from Washington, D.C., so that Bob could become vice president (and, later, president) of his parents' small company, which made acrylic furniture in a large, cheap space that was a whole floor of one of the old textile mills. We had just bought the big blue clapboard next door to Freddy Colvito's two-family house without my ever having seen it. Because I had a job tending a greenhouse in addition to my writing, I hadn't been able to take time off from work to go house hunting, so I had given Bob a short list of preferences and sent him north. I asked for a fireplace, a large kitchen, a sunny yard. I also said I wanted a neighborhood with sidewalks: I wanted to be within shouting distance of people, of *neighbors*, not out in the sticks.

Bob called two days into the hunt to say he had found a beautiful Victorian for virtually pennies—a jewel of a three-story house, with a wraparound porch, that hadn't been hideously updated, "modernized," or cut up into apartments. It had a fireplace with a ceramic-tile hearth, a large kitchen with the original wainscoting intact, hardwood floors, the original light fixtures (once gas, then—long ago—converted to electricity), even an old wooden icebox in the pantry by the back door, as well as a yard that was sunny in spite of the flaming red maple that graced it and that had purportedly come as a seedling from Harvard's Arnold Arboretum.

Were there sidewalks?

Yes, sidewalks, up and down and around the block.

And Lawrence. What kind of a place was Lawrence?

Bob described it as "interesting," not homogeneous like Andover ("Blandover"), where he had grown up. For many childhood years, he had been driven through Lawrence by his mother on the way to his piano lessons with Mrs. Liversidge, who lived in Methuen, another suburban border town but with none of the snob appeal of Andover or neighboring North Andover (because it's been populated largely by former Lawrencians?). He had been driven, in fact, along the very street where the house he had picked out for us stood.

Since Bob and I married, in 1973, I'd traveled often to his parents' house in Andover, and had even visited Lawrence two or three times, but always in the dark and for one purpose only: to have dinner at a locally famous Lebanese restaurant named Bishop's. I remembered how abruptly different everything was when we crossed the border into Lawrence, the scenery changing in an instant from boilerplate New England (white church steeples, footpaths crisscrossing the green lawns of the prep school) to a densely settled urban landscape. I must have seen the mill buildings but assumed they were old, decrepit office buildings. Or run-down department stores, maybe? At any rate, I was led to believe by members of my husband's family that Lawrence was not a place to be taken seriously. Just look at Bishop's itself, with its gaudily incongruous Taj Mahal architecture; its comically huge portions. And, for dessert, that Lebanese delicacy—baked Alaska.

Andover, by contrast, was a serious place. The Addison Gallery of American Art, at Phillips Academy, was a serious cultural institution. The town's gleaming new water-treatment plant was *dead* serious, open for tours, and we took one. We also hiked to the top of Holt Hill to glimpse a place even more serious than Andover—Boston, its skyline poking up beyond the treetops, the windows of its skyscrapers lit orange by the descending sun.

Accustomed solely to sights like these, I probably wouldn't have taken Lawrence seriously, either—but then I moved there.

Working-class and *blue-collar* are not the only terms used to describe the people who come from places like Lawrence. These days, they are also called "ethnics" or "hyphenated Americans"—as if, somehow, we all weren't.

Theoretically, I suppose, we are all in the working class, too, if we work. But of course *working* is not—and never has been—the full measure of the term. In a city like Lawrence, "working class" is a culture—though it's often defined by those outside it only by what it lacks.

"Where's she been?" asks my niece from the university community of Austin, Texas, when I tell her a Lawrence friend of mine, a woman with a bachelor's degree and a master's, didn't recognize the sliced avocado I put in the salad I was serving for dinner. "Lawrence," I reply.

On the other hand, my Lawrencian friends, even the least educated among them, have their own special knowledge of things my niece and I know nothing about and maybe never will.

"I dreamt you were pregnant," Lucille announced to me one morning as she hung her wet mop outside her kitchen door.

"Oh, no," I told her. "I don't want to be."

"Don't worry, honey." She smiled. "Whatever you dream, it means the opposite."

SOMETIMES IT'S HARD for me to remember that status in the working-class world is not derived from what one does for a living. Working-class people as a rule don't have "careers"; they have jobs, and their jobs are not the most interesting and important part of their lives.

A woman among many I came to know in Lawrence, of French-Canadian descent, fits the model. Charlene, a mill worker's daughter in her early fifties, lives in an aluminum-sided triple-decker—that is, a three-story tenement—which she owns, and which has a swimming pool in the ground alongside it. If the New England textile industry hadn't collapsed forty years ago, she would surely have gone into the mills to work herself. Instead, she gets forty dollars a morning cleaning houses in Andover.

"Their houses get just as dirty as mine," she reports, "and I've got a better vacuum cleaner.

"They think I'm destitute," she adds, laughing, "but I've got more freedom than they do."

Please do not ask her to feel sorry for the wife of someone with two kids at Ivy League colleges who, now out of work, was the vice president of a corporation (a scenario she saw on TV). "He was making what? A hundred thousand? Jimmy [her husband, an appliance repairman] makes in the thirties. Where did her money go? Her car is ten years old? I'm sorry. She made her choices."

Charlene, whose car is fourteen years old, has made hers, too. She may live in Lawrence, she may clean other people's kitchens and bathrooms for a living, but she also manages to play tennis nearly every day. Year in and year out, she competes at the top level at a club up the highway in Haverhill.

Charlene's former tenants, Paul and Carol Podposki, also belong to the club. Last year, they bought a condominium in Haverhill, but Charlene doesn't envy them. The rules at this condo prohibit the parking of trucks; owners may not even park them inside their own garages. Paul and Carol weren't aware of this restriction when they bought the place, however, and it does present a problem for them, since Paul, like Charlene's husband, drives a truck to work. So no matter what shift Paul happens to be working, Carol must get up with him and drive him to where he parks his truck, then pick him up there when work is over. "She can't hang clothes, either," notes Charlene, who, for that reason alone, says she could never live in such a place.

Or take Casparino Robito, who worked in the twist room of the Wood Mill as a young man in the 1940s and whose parents and grandparents all worked at the Wood Mill, too. ("No interview. Just start. Monday morning, six o'clock. July 25, 1945," he told a volunteer who tape-recorded his reminiscences and those of other former mill workers for the Immigrant City Archives, Lawrence's "historical society," in 1989.) He tended a machine that twisted strands of wool into weavable yarn. It was his living, but that wasn't what he lived for. "I had a lot of friends because my prestige was high, because I was a boxer," says Robito on the tape. "They liked me—a lot of my friends used to come to see me fight. I used to fight in Lawrence, and I fought in Boston. I fought in Providence, Rhode Island. I went through the Golden Gloves.

"I started fighting at the age of twelve," he goes on, a bit garrulous. "I kind of like fighting. I like to fight in a ring, and when I went into the Marine Corps, I went to boot camp, Parris Island, and they always had bulletins, what do you do best, so I applied for the boxing team and was interviewed, and I made it. In other words, my job at the Marine Corps at that time was Special Services Division, Boxing Team."

Until the Korean War broke out, he traveled all over Europe, boxing for the United States against the military teams of other countries. Then, in September 1950, he took part in the invasion of Inchon. In July 1952, he came home to Lawrence with a letter of commendation, and frostbite. ("I've seen guys frozen to death, and when a man dies of cold, he dies with a beautiful smile on his face, believe it or not. I've seen many dead. Marines.") Frostbite gave him the right to have a military honor guard at either his wedding or his funeral. He chose to have it at his wedding: "They sent me six men in blue and they were at my wedding with swords."

He didn't go back to work in the twist room or anywhere else in the Wood Mill, though. They weren't hiring. The mill was about to shut down. And Robito and eighty thousand other New England mill workers were on their way to becoming historical curiosities.

FROM THE TOP of my street in Lawrence, I got used to seeing another fact of working-class life, at least as it was once lived there; but tangible though it surely is, I still found it hard to comprehend. It is the Wood Mill itself, which, at the time of the New England textile industry's demise, was less than fifty years old. Lucille Piacenzo told me she was born the year the mill was built. "Nineteen-oh-five—in Tiano, near Naples. You can see the date right on there," she said, referring to the mill's cornerstone.

But the Wood is no quaint New England landmark you might happen upon by chance while rounding a bend in the roadway. Picture this: a skyscraper lying on its side, on a roiling river's weedy banks; beside it—between it and the river—is a parking lot that echoes its huge rectangular shape. The lot, in fact, lies where an identical prone skyscraper used to stand. The other half of the brick behemoth that was the Wood, it was torn down after being struck by fire in the sixties, and with it the cornerstone, alas.

The Empire State Building, at 1,250 feet, is not as tall as the Wood—the remaining half of it—is long. "The eye cannot see it all at once," Edward R. Murrow intoned for his CBS TV audience in 1953, the year he came to film the industry's final hours. "It's like trying to photograph the horizon." Once trumpeted as the largest mill building in the world, it employed ten thousand people, nearly a quarter of Lawrence's workforce.

There is a good chance that the women and girls who, in 1911, jumped to their deaths from the windows of the Triangle Shirtwaist Factory in New York had been sewing cloth made in the Wood Mill or elsewhere in Lawrence by William Madison Wood's American Woolen Company. That year, Lawrence was the cloth-making capital of the world, easily surpassing two of its early-day rivals—Manchester, New Hampshire, and Manchester, England—combined.

JUDGING FROM the way she talked about it, I could tell that Lucille felt proprietary toward the Wood Mill; she has good reason. Upon arrival in Lawrence, her father was hired to excavate for the mammoth construction; with other immigrants, he stood in a line in the mud, digging with nothing but a shovel. Every day, Lucille's mother wheeled her down to the site in a carriage, with her father's lunch pail.

As a child, Lucille also traveled several times to Italy with her mother, while her father stayed behind in Lawrence. Like many immigrants before and after her, Mrs. Maschiarello couldn't make up her mind about America. Finally, the entire Maschiarello family settled in Lawrence permanently in 1912. It was a year that was portentous for the whole city—for the whole country, in fact—because of the great strike. It's called Bread and Roses, though not by the Lawrencians whose parents or grandparents took part in it and who heard the stories from them. A friend who worked for social change in the 1970s in San Francisco once visited me in Lawrence and told me earnestly, "I used to know a lot of people who would be very impressed by your address." There is a song, "Bread and Roses," which this California friend sang for me:

As we come marching, marching in the beauty of the day,
A million darkened kitchens, a thousand mill lofts gray,

Are touched with all the radiance that a sudden sun
   discloses,
For the people hear us singing: "Bread and roses! Bread
   and roses!"

The phrase is a metaphor for the proposition that workers,
like the rest of us, do not live by bread alone. I've since
learned that the lyrics were first published as a poem in the
American Mercury in the year before the strike by James
Oppenheim, a member of the Industrial Workers of the World
(or IWW, or Wobblies—or "I Won't Work" union, as its de-
tractors called it), which wanted nothing less than to over-
throw the wage system in favor of worker ownership of
factories.

   People say the strikers did sing while they marched, but
not that song. Former Lawrence mayor John Joseph Buckley,
who was first elected in the early 1950s and reelected ten
more times, serving twenty-two years in all, puts it this way: "I
don't know about bread and roses—bread and blood is more
like it."

   Besides, Oppenheim's words weren't officially set to music,
at least in published form, until after World War II.

   One thing is not in dispute: that the great strike of 1912
was a high-water mark of the radical U.S. labor movement—as
well as the beginning of the end, of that phase of it, anyway.
If things had worked out differently, Lawrence would be one
of the sacred pieces of ground, one of the places where history
now would say the revolution began.

   Lucille's father probably took part in Bread and Roses.
Italians were at the forefront—"volatile," "excitable" Italians.
At least according to the press reports, which often used such
words to describe them, the Italians were the first to start running through one of the factories, shouting and breaking the
belts on the machines. But Lucille was told no stories. Or if

she was, she doesn't remember them. All she remembers now is that her mother tried to keep her out of school, but a truant officer came to the house, so off Lucille went to first grade. She spoke no English (she speaks it without an accent today) and though she says she tried hard, by the time she was legally allowed to quit, at age fourteen, she was still only in fifth grade. She began work at once, at the Washington Mills, where her mother and her sister Marie were already employed. Soon she went over to the Wood, where she stayed for the next forty years.

LUCILLE AND her mother both worked as jackspoolers, mother teaching daughter. A sit-down job, so it was prestigious—and a female mill worker's job exclusively. What did it involve? "You sat down and ran your hands across the spools to make sure there were no knots in them before they made the cloth," says Lucille, her tone implying, If you're so smart, college girl, then why don't you know that?

Burling, another sit-down job, was even more prestigious than jackspooling, I learned from those taped oral histories at the Immigrant City Archives, and at the Museum of American Textile History, in North Andover. Burlers found the knots in finished cloth, raised them, and eliminated them. Nell Gaudette, who burled for nineteen years: "At first I couldn't see the knots—they [the experienced burlers] would see them and you wouldn't. Now I could see a knot a mile away." (After the mills shut down, she worked as a missile-parts inspector in Quincy, near Boston.)

To sit wasn't the only luxury afforded by these so-called good jobs. Reduced noise was another. But to realize what a perk this was, you would first have to understand what the noise was like full force. You can get an idea by visiting the weave room in one of the old mills. A working one still exists in a textile museum in Lowell, another old mill town ten miles upstream from Lawrence on the Merrimack River, where eighty-eight power looms rhythmically slam their iron parts against one another. Have you ever lived near a construction site where a pile driver was in use? That's the sound, only at a faster clip. And at closer range. You are handed a set of disposable earplugs along with your ticket. The brochure says that in the original weave room the noise would have been greater still, because more machines would have been packed into the space. One does not "listen" to a sound like this. It vibrates not only your eardrums but your whole body, including your fingernails. The air positively shimmers with the din. You could swear it was visible. And think of this: at the museum, you are kept a good distance away from the machines, behind a railing. A woman I've met, Filomena Hebert, who is in her seventies and worked in the Lawrence mills for over thirty years, starting at age fourteen like Lucille, habitually stood as close to her machine as a woman ironing stands to an ironing board. "That's why I have this," she told me, pointing to her hearing aid.

"The weaver-god, he weaves; and by that weaving is he deafened," Melville wrote in *Moby-Dick*.

"Because of the noise, some ladies told me that's why they still talk so loud," says former mayor Buckley.

You must realize, too, that the rooms where the machinery clanged and pounded were stiflingly hot, the windows only grudgingly opened, and the humidity kept artificially high with steam, because the yarn required it. The heat, the moisture, kept the yarn supple, prevented it from breaking.

Hot and noisy, the mills were also dirty—unprocessed wool and cotton are full of dust—and so those "good" jobs were also relatively clean, because they did not require handling the raw material. The machinery was grimy, too; the debris that filled the air collected in its parts (it was a constant chore to keep it clean), and made breathing difficult and sometimes deadly.

I hasten to say, however, that some old textile workers get angry when they hear people deem their former jobs hellish. Mulespinners, for example, are a prideful lot; mulespinning, one of the most prestigious mill jobs for a man, was hardly a sit-down job, but the skill required to do it brought honor, and more pay. The machine, called a mule, looks like a plow with wheels, and is manipulated by reins, which the mulespinner would rhythmically let out and pull in, spinning the yarn onto dozens of bobbins simultaneously, walking forward and backward all the while, often covering the equivalent of eight miles in a day. It required not only physical vigor but exceptional dexterity and timing—and time to learn the job in the first place. "It took about five years to fully learn mulespinning," according to retired mulespinner Ernie Therrien. "After a while it got easier, because you got more skillful. Just like a ballplayer, a rookie, as good as he is, he doesn't reach his potential until he's all done."

Filomena Hebert, the woman who wears the hearing aid, is another former mill hand baffled by the complaints about the work, but her statement defending it falls short of pure enthusiasm: "First of all, I didn't know any other job," she says several times in different ways. On the other hand, Robito, who admits he hated mill work himself ("I hated being closed in"), seems to understand the so-called mill temperament better than many of those docile souls who apparently had it; and it's he who touches on the contentment—*happy* is the word he uses—that comes from resignation when there is no choice:

"You see, you gotta understand, most of these people came from the old country and they'd work like a dog, s'long as they had their big piece of bread, their cheese and their onion, and a bottle of wine. My grandfather's lunch was leftovers of what we ate the night before and he'd have a big pail and he'd put the leftovers in the pail. Most of these people, they never threw food away, never, like you see today in the barrels. It's a sin. They worked and they were happy at it. They were happy."

HOW IRONIC it is that, increasingly, work for members of the working class is not something on which to depend. *Deindustrialization* is not a word Robito, who later went into the dry-cleaning business, would use. But I think he knows, better than the scholars who invented it, what it means.

Even in supposedly good times in Lawrence, life was often unsettled, because the availability of work changed from week to week. "You know, people never worked fifty-two weeks a year," says former mayor Buckley, who had a job at the Wood Mill himself for a time, a short time, before a track scholarship to Georgetown University changed the course of his life for good. When a big order came in, they called the workers in; when there wasn't enough work to go around, they laid people off. "When textiles were off, everything was off," Buckley says. "And when there was a boom, everybody would be working in three shifts."

When asked about the rumor that the Ford Motor Company once wanted to establish a plant in Lawrence but mill owner Billy Wood wouldn't let them, Buckley says, "That rumor's been around here for years. Their claim is that Ford came to the chamber of commerce. But the chamber was controlled by the mills at that time, by textiles, and they always wanted to keep a pool of labor available for the third shift in case they got a big order. And that's the way it was. I don't know if they kept it that way, but that's the way it was. There was always a third shift here in case the textiles needed one." (The irony is, of course, that if Ford had located in Lawrence, they'd probably be pulling out now. The city's difficulties, in other words, would merely have been postponed.)

IS ANY JOB better than none? Conditions have improved over the decades for factory workers, even those few remaining in Lawrence. There are no sit-down jobs at Akko, Inc., which is the name of the furniture factory owned by my husband's family, but it is fairly clean, and the space is not airless or noisy, as it was when textile machinery pounded away there. In fact, it is rather quiet: on one of my visits, I heard Qwang, a young Vietnamese immigrant, softly singing as he worked (Springsteen's "Born in the U.S.A.").

Note, too, that Qwang wears safety glasses on the job— required gear for all (as a result, he, along with everyone else, looks oddly studious), though the work isn't at all dangerous. Textile work, on the other hand, certainly was. "I almost lost a finger once," mulespinner Ernie Therrien claims. "My wedding band saved my finger. [The machine] cut the ring right off. One kid got his head crushed under the mules while I was there. See, the spinner wants the machine to run, because when it's stopped, he's losing time. The kid had to get under it to clean the sticks. He didn't get out fast enough, or the guy probably didn't see the kid. He thought his brakes were on, and the mule went in."

At Akko, by contrast, the worker controls the machines and tools. Still, many of the workers' jobs, like those of hourly wage earners anywhere, are dead boring. Though, to my eye, the place looks more like a vast sculpture studio than a factory, with gleaming pieces of acrylic in various states of readiness at each workstation, the hours of hand-sanding and buffing and assembling required to produce the objects are not relieved by even momentary opportunities for creativity. There's no getting around it: the work is repetitious and tedious—often nerve-rackingly so, because if concentration lapses, costly mistakes can quickly be made. To ease their tedium, people are often moved from task to task. This is meant to be a plus, but some employees object: they value the tranquilizing effect of doing the same dull work day in and day out.

AT THE private secondary school in North Andover where I teach part-time, students needing discipline are assigned work detail—cleaning up the grounds and school buildings—at eight o'clock Sunday mornings. Two hundred and fifty-two acres, the campus is land that once belonged to the Russell family, which earned most of its fortune manufacturing paper in Lawrence. I once mentioned to a teacher at school that I thought such manual labor as punishment inadvertently but powerfully conveys to the students the idea that the members of the school's maintenance staff, many of whom live in Lawrence, must have done something *really* bad to have been relegated to doing manual labor for a living. I picked this teacher to share my thoughts with because she helps run an annual faculty seminar, called Valuing Differences, about race, gender, and class issues. The teacher said, "Well, it's not the work; it's the getting up Sunday morning to do it that the kids hate." But, she conceded, relations between staff and students are sometimes "strained." Relations between staff and faculty can be "a problem," too. And it's been discussed at the seminar, she said, but there is still a great deal of discussing to do. "Class," she sighed. "It's the one issue nobody wants to touch."

WINTER 1988. In the lunchroom of the local cable TV station, where I am waiting for a friend, I overhear some workers in blue-collar clothing who are on their break:

"When are you going to get hitched?" a young woman asks

the burly guy who has just come in with a fistful of hot dogs from Lawton's-by-the-Sea, a well-known diner on the north canal.

He says he is waiting to see what kind of earning power his girlfriend (a part-time student) will have before he agrees to marry her.

Meanwhile, they've been living together in her father's rental property in Lawrence for two years.

"Why don't you marry her to get the house?" the young woman asks.

Obviously he's considered this, but there's a problem: "It's on the market."

My eavesdropping also tells me that these are young people who buy diamond engagement rings and wedding bands on time (then punch a hole through the bathroom wall if the stone gets loose and ends up washed down the drain); who take the marriages of the soap-opera characters playing on the wall-mounted TV as seriously as they take their own.

"He's marrying *who? Her?*"

"It's not *fair.*"

"*Life's* unfair."

"Life *sucks.*"

Maybe the prospect of a fair fight is the root of the attraction many in the working class feel for sports—Charlene's tennis, Robito's boxing, ex-mayor Buckley's track—where rank is always determined by merit, by measurable results.

By the same token, one thing can be said in favor of manual labor: Unlike head work, hand work invariably yields a tangible product. It's the reason why many an overworked executive retreats to his woodworking shop in the basement on weekends. Who knows? The appeal of this aspect of working with one's hands may also be the reason for the founding of a certain home-improvement company whose ad I read in a playbill one night while sitting in a Cambridge theater:

When the wind is southerly, any carpenter knows a hawk
from a handsaw. . . .
So why not hire one who also knows Polonius from
Claudius?

Byggmeister introduces a new class: the blue-scholar
worker.

BYGGMEISTER
the finest in residential additions and alterations.

I suspect that if I had never lived in Lawrence, I'd have thought the Byggmeister ad was clever. I might even want "blue-scholar" workers working on my house. Instead, I am offended.

For the ad implies that the blue-scholar worker has made a conscious choice. (The blue-collar worker, with his blackened thumb, has not.) Mr. Blue Scholar could just as easily have a desk job—teaching English lit, perhaps; instead, he *wants* to work with his hands—with both mind *and* body engaged. And though he'd be superior to the blue-collar worker anyway (or so he thinks), now he's succeeded in beating him at his own game.

But why did it take living in Lawrence to make me sensitive to the insult the ad conveys? After all, though my father put on a tie to go to work when he was in his early forties, we were still very much a working-class family. Dad had been a carpenter (who actually does know his Shakespeare), a member of the United Brotherhood of Carpenters and Joiners of America; then he signed on with the town bureaucracy and became a building inspector. He traded his coveralls and pickup truck for a suit jacket and town car—a fumy Corvair, as it turned out, which gave him headaches. No matter: he would keep his fingernails clean, and my sister, Janet, and I would no longer have to take turns walking on his back to help relieve his persistent bursitis.

This was in a municipality so unlike Lawrence as to be its polar opposite: Greenwich, Connecticut, the moneyed suburb of Manhattan. I was born and raised in Greenwich—a place that makes even Lawrence's stylish neighboring towns seem shabby. Former president Bush may have prepped at Andover (class of 1942), but he grew up in Greenwich. (His mother, Dorothy Walker Bush, died there at age ninety-one in 1992; members of his extended family live there still, with their servants and dogs.) During the Depression, "Poppy," the son of Prescott Bush—who later became a U.S. senator—was driven by chauffeured limousine to Greenwich Country Day School.

Both sets of my grandparents came to Greenwich from Italy in the early 1900s and never left. Greenwich, for its part, needed its huge backcountry estates built and tended, and stone walls built around them. So they tolerated these immigrants and the multifamily homes they built, their elaborate, terraced gardens, their chickens and many children.

My mother's father was a gardener, who rode his bike to work; my mother's mother did housework (so did my grandmother's sister—my great aunt—who was employed as a domestic at Prescott Bush's house). The next generation, however, made sure it avoided servitude. My mother joined the U.S. Navy, and then, on the GI bill, went to a New York modeling school, though she never earned her living by her looks. Instead, she married Dad and became a private secretary, typing correspondence for a Greenwich interior decorator, whose maid served her lunch. Mom typed for many other people over the years, keeping up her shorthand by listening to records of a man's droning voice dictating business letters. After the big corporate headquarters started moving to town in the sixties, she became an executive secretary, with a boss who had a little chess set in his desk drawer, which he shut furtively when visitors called. Sitting uncomfortably idle at her own desk, Mom put Janet and me through college.

Thirty years later, in the aftermath of the eighties, many of those corporations have either left, been forced to downsize drastically, or been absorbed in takeovers by other corporations, leaving hundreds of empty office buildings all over Fairfield County. (At the start of 1993, the office vacancy rate was 24.5 percent.) The American Can Company headquarters, for example, built in 1970 on 150 acres of prime Greenwich woodlands, is empty. But the town, with its four-acre backcountry zoning and DUCK CROSSING signs, doesn't crumble. It can absorb such blows. The town planner's only lament, at least as reported by *The New York Times*: "It could have been a golf course, and what a magnificent thing that would have been."

Now my parents are retired. They live in Greenwich for five months of the year, and in Boca Raton, Florida, for the rest, playing golf and tennis and bridge. Thanks to real estate values, the modest house my father and his brothers and friends built for our family in 1952 for $12,000, including the quarter acre of land, is worth $300,000 or more, even in today's depressed market. The little Cape abuts a private golf course, and for decades my parents climbed over the country club's chain-link fence in the early evening to practice their putts and swings. Now, almost unwittingly, they are members of the leisure class. Once, however, arriving in Florida for a visit, I walked into the lobby of their condominium and saw my father on his knees, tending to something at baseboard level. He'd rather do the work himself than have the condo hire someone to do it, and not as well as he could. Besides, he has the time.

Later, I learn it was he who had wallpapered the lobby.

IF MY GRANDPARENTS had settled in Lawrence instead of Greenwich, how different everything would have been for them, for my parents, for me. Many such immigrants were supposedly lured to Lawrence by ads—posters printed by Billy Wood's American Woolen Company, showing cartoon caricatures of delighted workers leaving the factory gates toting bags full of money to the bank—though an actual poster of this sort has never been unearthed. If my grandparents had seen those ads or been taken in by rumors of riches to be earned in Lawrence; if their fellow villagers had been going there instead of to Greenwich; if my Grandparents Schinto and Biase had lived two houses apart on Common Street in Lawrence, instead of on Davis Avenue in Greenwich; if they and their children—my parents—had gone to work in the mills, starting, in many cases, like my neighbor Lucille, at age fourteen . . .

If, if, if . . . I turn away from the whole imagined scenario, my alternative family history. I want the images to disappear; it makes me shudder to see my family's faces superimposed upon the faces of hardscrabble Lawrence. At the same time, however, I am irresistibly attracted to these imaginary scenes. I suppose that's what fascinates me most of all about Lawrence. There, for the first time, I met the sort of people I came from, in a purer incarnation, less "assimilated." Or maybe I am only now willing to acknowledge them. . . . Did I actually once shun them? I certainly never intended to become one of them, at best a secretary like my mother, forever typing someone else's words instead of my own.

And another thing I know for sure: if I had been born in Lawrence, or in a place like it, I would never willingly have lived ten years of my adulthood there. No, I never would have agreed to move there when Bob proposed it.

Having done precisely that, however, I realize now that it was one of the best decisions I've ever made. In Lawrence, I learned more about life than in any other place I've ever called home; in Lawrence, too, I learned the most about myself.

"What can I give *you*?" I asked Lucille one day, after she had sent John to knock on my back door with yet another plate of her cooking.

"Just your friendship," she replied, knowing even then, I guess, that it would be the single thing she truly would need from me.

I wonder if she also knew it would be the thing I'd find the most difficult—and rewarding—to give.

CHAPTER 2

Aristocrats and Democrats

T HE VICTORIANS had a notion that an idle river was profane. In the opinion of that nervous era, busyness was beauty. As they saw it, the Boston businessmen who founded Lawrence in 1845 (the year Thoreau built his cabin on Walden Pond) were the Merrimack River Valley's saviors. Here is J. W. Meader, who wrote *The Merrimack: its source and its tributaries* (1869), on the subject of Lawrence:

"For two centuries, the river and the land literally ran to waste; but sparsely settled, in productiveness meagerly requiting the tiller's industry, it seemed destined, like other points of manufacturing interest along the Merrimack, to a career of barrenness and comparative worthlessness, until the splendid water power caught the eye of the sagacious manufacturer, when a change as rapid as wonderful, came over the scene: the desert waste grew green, active, busy life dispelled the unpleasant silence . . . as if by a touch of the enchanter's wand."

Wait a minute, now. The *desert waste* grew green when factories were built, dispelling the *unpleasant* silence? This, to my contemporary sensibility, is an astonishing notion, though in fact the river did grow green after the mills went up: green, purple, red, depending on the dye being used that week.

Former mayor Buckley remembers seeing the colors swirling below the Duck Bridge, which he used to cross as a boy on his way to and from school—the bridge so named for the duck cloth made in the mill alongside it, not the bird that idle children feed.

In 1924, on the silver anniversary of his American Woolen Company, textile magnate Billy Wood, who would plant so many bitter seeds in Lawrence—some of which are only now coming into inglorious flower—issued a series of published pamphlets that echo the sentiment that the mills brought life to the river. The authors deplore the "ugly stretch of wasteland" that the river valley used to be, "lying idle and unproductive," and hail the "efficient manufacturing unit built on faith, energy, and a belief in the future."

Ugly? Wasteland? My garden journal from the first spring after we moved to Lawrence reminds me that my yard had the best soil I'd ever encountered: "Rich and brown and fine as the finest ground coffee!"

Robert Frost, a poet we associate with silent, snowy evenings in New Hampshire woods, was valedictorian of the Lawrence High School class of 1892. His father, a newspaper reporter, had died of consumption at age thirty-four in San Francisco, Robert's birthplace, so Robert and his mother and younger sister came to Lawrence to live with his grandfather, who was an overseer in one of the mills. And though Lawrence hasn't a single bookstore in which to buy his poems, Frost endures as one of the city's very few local heroes. (Leonard Bernstein, who was born in Lawrence in 1918, is another; he moved away as a child, but Lawrencians still cling to him.) There is an elementary school named after Frost in south Lawrence, and a small abstract monument dedicated to him in the common across from city hall. (It's supposed to be a fountain, but I've never seen the water flowing.) One of Frost's less-known poems is called "A Brook in the City." Critics say it is about Lawrence and the Spicket River, a tributary of the Merrimack that snakes around and under Lawrence streets, crossed by dozens of now-crumbling bridges built by WPA workers in the 1930s.

Three rivers in all—the Merrimack, the Spicket, and another tributary, the Shawsheen—are symbolized on Lawrence's flag, which was designed for the fiftieth anniversary of its incorporation as a city, in 1853: three ribbons of white in a horizontal trident formation against a field of blue. A toothed gear and a smokestack also figured prominently in the design that was used on the programs for the event in 1903. Unlike these images, however, the Frost poem is hardly meant to glorify industrial progress; the brook that is the Spicket is forced to run "Deep in a sewer dungeon under stone," and the poet wonders how the inhabitants of this hastily "new-built city" can live knowing that there is a river trapped below them "in fetid darkness. . . . And all for nothing it had ever done / Except forget to go in fear perhaps."

SPRING 1987. The Merrimack is dangerously high, and the Spicket and Shawsheen have already overflowed their banks, flooding streets and nearby homes. The rain is still lightly falling as Bob and I drive down to the mill district to take a look. We find a spot to stand in an opening between two old Pacific Mills buildings, one of them where the furniture factory is located.

It is night, not a black night, but one colored curiously brown. Mud brown hills of water are rushing past us. Things, big things, including what appear to be whole young trees, are being carried along by this powerful current. Both sides of the mighty Merrimack are lined with mills, so that not only are we standing at the base of a huge wall of them; we face another long wall across the churning water. The windows are lit up, row upon row of them, and the water level is so high that the buildings actually appear to be floating, like ocean liners, docked. I think it is their smokestacks, too, that remind me of ships; Lawrence's sky is punctured by a series of these brick obelisks—monuments to the Industrial Revolution.

Another time, not long after the flood, Bob and I went at night to see a fire. One of the mills was burning, and mill fires are spectacular: the great structures always burn so willingly, their old wooden floors saturated with the lubricating oil that dripped for years from the textile machines. There were once small armies of young mill workers, called "oiler boys," who, like the poor soul in Charlie Chaplin's 1936 movie *Modern Times*, did nothing but go from machine to machine with big triggered cans, squirting shots of oil into gears and parts.

I know a retired Lawrence firefighter, Tom Troy, who fought lots of mill fires in his thirty-seven years with the department. He remembers one in the late sixties that burned for days; the ruin it left remains. "We went back there for a month, day in and day out," says Troy, who once worked as an oiler boy in the American Woolen Company's Ayer Mill, a structure only a little less gigantic than the Wood Mill, which is directly across the street from it. The year was 1939, and Troy was eighteen years old, a recent graduate of Lawrence High School. Day after day, hour after hour, from machine to machine, he went with his oilcan, as he had been instructed. And day after day, as soon as he had finished, the ladies in the spinning room would wipe the oil off, because they didn't want it to get on the cloth. "So all day they would be chasing you, telling you not to oil, and the section hand would be chasing you, telling you things weren't oiled enough." Typically, a Lawrencian like Troy would have stuck with mill work for life; Troy, however, made his decision to leave shortly after he spoke with another oiler boy who was actually a twenty-nine-year-old man; he had started as a teenager, same as Troy, and in all those dozen years he had never been promoted, never been given a raise.

THE METAMORPHOSIS of Lawrence from a rural outpost called Merrimack (and several other temporary names) to a teeming New England mill town of nearly 100,000 took all of sixty years, a fact noted with pride in the early histories of the city. Maurice B. Dorgan, a local attorney whose father owned a well-known barroom, and author of *History of Lawrence, Massachusetts*, published in 1924, marveled that, between 1845 and 1848, masons building Lawrence's first mills laid bricks at the rate of 100,000 to 200,000 a day in "the pursuit of civilization." And he was particularly enamored of the accomplishments of Billy Wood: "The most marked development in the industrial growth came in 1905," he wrote. "The building of the Wood Mills started a decade of mill construction in Lawrence such as has probably never been witnessed in any other textile center. . . . Not only is the plant of the Wood Worsted Mills the largest single mill plant in the world, but it has the distinction of having been erected in a shorter time than any other manufacturing establishment of magnitude. Conceived one day, it was, as it were, in operation the next. . . ."

The advent of river-powered textile technology in the 1840s transformed people's lives just as suddenly as it did their landscape. Women left their sheep and their gardens of flax, their spinning wheels and their hand looms, and went into the mills to work for wages, and, later, so did their husbands and children. The factories paid surer wages than farming did—at least for a while—but the newfound "security" harbored hidden costs. It was the end of self-sufficiency, of self-reliance, of silence. It was the beginning of the speeding up of the world.

The world is still speeding, but now it largely bypasses

Lawrence. Oh, the highway signs leading out of Boston still indicate NORTH with the city's name, but the choice is a remnant of another time, when places like Lawrence mattered. The highway is the equivalent of a new river, man-made, and travelers on their way to Maine merely skim across the city's surface. What do they think of Lawrence's cold smokestacks? The huge mills with their broken windows? On the elevated road, you are at eye level with them—a disconcerting sight among the billboards. (This view of the sweep of Lawrence's mills along the Merrimack was used in a scene in the 1992 movie *School Ties*. They're supposed to be the old silk factories along the Lackawanna River in Scranton, Pennsylvania, the place the blue-collar hero, who has won a scholarship to a fancy prep school, is leaving; one foundering industrial town interchangeable with another, in Hollywood's opinion.)

A small fraction of the city's cavernous mills are rented out dirt cheap to companies like the Frishmans', whose 29,000 square feet—almost two-thirds of a football field—costs only $2,500 a month. The rest—perhaps as many as 85 percent—are vacant or used only for storage. In 1989, a Lawrence man bought a small mill building by the north canal and used it to "store" his trash; actually, he filled it with old tires, scrap metal, wood, and other construction debris, then abandoned it; this was his solution to the problem of rising waste-disposal costs. And though he's pleaded guilty to illegal dumping in five other Massachusetts locales, he hasn't been charged for the Lawrence mess, which was set on fire by an arsonist on New Year's Eve 1993.

How perishable the monolithic mills seem at such moments. Despite the fires, however, despite the ramshackle appearance of most of those that remain, the mills impose themselves upon the city like natural phenomena—brick mountain ranges, say—and anyone who dreams of accomplishing anything there must take them into account; must go over, under, or around them. Or make them the plan's centerpiece. Or plot (somehow) to be rid of them completely.

They seem all the more monolithic because the city is so small—less than seven square miles. Subtract its rivers, its two canals, and its public spaces (one hundred acres of poorly designed and decaying parks and playgrounds, and another one hundred acres of scandalously unkempt cemeteries) and Lawrence would be even smaller: less than four miles square. It is quite possible to walk clear across the city in a morning. In a car, it takes a little longer than the few minutes you might expect, however, not only because of one-way streets and traffic but also because the Merrimack, like Dublin's Liffey, bisects the city. Four bridges traverse it, connecting north Lawrence with south, so that, between these and the spans over the Shawsheen and the Spicket, you are forever crossing bridges to get anywhere.

Still, unless there is a flood, it's easy to go days or weeks— even, perhaps, a contemporary Lawrence lifetime—without actually thinking about the water. The Merrimack itself matters not a jot in most Lawrencians' lives any longer. It might as well be a painting of a river. It might as well be what it was before Lawrence existed, just a little less than 150 years ago. Its work, at least in one sense of that word, is largely done.

LAWRENCE IS famous for its textiles no longer; instead, it is known for its urban blight. The crime rate per one thousand inhabitants is comparable to that of Boston. It's known nationally as one of the car-theft capitals of the country, second only to Newark, New Jersey; cars are more than twice as likely to be swiped there as in New York City. The same day that I read in the *The New York Times* that Lawrence was number two in auto thefts in 1992, I was unable to check another local statistic at the Lawrence Public Library because the reference librarian's car had been stolen and she hadn't been able to come to work.

Lawrence is also the place where, in 1974, Willie Horton committed the crime—the murder of a seventeen-year-old gas-station attendant—for which he was serving time in a Massachusetts prison when he escaped from his weekend furlough. Indeed, the world might not know Willie Horton's name if it were not for the two *Lawrence Eagle-Tribune* reporters who wrote the subsequent prison-furlough stories, winning (as many think) an election for George Bush and a Pulitzer Prize, as well.

Crime isn't Lawrence's only claim to national shame. In line at the grocery store one day, I was thumbing through *People* magazine when my eye was caught by a photo of Lawrence schoolchildren posing with writer Jonathan Kozol—an illustration for an article featuring *Savage Inequalities*, his 1991 book about the injustices inherent in a system of public education funded almost entirely by local property taxes. A while later, I heard Kozol, on National Public Radio, refer to Lawrence as "one big ghetto."

That's a harsh characterization, and not entirely accurate. After all, on that same day, I attended a friend's fiftieth birthday party in south Lawrence, in a sprawling neighborhood of 1950s-style single-family homes—anomalies for Lawrence, granted, but there they are nonetheless, many of them moved from elsewhere in the city when they were just a few years old, out of the path of one of those new interstates.

On the other hand, my friend and his wife send their daughter not to the Lawrence public schools or even to a Catholic school there, and the city has many. They send her instead to a Catholic school in Andover, St. Augustine's. "It's eight minutes away," they say. "St. Augustine's in Lawrence is eleven." But I know that a three-minute difference in travel time isn't the real reason behind their choice; so do they.

Sometimes the things that aren't said about Lawrence are worse than the things that are said. On New Year's Day 1991, the *Lawrence Eagle-Tribune* was suddenly simply the *Eagle-Tribune*, without a word of acknowledgment by the publishers. At least the paper's name no longer belies its current location: the main offices have been in North Andover for over twenty years. A market study from the mid-eighties strongly suggested that if the century-old paper hoped to survive, it had best offer regional coverage. Since then, it has been slighting Lawrence ever more blatantly, and having no trouble featuring it in a less than favorable light. For this reason, I find it alarming, as I occasionally ride my bike along the back roads of the Merrimack Valley three or four towns north of the city, to see the route lined with boxes marked *Eagle-Tribune* for the newspaper carriers. Do people really read the *Trib* all the way out there? What impression of Lawrence are they forming from it? Do they ever visit the city to see it firsthand? Or has the paper, with its police-blotter headlines, made them too afraid?

IN THE late eighties, Lawrence's rough reputation was part of the reason why the Museum of American Textile History bypassed the city when it was looking for a new home. For years, the small North Andover institution had been making plans to move its collection of textile machinery to larger quarters; ideally, they hoped to display it in actual mill space, the way it's done in Lowell. Lawrence beckoned. After all, the story of textiles was Lawrence's story; didn't it have the right to host the tellers of its tale? The museum even went so far as to purchase an old American Woolen Company mill building, but then the board of trustees changed its mind: its members rejected the Lawrence site and started their search all over again (eventually joining the other museums in Lowell). The word is that state and city politicians blew it; snobbery also seems to have played a role, however. "Our board is elitist," someone close to the controversy told me in confidence. "Some of the wives couldn't imagine going to Lawrence for functions."

It's not only elitists who don't think Lawrence merits a museum, however. It's not only outsiders who speak of Lawrence as if it had sunk into the river after the textile companies pulled out back in the fifties. "A museum? What good is it going to do?" one old-time Lawrencian scoffed. "They won't learn anything from the past," he added, politely excluding me as well as himself from that unregenerate "they."

LAWRENCE WAS once in the vanguard, a wonder of the Industrial Revolution in America, as remarkable as Detroit. Our country's economy was built on mass-production techniques forged in the textile mills, including the division of labor. The trouble is, this system, in which vast numbers of individual workers are responsible for making only a small piece of a standardized product, is proving dysfunctional in our contemporary world; the big industrial structures it requires are too inflexible to allow the sudden modifications dictated by rapid technological advances, changing tastes, and market conditions.

Many believe that if places like Lawrence have any hope of revival, it's small businesses like the Frishmans' that will provide it. With only thirty employees, Akko is nimble and able to stay au courant. Not in business to mass-produce anything, it prides itself on selling to people with cutting-edge tastes, ignoring the fact that its prices put most of its wares out of the reach of ordinary people, whatever their preferences (Bob and myself included). Looking through Bob's old files, I see that Yoko Ono, among many other celebrities, has made purchases—two custom typing tables for $325 each—and that another Akko piece was used as a prop in a photo in the magazine *Gourmet*. In March and April 1985, Bob designed a chair—the first all-acrylic folding chair, which he dubbed "Prima"—and that same spring it was selected by Tiffany & Company for an in-store display. Bob went to New York for the unveiling. "Breakfast at Tiffany's today," I noted in my journal; "Bob left for the airport at 5:45 a.m."

Late that night, back home, he told me what he'd seen: *his* chair—six of them, in fact—along with the latest deck furniture and patio tables set with china and silver, resting on a sandy beach hauled, at great expense, no doubt, to the second level of the Fifth Avenue store.

WHEN BOB'S FATHER, Daniel Frishman, founded the company in 1975, he probably couldn't have imagined that one day an Akko product would find its way into such a scenario; certainly he didn't consider the impact his company might have on that icon of the other end of the economic scale, Lawrence. In fact, he began by renting a small space in Andover; only after the business grew did he move it into the mill.

The Frishman family—Dan, his wife, Ruth, and Bob and his three older siblings—had moved to Andover originally in 1956 when Dan, a textile chemist, took a position at Malden Mills, in Lawrence, as director of research, inventing fake furs and the like (the company survived the textile industry's demise by diversifying; in fact, in the nineties it has thrived), then, later, wig fibers for Reid Meredith (another survivor not tied to textiles).

Dan did well and eventually became an independent consultant, while simultaneously dabbling in modern-art collecting; that interest spawned a gallery on Cape Cod, where he met an art student who was working with acrylic, heating sheets of it in his oven and bending them into hanging planters; soon after, Dan founded Akko, engaging the artist to design small gift items. Nine years later, the company was doing over $1 million in sales of much larger goods, and was profitable. It would have been even more profitable if, as Dan discovered that year, his bookkeeper hadn't been an embezzler. That's why Bob, who was finishing up his tenth year as a speechwriter and legislative aide on Capitol Hill, was asked to step in. He had no business experience, but he was kin; he was trustworthy. He could learn. For many years, Bob and I had privately pooh-poohed Dan's business; after all, we had come of age in the sixties, when "plastics" was the "one-word" career tip that sent the hero of the 1967 film *The Graduate* careening in the opposite direction. But we were tired of Washington and its masks and games; we wanted a change. And so we made our plans to leave.

Of course Bob's parents assumed that we would live in Andover. Certainly we wouldn't end up in Lawrence. Lawrence was ugly. It was dull. It was tacky. It wasn't "us."

But end up in Lawrence we did. What's more, Bob started coming home from "the factory" promptly at 5:15 most week nights. He and I ate supper shortly after his arrival (lunch had been early, and so had breakfast; Bob's workday started at 7:30), when most professionals were still at the office. Old friends, phoning, would be surprised to find us "finished" for the day, eating when the working class eats. What had happened to us?

The Frishmans weren't the only Andoverites perplexed by our decision to live in Lawrence. Quickly, I learned that my address raised eyebrows at Andover parties. At one small social gathering, I met a young woman who said she wanted to live cheaply so that she could write. She was looking in Andover for a rental because she wanted to be able to walk to the health-food store and the thrift shop, but was appalled that the best to be found so far was "a filthy room" for $450.

"Have you considered Lawrence?" I asked.

"*Lawrence?*" she squeaked. "I mean, I know you live there," she stammered, "but I wouldn't know where. I mean, *where* in Lawrence would I live?"

Was saying that I lived in Lawrence like a white person saying she lives in Harlem? Not quite. But close, and getting closer, perhaps, as Lawrence's population is increasingly made up of people other than Caucasians of mostly European descent. Puerto Ricans, Dominicans, Vietnamese, Cambodians, Argentineans, Guatemalans, Costa Ricans, El Salvadorans, Nicaraguans, Uruguayans, and Paraguayans (nineteen different countries come together for Hispanic Week on the common) now outnumber the uneasy descendants of the Italians, Lebanese, French-Canadians, Irish, Germans, Poles, and Lithuanians who made up earlier immigrant waves. (It is agreed that the descendants of the Russian Jews, constituting a large and active community, left Lawrence en masse in the decade between the mid-sixties and the mid-seventies, when they built a new temple in Andover. In years gone by, there had been "a gentleman's agreement," as it's called, in Andover—an invisible barrier, if not outright restricted areas; now those covenants, formal and informal, are gone; and, in an odd twist, Russians who immigrate to the region today are counseled to live anywhere but in Lawrence if they can; mostly they do, with the help of their suburban sponsors.)

A typical 120- or 130-member graduating class from Lawrence High will boast students of forty different national origins, with given names more likely to be Fiordaliza or Phu than Heather or Jason. This genuine ethnic mosaic is stunning, but it is also alarming, for it presents the educational system and social-service agencies with some daunting problems. Bob and I couldn't help but smile when, at some of those same Andover parties where we stopped the conversation with our Lawrence address, we heard that so-and-so's daughter had gone to Liberia to help the poor. Didn't she know that all she needed to do was drive to Lawrence to find the Third World?

HOW QUICKLY people forget that hundreds of thousands of new immigrants have made a start in "Immigrant City" and moved on. On the other hand, there is a widespread feeling that those who have not made their escape have somehow failed. Lawrence is a place to be *from*, not a place to grow old in. In her speech at the opening of the new campus of Lawrence's branch of Northern Essex Community College in May 1991, former state senator Patricia McGovern talked about the college being "the way out." "The way up and the way *out!*" she shouted, and it got her her biggest round of applause.

Where do you go when you leave Lawrence? I heard one wag quip that Methuen is an immigrant city, too, since so many Lawrencians have moved there. (I've also heard it mocked as "Lawrence with grass.") Salem, New Hampshire, one step over the Massachusetts line, is another desirable destination. North Andover is better still, and Andover is considered the crème de la crème.

Though many of their families originated in the mill city, and though they often proclaim to "love" Lawrence—its "local color"; its ten-screen movie theater (which Andover's strict zoning laws and ever-vigilant citizenry would never have allowed); its secondhand furniture stores and ethnic groceries— Andoverites have a reputation for being out of touch with Lawrence and Lawrencians. In *An Old New England School: A History of Phillips Academy Andover* (1917), a tome by headmaster Claude M. Fuess, Lawrence is given one paragraph. The text is about the Pemberton Mill disaster, which occurred on January 10, 1860. At 4:45 p.m., the five-story mill building collapsed, a swaying having been set up, one theory has it, by the rhythmic pounding of the textile machines throwing their shuttles back and forth. It took sixty seconds. Eighty-eight people were killed, and 116 were seriously injured or maimed for life in either the collapse or the fire that started during the rescue. All Fuess could muster is this sentimental sap: "Some of the Academy boys who ran to the scene still remember how the girls imprisoned in the flames sang 'Shall we gather at the river?' as death came nearer and nearer." Sentimental, and apocryphal: Robert Lowry didn't even write the song until four years later (and didn't publish it for another year), and if the boys did indeed "run" from campus, they did so for seven miles.

In 1912, the year of the great strike, an Andover librarian complained in her annual report to the town council that her child patrons were being "robbed of their childhood heritage of innocence, imagination, and ignorance," by the (in her view) "insidious, even subtlely immoral" juvenile books being offered by New York publishers. What seemed to irk her most was the "objectionable" choice of subject matter, and while the volumes to which she referred are unnamed, I suspect the books portrayed real life. Meanwhile, the childhood heritage of Lawrencian children was work in the mills, often at ages younger than the legal fourteen (fake documents were easy to secure and parents often needed their children's wages). Underage children hid behind mill machinery if the truant officer came looking. In and out of school, in and out of the mills, they often failed to excel or advance in either place.

Some Lawrence children lost more than their childhoods to mill work. Cotton and wool dust damaged young lungs, and accidents were common. In 1911, one girl, Camella Teoli, became famous when her hair got caught in the rollers of a twisting machine (like the one that amateur boxer Robito would later tend) and her scalp was pulled off. She was thirteen going on fourteen (she had gotten the job with a doctored birth certificate), and her story made the front page not only in

Lawrence—the *Lawrence Sunday Sentinel* insisting, as it often did, that mill accidents like Camella's were "the result of the excitable dispositions of some of our foreign populations"—but in New York and Washington. In 1912, she testified before Congress, at hearings called after the Bread and Roses strike. Mrs. William Howard Taft, who had read about Camella in the newspapers, sat in the front row, teary-eyed and appalled. Up until then, the enactment and enforcement of child-labor laws had been left to each individual state; the hearings were part of a decades-long push for a viable federal law, which finally passed in the 1940s. In the 1970s, a new street in Lawrence, created by urban renewal, was named Camella Teoli Way.

"EXCITABLE" foreigners never lived in great numbers in Andover. Just as Lawrence has no Colonial past, having been transformed from wilderness to a Victorian-era industrial city virtually overnight, Andover has no past that includes a major influx of post-Colonial immigrants from Europe or anywhere else. Like the rest of "old" New England, Andover's roots are English. Colonists settled it in the 1640s, two hundred years before Lawrence's founders stood on Phillips Hill and saw the land they wanted to develop into the textile city of their vision. At the turn of the century, the town's strict building code kept the triple-deckers out, and two-families to a minimum; it continues to do so today. Andover remains very much an Anglo world.

Perhaps it is at Christmastime that the cultural difference between the two places is most vividly on display. Lawrence's Christmas decorations are the colorful kind, some so elaborate that they are left up all year (though not lighted), because taking them down would be like trying to dismantle a spider's web. Several families use thousands of bulbs; their extravaganzas stop traffic as people come from miles around to see them. Driving past Andover houses, however, you will rarely see anything but tiny white lights flickering on the trees, or tasteful electric candles burning in the windows.

Yet genteel Andover is inextricably linked with its rude cousin, Lawrence. There is, for example, a beautiful English-style garden cemetery in Andover—sixty-seven acres' worth, one of many green spaces of the town. I wonder how many of the Andoverites who enjoy walking there know that the huge stone archway through which you enter and exit the cemetery and the pink granite cemetery wall, a mile long, were gifts to West Parish Congregational Church from Billy Wood, built by Lawrence laborers, and financed with profits from the mills.

Wood also donated to West Parish an elegant English-style stone chapel, set in the heart of the cemetery, to mark the graves of Wood himself, his wife, his parents, and his children. It has a water organ, an Italian Renaissance–style tile roof, and eight stained-glass windows created by Louis Comfort Tiffany. Even closer to Lawrence than West Parish—in fact, just a step over the Andover line—is another of Wood's legacies: an idyllic suburban neighborhood named Shawsheen Village.

Shawsheen makes Andover proud. Nothing even remotely like it graces Lawrence, or any other community in the United States, for that matter. It consists of two hundred two- and three-story houses, all architecturally alike, in the Colonial Revival style, but no two identical, the whole group of them divided by a busy main street into two distinct sections: Red and White. Red Shawsheen's houses are brick, White Shawsheen's are (or were, originally) white clapboard. Built between 1919 and 1924 by Wood's American Woolen Company, they were leased to AWC employees—the more substantial and elaborate brick to upper-echelon executives, most of whom were moving to Andover from Boston; the more modest (and much more numerous) wooden ones to those lower in the pecking order: overseers, bookkeepers, clerks, and (new concept) their nuclear families.

Hand it to Wood: housing for management was a novel idea. As the *Bulletin of the National Association of Wool Manufacturers* reported of Shawsheen Village in January 1924:

> While the great majority of [company housing developments] have . . . been undertaken for the purpose of giving better homes and living conditions to those engaged in mill or factory work, [the innovation of] the American Woolen Company was the transfer from the city to a newly created model village in the country for its executive force of men and women. . . . Here, it is hoped that the office force, removed from the city with its distractions, artificiality, and extravagance, will become attached to the country and learn its simplicity, its outdoor life, freedom, wholesomeness, and neighborliness.

Others did not see Shawsheen in quite those lofty terms. A labor-union newspaper referred to it as "Suckersvillage," a suburb for Billy Wood's "Lawrence Lickspittles," and described it as "an imitation feudal town" featuring "rows of artistic dwellings for his most faithful and intelligent slaves." (Perhaps this dyspepsia arose in part from contemplating what Wood did build for his thousands and thousands of mill "operatives": a token few streets' worth of row houses, in Lawrence. Today one remaining group of those homes, two-story brick and ugly as sin, could easily be mistaken for an unfortunate example of public housing.)

Wood's ambitious plans for Shawsheen called not only for the construction of homes, which he hoped would eventually number one thousand, but also for shops, a post office, a school, tennis courts, a golf course, a bowling green, and a garage—some of which were built and some of which were not, for by the mid-1920s, the decline of the American Woolen Company, and of Lawrence, had already begun. In fact, though it's not well known in Andover—or in Lawrence, either—the expense of building Shawsheen was one cause of the demise of Wood's empire, and so, therefore, of Lawrence's. Notwithstanding TV commentator Murrow's grainy black-and-white footage of the last Lawrencian mill operatives getting their paychecks in the fifties, the slide had begun thirty years earlier.

No mention of that, or of Shawsheen's role in it, however, by Mr. Murrow. Nor is Shawsheen's role in Lawrence's decline noted in the walking-tour pamphlet published by the Andover Historical Society. Oblivious, its author merely states with pride: "The entire Shawsheen Village plan emulated Anglo-American roots, and today its historical and architectural integrity have been nationally recognized by its inclusion on the National Register of Historic Places."

ONE DAY, listening to tapes at the Immigrant City Archives, I heard a woman, born in Lawrence in 1896, describe her Berkeley Street neighborhood, not far from the street where I used to live, and her words reminded me that members of different bourgeois occupations formerly lived in far closer proximity than they do today. Of her Lawrence neighbors, she said: "One was a dentist, one was a farmer, one ran a milk route, one was a carpenter—it was very mixed and very natural." Her own father was a lawyer.

Thomas W. Leavitt, the former director of the textile museum (who is now director of the Museum of Our National Heritage, in Lexington, Massachusetts), describes a similar miscellany living in close proximity during his boyhood in the late 1930s in Hopkinton, a "suburb" of Concord, New Hampshire, situated on another well-worn river, the Contoocook:

"It was a small town where the blue-collar working class, the middle-class technocrats, and the managers and professional people all knew each other and in fact knew each other so well that they fraternized with each other. So that in that town, the market farmer, whom I worked for as a high school kid, played cards every Saturday night with the local school superintendent and his wife, and the local doctor and his wife; and my mother [a bookkeeper] and stepfather [a machinist] played cards on Saturday night with the local owner of the lumber mill [for whom his mother worked], and the fellow who owned the small company that made frialators, and the fellow who had the big local apple orchard. So you had this degree of intimacy among people who had different economic and educational levels that you and I just don't experience."

Neither the turn-of-the-century Lawrencian nor Tom, the child of the thirties, however, remembers "a degree of intimacy" with any member of our country's most populous occupational group—the unskilled and semiskilled. Never part of the "natural" mix, in Lawrence these groups were isolated down in the mill district right from the start—ominously, one could say now, as, with the development of automobile culture, the separation between hilltop and bottomland has become the boundary between city and suburb.

That was why Bob and I sometimes seemed like eccentrics living in Lawrence; Tom still does seem that way: when he thought the museum would be relocating to Lawrence, he moved with his family from North Andover back to the city after an eighteen-year hiatus. At a party Tom gave at his house on New Year's Day 1992, he introduced Bob and me as "the *other* middle-class couple in Lawrence."

Was he boasting or asking his out-of-town guests to commiserate with us? A little of both, I guess.

One year, I saw him in the crowd at Lawrence's annual Feast of the Three Saints, a weekend-long Italian festival held in what used to be an Italian stronghold, with bakers and butchers and pizza makers, and wine makers in basements, but which is increasingly populated by Latinos and the accoutrements of their culture: at Bongi's Delicatessen, key rings bearing the flag of the Dominican Republic hang alongside the plastic red hot peppers that are a potent symbol for southern Italians, who use them to ward off the evil eye. It's also true that those who attend the festivities are increasingly from the suburbs—former Lawrencians returning nostalgically to the old neighborhood—so the event is less than bona fide.

A torchlight parade is the high point of the feast. Well, sort of torchlight. Actually, men carry road flares, and the acrid smell of the burning chemicals fills the air, along with the smells of fried dough and grilled sausage from the food stands, as the Sons of Italy band plays ponderous tunes and fireworks explode on the roofs of three-deckers, lighting up the mills a few streets beyond.

In the middle of all that, I encountered Tom, a tall, muscular man with a rather professorial air (he has taught college history). He had a stranger's child (Latino) straddling his shoulders, and a big grin on his face.

I knew why he was smiling; I'd felt it, too, if only briefly: "This is why you live in the city instead of the suburbs," said Tom, who had left his job at the textile museum, one he'd held twenty-eight years, when its move to Lawrence didn't occur. "This is the nitty-gritty."

But is it? Don't the event's modernizations imply the very opposite?

What is more, you don't have to live in Lawrence to partake: you can come by car to enjoy the local color for an hour or two—and then run.

Even worse, most of the participants, whether city dwellers or not, are middle-aged or older. Who will organize the feast when they are gone? The Latino boy sitting on Tom's shoulders certainly isn't going to carry on the tradition; he lives in Lawrence—he is a Lawrencian—but he has traditions of his own.

CHAPTER 3

Having Arrived at Last Where I Am

P EOPLE WHO know the insularity of such places must be wondering how I had the nerve to take on the subject of Lawrence. Even if I had decided to live there for the rest of my life, I would always have been an outsider, because I'm not a native—"a lifelong resident of Lawrence," as they say. I don't even pronounce Lawrence correctly ("Lahhhrence," through the nose). And yet everywhere I went in that city, I found myself being recognized for what, in Lawrence's eyes at least, I truly am.

"You Italian?" the clerk behind the counter at the Lawrence Public Library asked me out of the blue one day not long after I had moved there. She is dark-haired, delicate-looking, possibly (probably?) Italian herself.

What did her question mean? It couldn't have had anything to do with the books I had chosen to check out. I hadn't given her my library card yet, so she wasn't going by my name. She had obviously asked her question simply, solely, because of how I look. Was her curiosity supposed to be a compliment?

I told her, Yes, I am Italian, and she smiled, happy to have her hunch confirmed. And I, suddenly, was pleased to have my ethnic heritage acknowledged. In Washington, D.C., where I was a member of a much broader human category—white—and where there was only one large ethnic group—African-Americans—the question would never have been asked of me. In Greenwich, it wouldn't have been asked, either, because the answer wouldn't have been considered important information.

"What part of It-lee did your grandparents come from?" my next-door neighbor John asked me the day we met. "A suburb of Naples," I said, using a line of my father's. But John, born in Lawrence in 1906 to parents who had just arrived from the outskirts of Naples themselves, wasn't amused. He really wanted to know.

So I told him what I had heard in conversations when I was a child, about the two peasant villages—Castel Grande and Castel Franco (names I've seen on a very detailed map, using a powerful magnifying glass)—within the borders of a mountainous place called Benevento. Many families from that region, those villages, had settled in Greenwich together and had remained provincially rivalrous, in work, in play, for decades.

In the late fifties, driving in backcountry Greenwich with my mother, I remember seeing old Italian ladies who wouldn't have looked at all strange in Benevento looking strange indeed in my posh town. They were in a field, bent over, rumps high in the air as they moved along, pulling something from the earth and putting it into brown paper grocery bags. "Awk, that's so Italian," said Mom, clicking her tongue. They were gathering dandelions for salad, she explained. We never ate them at our table—I still haven't tasted them—and yet, pulling the jagged leaves out of my garden, I recall that day in Greenwich and think, I should be eating these for dinner instead.

It was John who pointed out to me another edible weed—a type of *broccoli di rape*—that grew on feathery stalks outside our back doors in Lawrence, sending seeds to lodge everywhere, cracks in the sidewalk included. I could tell he was miffed at my ignorance: what kind of Italian was I never to have heard of it before? (Afterward, I started to notice that the greens are sold in bunches at Italian grocery stores in Lawrence and elsewhere, and that there are recipes for it in Italian cookbooks I've owned for years.)

SOMETIMES WITH less restraint and finesse than the library clerk or John, other Lawrencians also tried to size me up, to decide where I belonged. One day while I was buying milk in the little variety store across the street from my house, the owner, Louie, working behind the counter, said to me, "I heard you had all the money in Lawrence."

"Who told you that?"

"A man comes in here, he told me, 'If I had their money . . .' "

"If he had my money, what?"

No reply, and Louie was looking sorry he had started the conversation.

If he had my money, he wouldn't live in Lawrence? Was that it? I didn't ask.

Louie is a small, gray-faced man with a smoker's cough. He once hit a would-be robber on the head with an electric space heater he kept on the floor behind the counter. That took courage, but Louie's health isn't the best, and soon afterward, the store, a small cinder-block structure squeezed between two triple-deckers, changed hands.

Another time, while shoveling snow, I had a talk with Rejean. A slender man in his forties who wears a ponytail and who used to live in the three-family house next door to me, on the side opposite John and Lucille, he works as a technician at the huge AT&T plant in North Andover. On this particular day, he was shoveling his aging landlord's driveway, grudgingly. He's a bitter man, I realized when he said, "I won't have to get my exercise at Cedardale tonight," referring to my health club—to which he does not belong.

Rejean wanted to leave Lawrence. I knew that from other conversations I'd had with him about the "Spanish." Once, he had hoped to buy the house he lived in from his landlords, Bruno and Jane Zwecki, old and ailing Polish-Americans who, in the reversal Rejean envisioned, would then have become Rejean's tenants. But the Zweckis were reluctant to let go. Maybe now Rejean is glad. Not long after our conversation in the snow, he and his family moved away—twenty miles from Lawrence—to Salisbury Beach, at the mouth of the Merrimack. No doubt he was plotting his escape even as we spoke (the first step—ironically, since he ended up at the water's edge—was to sell his beloved boat).

In the meantime, Rejean had seemed to enjoy tsk-tsking about the elderly woman who used to live alone in the big single-family Victorian like mine, one house down from his, and who was robbed around Christmas. (Was his enjoyment derived from the fact that he thought a tale of crime in close proximity might scare me? I tried to convey that my D.C. neighborhood was much "scarier," but he evidently wasn't impressed.) Seven o'clock in the morning, he told me, she comes down to her kitchen, to find a man standing there. She's living with a friend now. And two other elderly women, sisters in the Victorian next door to hers, are frightened and have put their names on a list to get into a home for the aged. And Freddy Colvito is putting in a new boiler. That means he plans to sell soon. All three of those houses will go on the market next year, Rejean predicted. Why don't you buy them up, he wanted to know, if you like Lawrence so much? And I wondered, Was it he who had said to Louie, "If I had their money . . ."?

———————

I GUESS Bob and I must have baffled a lot of other people on the block by living in Lawrence; we may even have made them feel as resentful as Rejean obviously felt. They knew at a glance that we were different from them, just as I knew instantly that they were not like me. So many of them smoked, for example, without apology, puffing on cigarettes as they walked to and from their parked cars. Their fashions and hairstyles were different, too: the men let their hair grow long, so they looked uncannily like hippies from the sixties; the women's hair, stiffened with mousse, fanned out atop their heads like tiaras.

Mrs. Brande, the old woman who lived in the two-family across the street from Rejean's old apartment, looked like Louhi the Witch, a character in a book I read aloud to a class one day at a public elementary school down the hill. She was hunched and had a hooked nose, and walked with a cane. She wore old bell-bottom pants (yet another remnant of the sixties to be found in Lawrence—thirty-year-old pants that just hadn't worn out yet?). But she was an energetic sweetie who'd had a long career down in the mills.

On Sunday afternoons, she got picked up by a church group in a big gray van, then was dropped off home again early Sunday night. One of her brothers lived with her; the other, who looked enough like him to be his twin, lived in the triple-decker between her house and the variety store that used to be Louie's. For a long time, I thought the two brothers were one man with two cars; then I saw them together. I guess that's a mistake a middle-class person might make more easily than a working-class one. Not every family in America can afford two cars.

Mrs. Brande, for her part, misconstrued the relationship between Bob and me, because we didn't fit into *her* worldview. For years, it seems, she believed that we were father and daughter. How else to provide a parent-child relationship to a household, like ours, that doesn't have one? I do look younger than Bob (though I'm a few weeks older). And I would often leave our Lawrence house with armfuls of books. But those facts don't really explain her mistake—or mine. We both saw what we expected to see.

The foursome that used to be Mrs. Brande's tenants upstairs is what I suppose she would consider a more "normal" family than ours, even though the man, who works with Rejean at AT&T, was separated from his wife and two children. He lived for a time in an apartment on a nearby side street, and the kids raced back and forth between the two houses. For a while, the furniture moved back and forth, as well; once, their stereo cabinet stood on the sidewalk for several days, atop a mound of dirty snow. Later, both parents and both kids—and all their furniture—moved away. I don't know where.

After they left, no one cut Mrs. Brande's lawn. She apologized to me about it, but I told her I didn't care. She had enough other troubles: when an ambulance came and took her away, I wondered if I'd ever see her again; a week or so passed, and then she returned, using a walker.

Soon after I moved into our house in Lawrence, Mrs. Brande told me that her cat was twenty-five. One day, I realized that I no longer saw it sitting in the window.

Mrs. Brande had a dog, too, but it never left her yard. Walking one's dog on a leash is, need I say, a very middle-class thing to do, and my dog-walking habit fostered yet another cultural misunderstanding. My route took me past many working-class dogs, like Mrs. Brande's, who barked at my German shepherd and me from behind chain-link fences. I had cleaned up after Heidi in D.C., and I did it in Lawrence, too, though it meant carrying the poop all the way home, because there were no trash receptacles on the streets. Nonetheless, on this particular day, a woman whose house we regularly passed came out her side door to chase us away. Toothless (her false teeth left on the bathroom sink?), hips padded with extra flesh, she brandished a rake.

"I clean up with newspaper! See?" I shook it at her.

But she didn't stop berating us. She wouldn't listen, refused to see how I was an asset to the neighborhood. I left in a huff, dragging my dog behind me.

Halfway down the hill, I came upon another old woman, also toothless, with a stain of food (something red—spaghetti sauce?) at the corner of her mouth. I walked toward her, shouting, "Do you live around here? Have you ever seen me walking my dog? If you have, you'll know that I clean up."

"I don't care—I'm afraid of dogs, anyway," the woman said.

"I clean up," I said again, tears welling.

I DON'T MEAN to imply that culture clashes between the working class and the middle class are anything novel. Nor were they new when I was a college student in the late sixties and hard hats did battle in the streets with antiwar protestors dressed in working-class blue jeans. After the war, however, I sort of forgot about the whole thing; in D.C., I lived in the Yuppie enclaves of Georgetown and Capitol Hill, where it was easy never to meet a working-class person. Then I moved to Lawrence, and even though many of my neighbors looked a lot like those student protestors—middle-class youth who donned blue-collar garb as a statement (or, even worse, a costume)—I began to realize in my gut what the statistics have been telling us all for several years now: that the gap has become wider, not narrower, over time.

In the fifties and sixties, my father didn't need a college degree to earn a decent income and to pay for the higher education of his kids. Even unskilled workers did all right on certain assembly-line jobs. Not so today. Wages for workers with no more than a high school diploma have been declining for two decades now, after adjustment for inflation, and working men like Rejean surely know it. As a union member, Rejean also must realize that organized labor's clout in the workplace and outside it has been badly eroded. Once, 34 percent of the private sector workforce was unionized; now it's only 12 percent. In fact, Rejean is lucky to have a job at all. The AT&T plant where he works employs six thousand, but that's down from the eleven thousand who worked there before Ma Bell was broken up in 1984.

In the late eighties, working-class resentment played a role when Boston's Emerson College tried to relocate in Lawrence. At the height of the real estate boom, the private liberal arts institution wanted to sell its pricey Back Bay properties and build a new campus on the banks of the Merrimack, becoming, in the process, one of the best-endowed colleges in the country. The way some people argued against this move, however, you would have thought Emerson, which finally decided to stay put, was a nuclear-waste dump. Phillips Academy sits on its sprawling Andover campus, the envy of many colleges, lending prestige to the town and upping its real estate values; but despite this example next door, many Lawrencians, including some well-organized senior-citizen groups, actually picketed to protest Emerson's projected relocation.

Rejean wasn't in favor of it, either, even though Lawrencians would have had a break on tuition—a perk that might have benefited his three teenagers. But the arrival of Emerson and its students (most of them certain to be outsiders) also would have upped his taxes, since the college was asking Lawrencians to help pay for the proposed site, which included land the city was going to take by eminent domain, and to accept all liability for any damages resulting from court challenges by the owners of those properties.

Understandably, the opposition saw this plan as less than fair and suspected it was unsound, as well. Never mind the prestige the college would bring, or the expected economic spin-offs, which were supposed to more than compensate for the extra expense at tax time. Nor were Emerson's foes much impressed by the art gallery and the theater for concerts and plays Emerson planned to build with its windfall. Those recreations had nothing to do with people like Rejean.

Still, there is regret in Rejean's voice when one day he tells me he wishes he had become a lawyer. Instead, he says, he fooled around at Lawrence High School. He probably *could* have been a lawyer if . . . *If, if, if* . . .

I have heard regret, too, in the voice of a leader of the opposition to Emerson, who told me that if there had been more sensitivity on the part of the college and its allies, a fairer, sounder plan might have been worked out.

It's also true that when the Lawrence campus of Northern Essex Community College opened, a few years after the Emerson deal had died, Lawrencians didn't object; in fact, they welcomed it. For one thing, they weren't being asked to float a bond to help fund it; for another, they believed the state institution, with its remedial English-language classes and certificate programs in machine tooling, welding, and electronics—offered in addition to its regular college-credit classes— would be more attuned to the needs of their citizenry than Emerson would have been.

In the end, then, perhaps the failure of the Emerson College project boils down to a failure of communication—a cultural gap so wide that a college whose specialty is the communications field could not communicate with blue-collar Lawrence.

WHEN IT COMES right down to it, where you will be happy living depends on where you are most comfortable; not where you belong according to some "rule" about work or class, but where you *feel* you belong—which is usually the place where you feel free to be yourself.

In Lawrence and other communities like it, your immediate neighbors are the ones who give you that freedom and that sense of belonging, or not. You cannot ignore one another: your houses are too close together—huddled, so to speak. Privacy—acreage—costs money. Even a middle-class high-rise, if it is well designed, affords more seclusion than most Lawrencians have.

And so, I could hear the arguments of my Lawrencian neighbors, and their sweet talk. (As they, no doubt, heard mine.) On certain weekday evenings, I heard my neighbor Frank and his friends shuffling and cutting a deck of cards on Frank's kitchen table. I heard another neighbor, Kerry, routinely reprimanding his Doberman: "Apollo! Git over here!" And every night without fail, I heard the blaring television of my neighbor Skip: his wheelchair-bound mother was very hard of hearing.

FBI agents doing a background check wouldn't learn half of what I learned in warm weather, when everybody's windows were open. I even spied on Lucille. When I was with her, I found it excruciating to watch her walk. Her arthritis made it difficult for her to bend her knees, so she moved like a stiff-legged doll, though surprisingly fast, particularly around her kitchen. Yet, standing at my window early one morning, I watched as she went fairly easily down her two back steps into her garden to check on her basil plants, and I asked myself, Is she simply having an easier time of it today? Or does she exaggerate her pain and ask me or John to fetch things for her because, after so many years of factory work and being told what to do, she likes to give a few orders herself?

Of course, Lucille spied on me, too: there was hardly a thing I could tell her without her saying, "I know." ("I know, I saw you leaving." "I know, I saw them arrive.") We were neighbors, after all—and neighbors keep an eye on one another.

Yet, despite our proximity, Bob and I didn't actually socialize with John and Lucille any more than we did with Rejean and his wife, or with Mrs. Brande or Frank or Kerry or Skip or any of the others. Lucille gave me all that delicious food, but we never once ate any of it together, neither she and John at our house nor we at theirs.

Sometimes we *sounded* like friends. ("My hair is a mess," she'd tell me. "That's why I'm wearing my wig, and my sister is coming to set it for me. I used to be so thin, like a whisper. You should see my tiny dresses.") And I believe we were, though we never got to know each other the way certain other friends and I have, anticipating each other's wants and needs. In those friendships, moments of synchronicity are commonplace; awkward moments nonexistent. That wasn't the way it was with Lucille and me during those years that we lived so close by and grew close as a result.

Summer 1986. "You shouldn't have done that," she says, seriously angry, shaking her finger at me out her back door.

This in response to the gallon of olive oil and the hunk of Parmesan cheese from Boston's North End that I had sent Bob over with.

"And you shouldn't do what you do for us," I shrug from my door.

And we both stand there shrugging and eventually smiling tentatively at each other across the shared yard.

"Awk, that's so Italian," my mother said when I told her of Lucille's generosity.

IF IN LAWRENCE great numbers of people who are unlike me did not become my bosom buddies, at least people who shared my tastes in books, movies, and politicians did—Tom Leavitt, for example. So I thought I had my social situation figured out—until, that is, I would have an encounter like this one at a used-book store in Andover.

Fall 1989. The shop is owned by a very good friend, so I am hanging around like a member of the family, thumbing through books and talking to the clerk, Jane, when a customer comes in and with a credit card buys a biography of Auden and tapes of Vivaldi and Chopin. Both Jane and I are surprised to hear him give his address as Broadway in Lawrence.

Not a typical Lawrencian, to be sure. (No more than I am or ever was or will be.) He's in his late thirties or forties. Is he middle-class like me? Or a working-class man with erudite tastes? I can't tell. His nondescript clothing provides no clue, and I can't get a good look at his face: he has his back to me as he conducts his transaction with Jane. Maybe if he'd say a few more words. Our speech gives us away.

As if reading my mind, Jane tries to strike up a conversation. Looking beyond him to me, she exclaims, "He's from your town!" as if it were hundreds of miles away.

Brightly I say, "I'm from Lawrence, too. Don't you wish we had a bookstore like this there?"

"It's close enough," he replies coolly, and walks out.

Why the snub? Is he merely shy? Or is there more to it? Why is he treating me like someone who lives in Andover? It's bad enough when, traveling between Lawrence and the Andovers (between one social class and the other), I feel like a person with dual citizenship; this guy has made me feel as though I have none.

THE FEAR of getting caught between worlds—of feeling as if you belong *nowhere*—isn't this what keeps so many people "in their place," which often translates into "where they started from"? Isn't it what might have but didn't prevent my father from leaving carpentry for the town of Greenwich bureaucracy when he switched careers in the sixties? Yet Dad, who gradually learned the language of the architects and attorneys who came to his office at the Building Department with their upscale clients' plans and pleas, *did* sometimes try to hide his polish when he was around those he had left behind in the building trades. "I should have went," I have heard him say to certain people, though he was the one who always corrected me when, as a kid, I said "these kind" or "It's me." He knows English grammar perfectly, but sometimes chooses not to use it, if he doesn't want people to feel their own lack of polish. My mother, who never played this game (she taught us to call our knee scrapes "lacerations," much to my aunt Anne's amazement), claims that when Dad talks on the phone, she can tell the social station of the caller from the way he speaks.

Is it hypocritical for my father to customize his speech this way, a kind of lie? Or is it the way he keeps in touch with "where he started from"? A little of each, I'd say.

Sometimes I find myself telling middle-class acquaintances the "truth" about my working-class family background. I do it most often to correct the assumptions people tend to make when I say I'm from Greenwich; for to leave it at that, without clarification, would be a kind of lie. Wouldn't it?

Do I also make this "admission" because I think it reveals something about me—how far I've come? Or, conversely, because it's a handy excuse—the reason I haven't gone further? I suspect that, if they're honest, many Lawrencians who are now Andoverites would admit to making a comparable couplet

of unspoken statements with the words: "You know, my grandparents worked in the mills."

But how many of us make these pronouncements to people who still work with their hands? And what would our
words imply to them? "I understand"? But we don't. Intellec-
tually perhaps we do, but that's different from visceral knowledge. If we really understood, we wouldn't have to say it in so
many words: like my father's colloquial speech, it would simply
show. Like real friends or even strangers who happen to discover a shared experience, particularly an arduous one, we'd
speak *without* words; with only a look, we'd understand each
other as easily as we understand ourselves.

AFTER WE MOVED to Lawrence, Bob also started tailoring
his speech to suit his listener. I called him a chameleon, but
maybe instead I should have praised him for being a good
manager. For it was at the factory, where he had to communicate his wishes quickly and effectively to people with backgrounds very unlike his own, without stirring up resentment,
that he used different idioms and intonations.

I had a chance to see just how difficult it was to establish
rapport with some of the people at Akko when Bob asked me
once to help out at the office, doing filing and other tasks.
Shawn and Dee, the two regular office "girls," were friendly
enough, but I felt a gulf between them and me as they drank
their coffee, ate their doughnuts, smoked their cigarettes, and
not simply because I was the boss's wife. I know it would have
existed anyway.

Christmas 1986. I feel the tension between "us" and
"them" even more profoundly. I am standing in the middle of
a Lawrence kitchen in an apartment above a pizza parlor. The
home of someone who works in the factory, the place is
sparsely furnished despite the just-rented sofa and chairs in

the living room. A thin young woman known at the factory to use drugs is flirting with Bob. In an ironic twist, we are dressed nearly alike, in black skirts and white blouses. The lasagna goes untouched. There's a cocaine mirror under a washcloth in the bathroom, but mainly people are drinking beer, or Kahlúa and cream. A drunk is spitting words into my face, describing his expertise at making "doughnuts" (circular skid marks) in the road. (Some days later, he will slam into a car in the Akko parking lot.) This young man and his brother, who is also at the party, are both insistent, poking fingers at me: they come from *south* Lawrence, near the Andover line, not Lawrence downtown, not *north*, which is where all the mills are; which is where the Akko factory is; which is where my own house is; which is where this party is being held tonight.

"DRINKING on the job" was not infrequently the final notation Bob made on the index card he kept for each employee. "Unexcused absenteeism" was the most common reason given for why people were terminated, but the cards recorded other reasons that cumulatively tell a sad tale: "Resigned after violent argument with Maria"; "fired for poor, slow work and suspicion of vandalizing the men's room"; "back to P.R., abused by husband"; "fired for punching Rafael"; "left to care for ill brother"; "left midday w/o notice, assume resignation"; "fired—only 15 years old, lied on application" . . .

Bob made notations of another kind on scraps of paper he kept in his desk. They recorded the amounts of money he loaned many of his workers and the dates they paid him back; and repay him they did: only one woman disappeared without paying off her four-hundred-dollar debt.

The loans became part of an informal wage system, because the formal one was often inadequate: between five and ten dollars an hour, depending upon an employee's skill and length of service. Lawrence is not Detroit (or even Lawrence anymore, as it was in its heyday); nobody's unionized there, and if they were, Akko would fold. Yet, these wages are adequate only if a worker's personal life runs smoothly; if it doesn't—if an eviction, or an illness, or some other crisis comes—the scrambling for an infusion of cash before payday starts; when Bob was at Akko, it often led to him, the boss, who had a middle-class salary—not that he could help everyone who asked. His pay—something over forty thousand dollars by the time he left Akko—was far from munificent, though, of course, as a stockholder, it was possible that he would make much more if the business did well—a big "if." (In fact, he never did earn anything extra.)

TO WIN the lottery (Massachusetts Megabucks, it's called) or to deal drugs: are these the only routes to "the good life" left for Lawrencians today? As wages fall and living costs climb, it's easy to draw that conclusion, and the effects of such thinking can devastate a neighborhood like the one where I lived. Take the building next door to Louie's. When we first arrived in Lawrence, this triple-decker was inhabited, and constant trouble: guys with no shirts would come screaming out the front door at all hours of the night. Beer bottles came crashing. Windows were broken. A sign in the front picture window (an incongruous touch on a nineteenth-century building) read PO-LICE TAKE NOTICE NO LOITERING. Did any of these young men have jobs? Seeing them emerge from their front door groggy at noon, I doubted it. My suspicions were confirmed when Louie told me they used to buy gum and cigarettes from him with bills pulled from big wads of cash.

Finally, they were evicted, but no new tenants took their place. The building was emptied and later its absentee landlords, who apparently could no longer afford either the mortgage payments or the perpetual repairs, boarded it up and walked away. No bank seemed interested in claiming the wreckage. One night, walking to my car, parked at curbside, I saw some teenage kids spray-painting the plywood door. That was the first (and only) time I had ever seen graffiti in the moment of their application, and though I felt oddly privileged, I drove away hoping the kids wouldn't do my white picket fence (one of the rare fences in the neighborhood that isn't chainlink). As it turned out, they didn't.

I realized later, however, that the squiggles and flourishes were the insignia of a gang. Then I began to see those same wordless symbols on other buildings, abandoned and otherwise, up and down the street. This was not the handiwork of blue-collar kids, but of kids who have parents with no work, no hope.

WHEN BOB and I moved to Lawrence, we didn't really think about whether we'd stay forever. We didn't plan that far in advance. It was the way we decided to get married, too: "What if we got married?" "Sure." "Okay." (So we called our friend the Jesuit and here we are twenty-odd years later.)

We often heard it said in those days: "Lawrence can go either way at this point." And we didn't really think too hard about what people were saying or what they meant. Later, I admitted to myself that they meant "up" or "down." "Up" meant gentrification, more middle-class folks like us moving in, and I could picture that. But "down"? I couldn't imagine it. If anything, I thought people were simply being racist, saying that the city's complexion would change. Since we had just moved from a city with a very large black population, this prospect held no terror (though, of course, our black friends from Washington are middle-class).

Anyway, "up" seemed a safe bet. Emerson had just bought

land for the college, and I didn't realize that it could so easily be returned—sold back to the city for a dollar—even after millions had been spent.

Gradually, after that, "down" seemed the surer shot. And we began to see how easily Lawrence could devolve from a working-class world to an underclass one; in fact, there were signs—like the graffiti—that the change was already under way. By the time we moved out, Louie's itself, after a series of new owners went out of business, was abandoned, too.

IN THE *Eagle-Tribune*, I regularly see ads like this one:

> St. Jude's Novena. May the Sacred Heart of Jesus be adored, glorified, loved and preserved throughout the world now and forever. Sacred Heart of Jesus, pray for us. St. Jude, pray for us. Say this prayer 9 times a day, by the 8th day your prayer will be answered. My prayers have been answered. Publication must be promised. Signed C.F.G.

Could even St. Jude, worker of miracles—patron saint of lost causes—reverse the fortunes of Lawrence? To pray for this, though I no longer live there, would be no altruistic petition. For try as we may to isolate the acute social and economic ills that are devastating cities like Lawrence, the effects of these troubles have a way of vaulting even the most closely guarded perimeters. We know this, and yet it seems we do little except build the barriers higher.

I happened to see one of Rejean's daughters five years after her family's move away from Lawrence and in the month of our own departure. I was a few towns north of the city, killing time during the auction of some of our antique furniture, which we had to sell, because the new house we had bought was smaller than the one in Lawrence. Tracy was the cashier at a stationery store on the same block as the auction gallery,

I discovered when I went there to buy a newspaper. She was newly married to a short-order cook and they were living above the store (he was, in fact, also a runner at the auction). She was curious to know about the old neighborhood. When she heard that we were moving, her face brightened—I guess because she finally felt free to speak her mind. "It's really gone downhill, huh?" she said chummily. "My mother won't even drive through Lawrence anymore," she added. I imagined that Tracy couldn't wait to call her parents to say that even we had been defeated by the place.

No wonder I'm inclined to prayer.

For the bad times to end, for things to start looking up in Lawrence, for all the nation's Lawrences to recover a prideful and cohesive sense of themselves, we may well need something of a miracle. After all, it was just such a "miracle"—or so it was called—that started the American Industrial Revolution here in the Merrimack Valley.

PART II

BELL-TIME

CHAPTER 4

Streets

W HAT FAMOUS LAWRENCIAN missed becoming Vice President of the United States by only one vote?" The question was put to his listeners by the affable director of the Lawrence Public Library, Joseph R. Dionne, during a local radio call-in show he designed and hosted one summer afternoon to drum up publicity and perhaps philanthropy for his always-ailing institution. I knew the answer Joe wanted— Abbott Lawrence—though, being lazy, I didn't phone in. (As it turned out, no one did.) At the Whig party's convention in Philadelphia in 1848, Lawrence, who had been a member of the U.S. Congress from 1835 to 1837 and from 1839 to 1840, lost out to Millard Fillmore in the race to be Zachary Taylor's running mate.

Actually, of course, Lawrence missed a chance to be *President*, since Taylor died of cholera morbus sixteen months after taking office. And Abbott Lawrence never really was a Lawrencian. Though a street is named for him—Lawrence Street (on which the library sits)—and though the city itself is his (and his brothers') namesake, he never lived there. Nor did any of the other Boston businessmen who, along with Abbott, Amos, and Samuel Lawrence, founded the city and for whom streets are also named: among them, Appleton Way for Nathan Appleton; Jackson Street and Jackson Terrace for Patrick Tracy

Jackson; Storrow Street and Storrow Terrace (as well as sorry-looking Storrow Park) for Charles S. Storrow.

In all, about a dozen men, possessors of some of the oldest and most distinguished family names in New England, put up $1 million for the initial investment. At the time, it was something new to pool one's money with that of others, as they did; they called themselves the Essex Company and named Abbott Lawrence their president (probably because his investment of $100,000 was twice that of anyone else). Striking their deal over dinner on March 20, 1845, they formed one of the first corporations in America and, unfortunately for Lawrence, one that never for a moment intended to spend its profits in the city where those profits were made.

Charles Storrow, not Abbott Lawrence, was appointed the Essex Company's resident manager; in 1853, he was elected the city's first mayor by the voting few (3,066 male taxpayers, aged twenty-one or over, out of a total population of 12,147). But I doubt his family lived there with him while he supervised the building of Lawrence and later briefly governed it; even if they did, no one would ever mistake this well-known Boston engineer for a Lawrencian. (Nor his wife: née Lydia Cabot, of the Cabots who spoke only to the Lodges, who spoke only to God.) In any case, no Storrow family ever established itself in the city, and there are no Storrows in the local phone book today. As for the Lawrences, there are four in the 1994–1995 city directory, and one of them is an African-American friend of mine with, as far as he knows, no claim to any family connection with Abbott Lawrence.

THE PRINCIPALS of the Essex Company ate their kickoff meal in Lowell. Ten miles to the southwest, ten miles closer to Boston, that other textile mill town on the Merrimack (where the noisy working weave room is now part of a museum) had been developed in 1822 by many of the same men who had decided to found Lawrence; its streets bear their names, just as Lawrence's do; and its namesake, Francis Cabot Lowell, put his mark on Lawrence as surely as he put it on Lowell. He put it, in fact, upon the whole country: a successful merchant from a branch of the prominent family (his father, John Lowell, was one of the drafters of the U.S. Constitution), Francis Cabot Lowell is credited—or discredited—with bringing the factory system to America.

Before any textile mills had been built on this side of the Atlantic, if cloth wasn't handwoven at home, it was imported, usually from England, where, since 1803, factories equipped with power looms had been unfurling mile after mile of cotton and wool cloth. No textile machinery, plans, or models were permitted to leave the country, however, and neither could skilled textile workers. That is why, in 1811, Francis Cabot Lowell decided to go to England and commit his infamous act of industrial piracy, which not only broke John Bull's monopoly but also changed the nature of work in America, and America itself, for good.

Lowell was in his mid-thirties when he arranged the trip that his biographers so delight in recounting: how he cunningly made his journey resemble a family pleasure tour by taking his wife and two young sons with him; and how, at their stop in Lancashire, he persuaded some mill owners to let him observe their machines in operation. Imagine him with his hands clasped behind his back as he obeyed the mill rule that he take no notes and make no sketches; imagine him, also, as, homeward-bound, he waited on the quay for the British to search his luggage, twice, to no avail: Lowell, who had entered Harvard's class of 1793 at age fourteen, carried the precious cargo out the factory gates and across the ocean in his prodigious memory.

During his stay in Lancashire, Lowell had gotten an eyeful

of something else besides the new machines. The ragged, lice-infested workers, many of them children, made a deep impression, as did the beggars and thieves living among them, and the whole horrible scene had started him wondering: Did using machines to do work previously done by hand somehow curdle people morally? Would the power loom breed similar degradation and social ills in America? He was determined that it would not. And so he built a moral vision into his plan to pioneer the new technology back home.

He established the country's first textile mill—the prototypical American factory—in 1814, in Waltham, Massachusetts, on the Charles River. The technology worked. But would the rest of his plan? Lowell died by the time his business associates founded the full-fledged mill city they named for him, where brick boardinghouses went up alongside the brick mills. The famous Lowell "mill girls," all of them single and most of them between ages fifteen and twenty-five, lived in those dormitories with a watchful housemother, who cooked their meals and made sure they were tucked in when the clock struck their curfew hour.

It is widely recognized that Lowell's plan called for the employment of virginal young women because he thought mill owners should hire only those whose moral behavior they had the best chance of regulating; it is less well known that Lowell believed mill employees should be temporary workers only. Toil in a factory for life? That would be akin to a life sentence to prison. No wonder the morals of British mill workers were low-down. Accordingly, Lowell's mills would employ a succession of innocents, one group following another into the factory "finishing schools," where, at least initially, four and a half years was the average tenure.

The mill owners monitored the moral lives of their mill girls so assiduously because these men of God felt responsible for them—in their view, it would have been un-American to feel anything else. But the precautions also made good business sense. After all, single females in the mid-nineteenth century did not ordinarily live apart from their parents, who needed to be assured that their daughters would be safe before letting them go. Never mind that factory girls earned more than the schoolteachers of their day; if the girls ran the risk of being "sullied," few parents would have been willing to put their Sarahs and Abigails aboard the wagons that cruised the New England countryside looking for recruits.

And 99.9 percent of the girls apparently did remain pure. While the heroine of Judith Rossner's 1980 novel, *Emmeline*, is a Lowell mill girl who gets pregnant out of wedlock and leaves the city in secrecy and shame, the worst reported of the typical *real* mill girl was that she'd been caught reading her Bible instead of tending her loom. Nancy Zaroulis's 1979 novel, *Call the Darkness Light*, captures precisely (and somewhat satirically) the chaste image of the Lowell girls in this fictionalized account of President Andrew Jackson's visit to the city then being billed as "the eighth wonder of the civilized world":

"The proprietors of the mills paraded their female operatives for Old Hickory and he marveled to see them, a mile and more of lovely women, all in white, each carrying a green parasol, preceded by a banner bearing the motto: 'Protection of American Industry.' He enjoyed himself immensely, so it was said. Never had he imagined such a spectacle. They walk! They talk! And they spin and weave twelve hours a day for the greater profit of the Corporations! And glory to God, hardly a one has lost her virtue."

Not only were they virtuous; some even were clever. In 1842, a minister began publishing their writings in a magazine called the *Lowell Offering*. Frequent contributor Lucy Larcom became famous for her inspirational observations of mill-girl life and her word portraits of heroines like Joan of Arc. In her unpublished memoirs, Elizabeth Sweeney Schneider, a Lawrencian born in 1854, reports that Larcom's name came up in her childhood games of "Authors" as frequently as Longfellow's and Whittier's. Today there is a park named after her in Lowell. Whittier, a lifelong friend of Larcom, was annoyed by the manner in which she had achieved her fame, however: why was it so amazing to people, he rhetorically asked, that essays could be written and cloth woven by the same set of fingers?

THE *Lowell Offering* ceased publication in 1845, the same year Lawrence was founded. Coincidence? No doubt. But the fact is, there would never be anything like the *Lowell Offering* in Lawrence. Though the Lowell experiment had been not only a moral success but a financial one as well, crucial changes were introduced into the new project downstream. And though these changes would be differences in degree, in scale, the end result would be an alteration in kind, as occurs when a drizzle becomes a downpour, a trickle becomes a torrent.

In Lowell, there had been good pay and high morale as a result of mill-owner scruples; Lawrence was strictly a money-making venture with no noblesse about it. Many a girl from the hinterlands of New England had yearned to go to the exciting new city of Lowell, where freedom from the drudgery of farmwork awaited her; in Lawrence, a new kind of drudgery was being invented (actually, it was old, the very Dickensian model Francis Cabot Lowell had abhorred, reincarnated in the New World after all), and many would suffer and some would even die as a result of it.

That nothing more noble than profit was intended in Lawrence may perhaps be discerned from the outset: in the 1830s, Essex Company agents quietly began purchasing plots of farmland along the Merrimack north of Lowell without telling the farmers and landowners who sold to them what was planned for the acreage. When their shopping spree was over, they had title to 2,300 lush acres on both sides of the river—two and a half square miles of Andover (which included North Andover in those days) and three and a half square miles of Methuen. Lawrence, the legal and political jurisdiction, didn't exist yet— not until the Essex Company petitioned the state legislature to make the new territory a separate municipality. The investors were politically well connected and the petition passed handily. Lawrence was incorporated, though not without loud protests from the two border towns—a brouhaha it amuses me to imagine, considering what the reaction in these border towns would be today if anyone suggested that the two ribs of contemporary Lawrence be returned to their former bodies.

The area measured only about half the size of Lowell, which is some twelve miles square, but ambitious plans were made for it. The men of the Essex Company had dammed the river in Lowell; they would dam it in Lawrence, too, but much more massively. The Great Stone Dam is what they called their construction, and while it doesn't look all that "great" to twentieth-century eyes, it was a colossus in its time, built of huge granite blocks set at an angle from riverbank to riverbank—a wall spanning a third of a mile and holding back water calculated to produce 10,000 horsepower.

The dam wasn't the only oversized construction in Lawrence. Lowell's mills were big; Lawrence's mills would be bigger, and more numerous, with less space between them. At the start, eleven were built there—compared with Lowell's initial two—plus a machine shop and foundry for repairs. As to their relative size: one of Lowell's early mills was named the Merrimack, for the river; two of Lawrence's were named for oceans—the Atlantic and the Pacific.

The new mills were built big because mill machinery had

grown bigger, and heavier, in the years since the Lowell factories had gone up—and because ambition and the pursuit of
profit required that the latest machines be used. This was
progress. It was also the death knell for the social vision that
had been the other legacy of Francis Cabot Lowell.

In the beginning, mill work was suited to girls who had
done hand weaving at home, delicately. The new machinery
required more lifting and maneuvering of heavy metal parts,
so men had to be employed; the mill girls would work alongside them, and no longer be quite so innocent. Some new girls
were Irish immigrants, and mill owners weren't as concerned
about the moral uplift of them. In fact, as profits accrued, the
owners forgot about morals altogether. Boardinghouse construction, which lagged behind mill construction from the start
in Lawrence, was eventually abandoned: even if they had
wanted to, the mill owners couldn't have kept up with the demand. The girls were on their own (as they were, increasingly,
in Lowell, too), and many never did return to their families.

Like industrial-age machinery itself, which transferred
power from water turbines to leather belts to gear teeth, these
technical changes bred still others, even more nefarious. The
switch from cam-driven to crank-driven looms, for example,
made the lint fly faster and thicker—so the rates of respiratory
ailments increased. Decibel levels also rose. Mill owners
lengthened the work week from seventy hours to eighty-four.
Speedups increased machine speed; stretch-outs increased the
number of machines a worker tended. In the 1820s, one
worker tended one or two machines; now one worker tended
three or four, racing back and forth among them. They were
also earning less. And if you couldn't keep up, if you made
mistakes, your already-shrunken pay would be smaller still.

But management made mistakes, too—big ones, which
were magnified by the massive scale of their operations. To
keep the new mills running required the wool shorn from

millions of sheep, the cotton grown on scores of plantations from Norfolk to Natchez. When sheep got sick, when weevils struck, the effect was financial disaster.

The panic of 1857 affected the whole country, but Lawrence found itself in particularly serious trouble. Two of the big mills failed outright; two more, the Atlantic and the Pacific, came close to failing. The foundry also failed, and its treasurer, J. H. W. Paige, knew why: "Two years' experience and observation have brought me to the conclusion that, while Lawrence needed a machine shop of moderate capacity, the wants of neither that city nor the vicinity nor the country required none of so great cost and such vast extent. . . . This company started on a scale which nothing but long-continued and well-established success could justify or bear. . . . The result of all is a debt. . . . The interest on that debt and the interest on and deterioration of machinery on hand absorb all the profit that can be made."

Lawrence's first newspaper publisher, J. F. C. Hayes, agreed with Paige. "It is easy for a joint stock company to build a gigantic factory, fill it with costly machinery, and say to themselves, we will make this, and we will make that, and above all, we will make money," he wrote in his *History of the City of Lawrence, Massachusetts* (1868). "But are they sure of that? Does the history of the large corporation in Lawrence not show most conclusively that these calculations have been illusive?"

Ill-conceived calculations of another kind were the cause of the literal collapse of the Pemberton Mill that terrible day in January 1860; yet the tragedy was as much the result of the ambitiousness of Lawrence's absentee investors as the financial failures were. Engineered by Essex Company member Charles Bigelow, who also engineered the dam, the building was eighty-four feet wide, nearly twice the width of the older factories in Lowell. The design meant that windows had to be especially large so light could reach the innermost rows of workers at their looms; larger windows meant weaker walls. Moreover, the vast floors were supported not by traditional columns but by newfangled cast-iron pillars—a brittle substance at best—and the record shows that as early as 1854 the Pemberton's pillars were discovered to be defective. The mill owners gambled that the floors would nonetheless be able to bear the weight of the heavy machines, even machines that violently hurled hundreds of shuttles, like miniature torpedoes, back and forth, hour after hour, day after day. When the gamble was lost, the disaster landed hastily built Lawrence on the cover of *Harper's Weekly*, which showed a single smokestack still standing like a cenotaph amid a gruesome rubble of brick and blood, broken metal and bodies.

The local coroner, Dr. William Lamb, summoned a jury and, after hearing the evidence of eyewitnesses and experts, ruled that the cause of the disaster had been the use of pillars too weak to support the immense weight placed upon them. Charles Bigelow was cited for "negligence" and censured; beyond that, responsibility wasn't assigned. Certainly no one discussed hubris or the overlarge visions of the men who had built the mill; and a new Pemberton Mill was erected the following year on the same site. But if its designers were not sentimental, they seem to have learned a lesson: the "new" Pemberton still stands solidly today, a documents-storage warehouse, at the edge of the Merrimack.

In 1868, Lawrence was featured by *Harper's* again, this time with a woodcut by Winslow Homer in the centerfold. Called *Bell-Time*, it depicts a scene that is a far cry from the initial social vision of Mr. Lowell: textile workers—men, women, and small children—shuffling along the canal with their empty lunch pails at the end of their exhausting day. The caption lays upon this city's shoulders the woes of every other mill town on every other river in the Northeast: ". . . the same faces, the same costumes, the same characters may be seen at 'bell-time' in the streets of every great manufacturing town in New England. . . ."

Look closely and you will see a ghostly figure among the crowd, an older woman with a crooking finger; she seems to be trying to engage in conversation the startled younger woman walking ahead of her. What is this all about? Is she trying to warn her of something? Early death perhaps? The accompanying text doesn't say. In fact, it doesn't illuminate the scene at all; instead, it consists of a rehash of Dickens's outdated *American Notes* (1842), which guardedly praised Lowell and its mill girls. This is a shame: if the magazine had meant to make a political statement by running the print in the first place, the editors missed their chance to make it much more forcefully. They could have commented that the short-lived mill-girl era, shamelessly patriarchal though it was, had evolved from good intentions into a system that, just like Britain's, was creating a permanent working class—one, in fact, that could be viewed as even sorrier than England's, for, increasingly, it was made up of immigrants who had supposed that in coming to the land of the free, where all men were created equal, they had left the Old World behind them.

AS THE WORKING CLASS was born, so was an American upper class born from profits made by the Essex Company's owners. Francis Cabot Lowell and his business partners had hoped to forestall this division; Alexis de Tocqueville, whose American tour of 1831–1832 took him briefly to Lowell, anticipated its inevitability. *Democracy in America* warns that workers who confined themselves to earning wages with factory skills and who forgot how to build their own houses, grow their own food, and weave their own cloth would be "weaker, more limited, and more dependent." Even in the thriving democracy that America professed to be, the mill worker assigned a certain task would simultaneously be assigned a low position in society that would not easily be surmounted. Moreover, Tocqueville observed, while "industrial science constantly lowers the standing of the working class, it raises that of the masters." The minds of the men who ran these huge enterprises were being stretched, he warned, even as the minds of those who worked the machinery shrank: "While the workman confines his intelligence more and more to studying one single detail, the master daily embraces a vast field in his vision, and his mind expands as fast as the other's contracts." Soon, Tocqueville predicted, the former would need only bodily strength, while the latter would need "almost genius."

And so the Frenchman urged all who called themselves "friends of democracy" to be vigilant, to watch closely this American "manufacturing aristocracy" made up of rich, well-educated men who had been attracted by "the scale of the efforts." "For if ever again permanent inequality of conditions and aristocracy make their way into the world," Tocqueville wrote, "it will have been by that door that they entered."

Despite Tocqueville's admonitions, enter they did, and by the very door he'd warned us to guard, according to Robert F. Dalzell, Jr.'s book *Enterprising Elites: The Boston Associates and the World They Made* (1987). While some scholars struggle to prove that class distinctions don't exist in America, this professor of American Studies at Williams College makes a convincing case that a class system not only thrives but that the Boston textile entrepreneurs helped create it.

"Certainly they themselves never said so and would have resisted such an interpretation if confronted with it," Dalzell writes. "It smacked, after all, of a kind of class consciousness few members of the group could have acknowledged with anything but anxiety. They were accustomed to thinking of themselves as prosperous merchants with important common interests. In their quest for security for themselves and their children the perils they confronted had been those of the marketplace—impersonal and anonymous. They even, for the present, continued to admit newcomers into their ranks with surprising frequency."

But year by year, as Dalzell shows, they reinvested their immense textile profits in real estate, banking, railroads, and insurance, hoping to preserve "fortunes already made, positions already won. . . . As joint ventures grew in number and scale, as the mechanisms of collective control bound members of the group more and more tightly together, and above all as plans were made to transmit the benefits—and the power—to subsequent generations, something very like a distinct class evolved."

Lowell, Appleton, and the others had feared that the factory system would unmoor traditional society, causing social upheaval and strife; and it did. They had hoped to industrialize America while preserving society as they knew it; and they did—but for those in their world only. As Dalzell's book concludes, mill owners made the country more secure "for people like themselves" but harsher for those outside their closed circle. Lawrence didn't just grow a working class, then; it grew a leisure class, too—people living elsewhere who were blessed with comfort and opportunity *because* Lawrencians were so work-weary. And it happened because the mill owners, living elsewhere themselves, often ignored the moral and social costs of their enterprises.

WHILE MILL OWNERS may have remorselessly ignored the plight of their own workers, slavery was one moral issue they couldn't disregard. Historically, it's a southern shame, but the men who made their fortunes in northern textile towns made them on the backs of African slaves as surely as did the plantation owners below the Mason-Dixon line. The "lords of the loom" and the "lords of the lash" (twin terms coined by abolitionist Charles Sumner in a speech he gave in Worcester, Massachusetts, in 1848) were doubles. As Ralph Waldo Emerson somberly wrote in his journal on May 23, 1846: "Cotton thread holds the union together; unites John C. Calhoun and Abbott Lawrence. Patriotism for holidays and summer evenings, with music and rockets, but cotton thread is the union."

Apparently, the mill owners were able to square with their moral selves the contradiction inherent in the idea of condemning slavery while being economically dependent on it. Abbott Lawrence's nephew Amos Adams Lawrence, for example, on a tour of the South a decade before the Civil War, wrote that he hoped this "inexhaustible source of wealth [i.e., cotton] could forever be diverted to our city"; yet, he is known as an abolitionist. The Massachusetts Emigrant Aid Company, which he generously funded, provided a flood of Free Staters to the new territory of Kansas. The city of Lawrence, Kansas, was named for him in 1854.

It's also true that, when Senator Calhoun proposed an alliance between "gentlemen" of the North and South, whereby the southerners would help fight labor agitation in return for Northern help in fighting the abolitionists, the Essex Company members declined; however, Abbott Lawrence, Nathan Appleton, and other politically powerful Yankee textile tycoons approved the entrance of Texas into the union as a slave state and supported the Compromise of 1850, with its rigorous Fugitive Slave Act.

When the fighting started, Lawrence was Union, of course, enthusiastically sending men and money to the front as its factories churned out cloth for government-issue blankets, working itself out of its economic slump. Lawrence memoirist Elizabeth Sweeney Schneider remembers that Union war songs—ballads printed on cheap paper, with fancy borders—

were displayed in bunches on the walls of a stationery store on Essex Street and that General Ulysses S. Grant and his family visited the city and were tendered a banquet at city hall (the plate that he ate from was auctioned off for ten dollars). Every time there was a Union victory, cannons were fired on Lawrence's common, even at night.

When the war was over, the soldiers returned "sunburnt and shabby," Schneider tells us. She watched them being welcomed on the common. Some wore the gray Confederate uniforms they had taken from the enemy, which struck her as ironic. What I find more ironic is that the men who had fought to free the slaves came home to a city where the term *wage-slave* was being defined.

THE ESSEX COMPANY gave Lawrence its common. Seventeen and a half acres of parkland in the middle of downtown, it is crisscrossed with paths pleasantly lined with big old trees. A busy little playground sits at the Jackson Street end of it; a well-worn softball field lies closer to Lawrence Street. The high school band holds its practices there, with drumbeats and trumpet blasts echoing off city hall. It is the setting for the annual Hispanic Festival, too, which yearly brings a protest from the old Italians who still live in and around the Three Saints Festival area nearby; they claim it's noisy, though they don't seem to mind the noise of their own feast. (An Irish-American friend of mine observed sardonically, "The Three Saints are very quiet saints.") There is also a Labor Day celebration held in memory of the great strike, an annual weekend-long event that was first held in 1985 and that has attracted such headliners as Pete Seeger, Arlo Guthrie, and Judy Collins (they are virtually the only celebrities who have been to Lawrence in years). Since the 1940s, Campagnone Common has been the official name of this public space, in honor of three brothers killed in World War II. Lawrence's Latinos call it *el parque de las ardillas*—the park of the squirrels.

I suppose Lawrencians should be thankful for this verdant crumb tossed to it so long ago with the sole stipulation that three hundred dollars be spent yearly on its upkeep and that no laundry be hung on its iron-fence perimeter (which has since been replaced by granite curbing), for there is precious little other open green space in the city. In the 1960s and 1970s, however, some people, hoping to revive downtown shopping on nearby Essex Street, Lawrence's main drag, proposed that the common be paved and made into a giant parking lot. Even today, that desperate idea is sometimes reintroduced at public meetings.

ESSEX STREET parallels the curving flow of the river, though the water is hidden from view, first by a solid wall of office buildings and storefronts and then by a second wall comprised of the monolithic mills. (The best view you're apt to get of the Merrimack is through a factory window.) As I write this, however, many of the storefronts are empty—boarded up, posted with real-estate agents' signs—and trash rustles around in their doorways. Some have been leveled by arson fires, leaving weedy gaps. Not a few of the remaining structures are storefront churches, their signs hand-lettered: YGLESIA DE DIOS. A temporary, flea-market feeling prevails in some of the newer places that have cropped up: for sale, in unruly heaps, are throwaway foil cooking pans, toilet seats, and bedding—all the things you would need to start a household if you arrived in Lawrence with nothing. An establishment called Rent-A-Center, another of the newer, slicker businesses, will lease you just about anything, from a refrigerator to a love seat, for extortionary amounts a week. While I was standing in front of that place one morning, a taxi driver pulled up and leapt out of his cab. "They're not open?" he asked, then pushed his check through the mail slot in the door. "That's better for me. I'm late, and it costs more if you're late."

Downtown is not all cause for despair. There are also some new businesses with a bit of genuine flair—for example, La Moda, selling Latino-styled party clothes for women and children, bright and frilly and stiff with crinoline, and in all the colors of tropical birds; Humberto's, a Latino barbershop, with its shiny back-and-white linoleum-tile floor; take-out food shops selling fried sweet potatoes, fried bananas, and pig-thigh soup; and a company that wires money to or from "N.Y., Dom. Rep., P.R." There is even a little Latino grocery store that delivers—providing exactly the service that the old Irish, Polish, and Italian markets used to provide to their customers.

But this is very different from the Essex Street that many people describe when they're trying to impress you with details of Lawrence's "glory days" two or three decades ago; the Essex Street where, on a Tuesday or a Friday night, "you'd have to walk in the street to avoid the crowds!" Wistfully they will catalog the full-service department stores that used to be—the Sears Roebuck, for instance, where their father bought them their first bike or the family's Ping-Pong table (the building is now rented by the Social Security Administration). Or they will speak of smaller specialty shops, like one called The Taylor Shop, where they got their going-away dress as a young bride. Or they will talk of vanished butchers and bakers, and of walking downtown with their mother for lunch at the diner-style Blue Bonnet Restaurant.

In 1991, a researcher named Kim Stevenson conducted a revealing survey of attitudes toward Essex Street. At the time a graduate student at the Massachusetts Institute of Technology's Department of Urban Studies and Planning who was interning at Lawrence's Planning and Community Development Office, Stevenson polled Latinos and non-Latinos on their impressions of the main shopping thoroughfare. From the non-Latinos, the overwhelming majority of comments were negative: "Essex Street is dead and dying." "I don't like Essex Street. I'm afraid of being attacked. It's depressing." "I do most of my shopping at the malls. Even if the same stores were in downtown Lawrence, I would not shop on Essex Street. I don't like downtown Lawrence. The crime rate is high and there are a lot of strange characters walking around. Lawrence probably had a beautiful downtown at one time, but not anymore. It has been ruined. It's too bad." The Latinos, on the other hand, described Essex Street in overwhelmingly positive terms: "nice," "clean," "relaxing," "lovely," "quiet," and "pretty." "One of my favorite pastimes during the day is to walk along Essex Street from Union Street to Broadway," a Latino respondent said; interestingly, it's the same route former mayor Buckley has taken on his daily constitutional for years without incident, though he says many people have told him he is crazy to walk in downtown Lawrence. (The only Latino polled by Stevenson who thought Essex Street was "scary" described an episode of harassment by the local police.)

Failing to see that the new Latino-oriented shops are heralding a new era (or maybe seeing it but wishing that they didn't), members of Lawrence's dwindling old guard tend to deny that maybe it's the few remaining businesses hanging on from the days gone by that are out of synch now. Take the Blue Bonnet Restaurant, put out of business in 1993 by a trash fire set in the alley behind it. One noontime shortly before it burned, I and a friend whose husband had lunched there as a boy took a walk down there. Peering inside, we saw that it was poorly lit and pretty dingy, with a few customers eating at the counter. A heavily iced birthday cake—its white buttercream frosting yellowed, crumbs piled around its paper doily base like sand—was on display behind the greasy front window. We were about to step inside when my friend groaned and directed my attention to the cake again. I looked closer and saw what she had seen: the tiny ants that had made those crumbs busily tunneling, feasting on a treat that had once been for sale.

IN 1991, the modern-day Essex Company gave Lawrencians another gift of sorts. Yes, even after the textile industry died, the company lived on, continuing to operate the dam, selling the water power and, lately (from the time of the energy crisis of the late 1970s), the hydroelectric power it generates. In 1986, however, it was bought by a firm called Consolidated Hydro, Inc.; it was then that plans were made to bestow the so-called gift, for Consolidated, which operates some seventy hydropower plants in fourteen states around the country, wasn't at all interested in owning hundreds of Lawrence's back alleyways, garbage-strewn and deeply rutted, to which the Essex Company still retained title, and they set their attorney to work getting rid of them. Fearing liability in personal-injury lawsuits, they hoped to turn them over to the city or to the owners of abutting property, neither of which wanted them, of course. Then, lo and behold, fortune smiled: the attorney discovered a right-of-way law from the 1970s that allowed Consolidated to claim that the Essex Company had forfeited ownership of those alleys years before and that they already belonged to the abutters or the city. So the company's latest gift was not really a gift at all, only the finalizing of an abandonment.

Though it has rid itself of the alleys, Consolidated still owns the canals and most of the roadways alongside them. One of these is Island Street, which runs parallel to the north canal. A sign posted at one end of it reads WARNING / PRIVATE PROPERTY / TRAVEL AT YOUR OWN RISK / THE ESSEX COMPANY. The roadway is so worn in places that the original cobblestone paving shows beneath the blacktop, the depressions sometimes filled with oily rainwater. Old train tracks also show through in some places. During Lawrence's textile days, cotton and wool used to come by rail; almost daily the trains pulled up directly alongside the mills and were unloaded as fast as men could work.

A couple of old mills still stand edgily on Island Street, facing the murky canal. A women's clothing manufacturer has renovated the one that is called the Kundhardt Mills, and that's a hopeful sign. But during the long years before the building was bought and the work began, it was Labell's Furniture, a dingy warehouse of cheap sofas and dinettes, its windows blocked by illegal signage proclaiming WATER BED SALE.

Island Street is also the one you take to get to Grieco Brothers, a manufacturer of men's clothing, including fine Southwick suits (worn by Presidents Clinton, Bush, and Kennedy, the company claims). Here, in July 1991, there was a pitiful labor strike, organized by the Amalgamated Clothing and Textile Workers Union—pitiful by any city's standards, much less Lawrence's. Three hundred people walked out; a handful at a time listlessly showed their signs to the passing traffic; three weeks after the action began, all three hundred walked back, having agreed to a 4 percent wage cut and the withholding of payments to their pension plan for a year. When the year ended, neither the wage rate nor the pension-fund payment was restored.

A wooden fence runs along the canal side of Island Street. It is broken-down, at one point no fence at all. A car could easily drive through it into the canal. Up and down both sides of both canals, north and south, it's the same story—encroaching weeds, decaying wooden locks, rust-frozen gears. A tubular bowstring bridge stretches across the north waterway, graceful even in its decay. According to the North Andover textile museum, it was built in 1864 and is one of the last of its kind in the United States.

In the late 1960s, Tom Leavitt initiated the first survey of historic sites and buildings in Lawrence and assigned his chief curator the task of doing the research and fieldwork necessary to put the Great Stone Dam and its canals and bowstring bridge on the National Register of Historic Places. The dam was finally listed in 1977; the canals and their structures remain unprotected.

SPRING 1992. I have come to the gatekeeper's house at the dam, just off busy Broadway—Lawrence's other main street, which runs perpendicular to Essex—to find a representative of the modern-day Essex Company. Up here, close to the dam, there's a nautical feel. The waterfall throws mist into the air, and the little Greek Revival gatekeeper's house looks like a transplant from a New England port. Built in 1846, it is one of the oldest structures in the city, its clapboards painted gray, with white trim. In another city—or, more likely, town (one of Lawrence's bordering towns, for example)—a sign would be affixed to the side of this building noting its historical significance: HERE IS WHERE LAWRENCE BEGAN. Schoolchildren would tramp through it, or at least past it. But that doesn't happen in Lawrence, and there is no sign of any kind posted on the building. (In fact, by law there should be a sign and more. As part of their 1979 federal licensing agreement, Consolidated's subsidiary, Lawrence Hydroelectric Associates, promised to erect a visitors' center of some kind near the falls; it's been in the so-called planning stages for all these years.)

I've been told to ask for Mel Lezberg, and here he is, bent over a table, looking at a plan. A slender, middle-aged mechanical engineer dressed in workman's clothes, he strikes me as someone you wouldn't want to come to with excuses. His title is regional manager for Consolidated; he is, as well, vice president of the Essex Company, and he lets me in on a secret.

"The secret to what we're doing is economies of scale," he says. "If you're running a single plant, you need a specific organization to do it. That same organization could probably run a number of plants. So that's really what Consolidated is all about."

I mention the rickety fencing along the canal on Island Street.

"Island Street is a private street," he says. "We sold a piece of that not too long ago, and we're in the process of giving the balance to the city." The company's motive is not largesse, of course, but the same that sent it looking to get rid of the alleyways it owned: fear of being sued.

And where is Consolidated headquartered?

"Greenwich, Connecticut," Lezberg tells me.

My old hometown. Why am I not surprised? I ask for the name of the president of the company and his office address. The zip code is my old zip code, my parents' zip code still.

I write to him—his name is Olof Nelson—to ask what he knows about what he has bought. Does he know the history of the Essex Company? Does he know the history of Lawrence?

"I am flattered by your interest," Olof Nelson writes back, but brushes me off, saying he knows only what he has heard "via word of mouth" about Lawrence.

I write him again, asking if that means it is correct to assume that he has never visited the city.

He scrawls in the margin of my letter: "No it is not correct."

I get the Dun & Bradstreet report on Consolidated for 1991, the year they gave their alleyways to the city, and see that, according to the document, it lost $500,000 in the twelve-month period. So much for economies of scale, especially in the recessionary early nineties.

Maybe that's one reason why the company has not yet fulfilled the part of its 1979 federal licensing agreement that mandated a visitors' center at the dam. In the *Eagle-Tribune*, Mel Lezberg has been quoted as saying that the location of the center is set but the time of its opening and the cost and the details of the exhibit have not been worked out. (As this book goes to press, on the eve of the dam's 150th birthday and nearly seventeen years after the federal license was issued, the visitors' center is finally nearing completion.)

I call my parents and ask them to look up Olof Nelson in the Greenwich phone book. I am curious about his home life. Does he actually live in Greenwich? And if so, what part? Backcountry? By the shore, so well protected in most parts of town by private roads, private property? (I lived within walking distance of the beach for all the seventeen years I lived in Greenwich but never once put my toes into that nearby water.) Or does Olof Nelson live in one of the mansions closer to the main shopping district?

"Forty-four Patterson Avenue," says my dad. It's an in-town address that abuts the rolling green campus of Greenwich Academy, a private school for girls. "That means it's pretty ritzy—"

"I know the street," I tell him sharply.

CHAPTER 5

Heights

A S LUCK would have it (if luck is the word), the great famine in Ireland coincided exactly with the founding of Lawrence. The story has been told many times, but that doesn't make it any less grim: the potatoes, planted on such a huge scale and from seeds of so few strains, were diseased, but their condition wasn't immediately apparent at harvest time; and so the millions and millions of tubers were dug and stored. And then they rotted in their bins, oozing a putrid black liquid. People tried to eat them, and they died. Eat them or not, they died, unless they fled.

Between 1845 and 1849, more than two thousand Irish found their way to Lawrence, making up over a third of the city's total population. They were put to work immediately, for seventy to eighty cents a day—Yankees were paid a dollar—building the granite-faced dam and digging the canals, and then constructing the mills that would be powered by the river water. To house themselves, they erected shanties—rude shacks of scavenged wood scraps. Thoreau built his cabin at Walden Pond from parts of a dismantled shanty he bought for $4.25 from an Irishman named James Collins, who had worked on the Fitchburg Railroad.

Thoreau's shanty was held together with nails, however; the

shanties of the Irish in Lawrence were held together by sod, or more plainly, mud mixed and applied with bare hands. Though strictly one-room affairs, those dwellings could be as big as one hundred by twenty feet and house dozens of people. Generally, there was a fireplace for cooking and a chimney of sorts protruding from the roof. They could be found in great profusion in the fields near the dam or near where the common is now, in a wide, flat, open space called the Plains. South Lawrence, another place for shanties, was known in those years as "Dublin." These plots of land were not rent-free. The inhabitants leased them from—who else?—the Essex Company.

Patrick Sweeney, father of memoirist Elizabeth Sweeney Schneider, arrived in Lawrence from Ireland right at the start, when the city was one huge construction site, dust and sand blowing everywhere, blinding your eyes, clogging nose and ears, making food gritty. An "eminent lady writer" described it this way for a Boston newspaper in 1860:

> The City of Lawrence is unique in its way. It is notable for simoons that scorch and tempests that freeze you; . . . for unexpected corners where tornadoes lie in wait; for bleak, uncomfortable sidewalks; where winds and dust clouds chase you, dog you, confront you, strangle you, twist you, blind you, and turn your umbrella wrong side out; . . . for uncleared ruins, and mills that spring up in a night, for jaded faces and busy feet; for an air of youth and incompleteness at which you laugh, and a consciousness of growth and greatness which you respect.

It was also a place where you could work yourself to death. The Essex Company needed strong backs—and, for the moment, nobody cared to whom they belonged. This attitude accommodated the Irish, whose drinking and brawling were attributed to a flawed national character; post-traumatic stress syndrome, which was no doubt prevalent, since most of these economic refugees had lost family members in the famine, hadn't been invented.

Young Sweeney helped dig the north canal. At night, he slept in a shanty he had built on a knoll behind the common. During his first winter in Lawrence, he experienced some delay in getting paid for the work he'd done, so when he finally got what was owed him, it came in a lump sum. With it, he wisely decided to buy real estate. He bought it from the Essex Company, which, during its first ten years, periodically auctioned off parcels of Lawrence land at huge profits. Sweeney built tenements on his land and became a landlord. But though he might have been on his way to prosperity, he still kept a habit of his homeland: in his spare time, particularly in the early evening, until dark, he tended a garden patch in a vacant lot near the Spicket River, where he grew potatoes.

THE IRISH POTATO FAMINE occurred despite an abundance of other foods. Harvests of Irish grain went on as usual throughout the famine years—and as usual were exported to England. What have been euphemistically called "antiexport disturbances" occurred on the docks as the grain was loaded aboard ships set to sail. And the only surprising part about those riots is that there weren't more of them. But I imagine the Irish were hunger-weakened.

If Sweeney thought that by coming to the United States he had left his English enemies behind, he was mistaken. I tend to forget that all English immigrants who came to America didn't arrive on the *Mayflower*. In fact, many emigrated in the nineteenth century right along with the Irish. Some of these were the skilled textile workers who, in Francis Cabot Lowell's day, had been forbidden to leave the country. Now, as British textile factory jobs became scarcer and wages fell due to increased mechanization—to say nothing of the effects of the broken monopoly—no one stopped them. Maybe England was glad to see them go: in at least one English mill town— Huddersfield, northeast of Manchester—riots occurred when factory owners introduced machinery to replace the hand shears that workers had traditionally used to finish cloth.

The mills in Lawrence, on the other hand, were actively recruiting. The Pacific Mills, among others, not only guaranteed jobs; the company also paid passage for these skilled workers and their families. Two and three in the same household often would be employed in the mill—husband, wife, an in-law, even a child or two. When I spoke with her in the spring of 1992, Elspeth Kepple was a nonagenarian who would soon decide to sell her neat but rather run-down old house on Tower Hill in Lawrence and move into a retirement home not far from there. As she sat with her white toy poodle on her lap, she told me she had never worked in the mills but that her English-born mother had. Arriving at age ten from the textile mill town northeast of Manchester named Bradford, she had gone to work immediately as a bobbin girl. "She wore a tray like a cigarette girl, with the band around her shoulders and back," said Miss Kepple. "When anyone needed a bobbin changed, she would go and give them one."

Miss Kepple's father's family had come from England, as well—not the textile region, but a little coal-mining town farther north. "One of my great uncles had died of black lung disease," Miss Kepple said, "and my grandfather was determined that neither he nor his sons would follow suit. So he came to Lawrence, bought land, and built a number of houses on Buswell, Trenton, and Lexington streets. His children bought most of those houses. We'd go over Sundays to visit. Dad called it Keppleville."

Miss Kepple's mother apparently had done well to marry a son of Grandfather Kepple, who'd been able to buy land so soon after arrival. But both English families were initially far better off than any of their Irish counterparts. Not only did the English come with more cash; they were given the better-paying jobs. They never lived in shanties; instead, they rather promptly moved into the kind of place that Kepple built. Many still stand today—large Victorian houses with fancy-cut shingles and wraparound porches on a slope called Clover Hill. In fact, the English joined the native-born Americans on all three hills overlooking the rest of the city—Clover, Tower, and my own former home, Prospect Hill. Meanwhile, the Irish were multiplying in the valley below and many were slowly realizing a terrible truth: in building the mills, they had built their own veritable prisons. Little but the lowest-paying mill work was available in Lawrence for these transplanted farmers now. Unless you were as enterprising as Sweeney, into the mills you went, where your bosses, who lived on those hills above you, would be the old familiar oppressors with English surnames.

There were new oppressors, as well: the Germans who had come to Lawrence, like the English, because their textile towns had foundered. They, too, settled on the slopes. Saxonia, Bavaria, and Silesia—German textile areas—are street names on Prospect Hill. (The German Old Folks Home is there, too, no longer ethnically exclusive; but the designation above the front door in old-world script remains.) The Germans were welcomed by the native-born Americans because, although they spoke a foreign tongue, they weren't poor and uneducated like the Irish; they were skilled workers, like the English, and most of them worshiped at the same Protestant churches.

Eventually, during the decade preceding the Civil War, it wasn't just that the English and Germans were favored, but that the Irish were blatantly persecuted. In Lawrence today, when people refer to the "riot," they mean the two days of skirmishes that began one August night in 1984 over a name-calling incident between Latinos and French-Canadians who had been living uneasily together in tenements and in the public-housing project at the foot of Tower Hill. In the 1850s and 1860s, they would have been talking about the rock throwing that erupted on the Plains in July 1854 between the Irish and a mob of Know-Nothing Yankees (anti-Irish, anti-Catholic, anti-immigrant) over a rumor that an Irishman had raised an American flag upside down. (He had, but accidentally, according to local historians.) Evidence of lingering nativist feelings can be found in a Lawrence city directory published some twenty years later: the place of birth of a shopkeeper— "Massachusetts," "Vermont," "Ireland" . . . —is listed along with the address of his shop.

Not everyone wished the Irish otherwhere. Massachusetts educator and statesman Edward Everett argued—backhandedly—that the Irish were an asset. "Their inferiority as a race compels them to go to the bottom of the occupational scale," he wrote, "and the consequence is that we are all, all of us, the higher lifted because they are here." As the Irish filled the dirty-work slots, the native-born and others ascended into the managerial class. They did not simply pull themselves up by their own bootstraps, then; many were boosted from below by those whose presence demanded such newly coined job titles as foreman, overseer, and superintendent. In Everett's opinion, these people who were paid to see that others worked should be grateful to Irishmen for their heightened status, not to mention their improved wages.

Slowly, slowly, some Irish joined the ranks of this burgeoning middle class. By 1871, Patrick Sweeney, for one, was not only a landlord but also the owner of a furniture store on Essex Street, selling parlor sets, oil paintings in showy frames, feather beds, china and crockery—furnishings for the sort of house in which he himself now lived, at 124 Newbury Street, not far from the site of his old mud shack. "The wallpaper in the parlor was a pattern of large interwoven figures of blue and brown on a white ground," wrote his daughter, Elizabeth. "The carpet was brown and white, a large involved design. There were haircloth sofas and chairs, black upholstery and walnut frames." What a Victorian delight—busy, busy and darkly oppressive in exactly the style of the day. It must have pleased the up-and-coming Sweeney, who later bought a newspaper—the *Lawrence Journal*—and once boasted that he paid more taxes than any other private citizen in Lawrence.

Not only material goods but also cultural riches were within reach of the Sweeneys now. In 1872, Elizabeth was salutatorian of her graduating class at the high school, where she gave a short speech in Latin at the ceremony. She claims to have been "the first girl of Irish extraction and Catholic religion to graduate from L.H.S."

Elizabeth's brother, John, not only graduated from high school; by the mid-1880s, he was well established as a lawyer, with offices in the Central Building on Essex Street, which, by then, the Sweeney family owned. When he married, John built a house on Berkeley Street, up on Clover Hill. The distance from Newbury to Berkeley isn't great, but John's arrival at that destination must have represented a milestone to the Sweeneys: one of their own at last had made it to the top of the slopes with the Yankees.

John Sweeney didn't stay on Clover Hill for very long— perhaps not more than a year. When the lot next door was sold to a man who began building too close to his property, Sweeney jacked up his own house, put rollers under it, and trundled it across the city line into the open fields of Methuen—prefiguring all those movers who have left Lawrence and its "huddled masses" when they "bettered" themselves.

This was fine for the Sweeney clan, but how did Lawrence look upon the loss? At the turn of the century, it didn't matter if middle-class people moved out; there were still plenty of other members of the bourgeoisie left behind.

John's daughter Alice, going even further than her father had, attended Abbot Academy in Andover, Phillips's sister school (the two institutions merged in the 1970s), and graduated from Vassar with the class of 1918. For several years after college, Alice was paid to read aloud to a rich widow, with whom she traveled to New York, Paris, and elsewhere. Later still, she got a job teaching at her old prep school and passed down the cushy reading job to her younger sister.

How far from mill work (some would say "real" work) the Sweeneys had come.

IN 1879, a new English family joined other upwardly mobile families of overseers, small businessmen, and professionals on Prospect Hill. They were the John Barkers, who came, like Elspeth Kepple's mother, from Bradford, and were, like her grandfather Kepple, already middle-class. The Kepples and the Barkers befriended one another, and when I told Miss Kepple my address, she recognized it immediately. "You're living in Marion Barker's place," she said, her tone part suspicion, part envy.

Marion Barker's paternal grandfather, John, had learned spinning in Bradford as a boy. He'd even owned a modest mill. Gradually, though, small independent mills were picked off by the larger, more mechanized ones, and Barker's mill went under. So it was natural for him to decide to emigrate—a man of forty with a wife and five children to support, and valuable experience to tender. It was a good move. The golden door was indeed golden for John Barker: he was hired as overseer of worsted spinning for the Pacific Mills (where Akko rents space today), and the family moved to the slopes at once, into 175 Prospect Street, the big three-storied Victorian house right next door to the one where I would live decades later (which hadn't yet been built). In the late thirties, Freddy Colvito would buy that house from John Barker's son (Marion's father), live on the second and third floors with his family, and rent the ground floor to a variety of tenants, including John and Lucille Piacenzo. (It's the place where John would take his own life.) Once clapboard, now covered with wooden shingles, its stained-glass windows intact, it is still owned by the suburban daughters of Freddy Colvito, who continue to rent out both apartments to various tenants (including, for a couple of years, two Akko employees).

At the top of Grove Street, there is another stately house, its shrubberies clipped by a caring hand. It, too, was converted into a duplex years ago; two men in their thirties are its owner-occupants today. In the 1880s, however, it was the home of the Lord family, including a son, John T., who grew up to become a clerk in the same Pacific Mills complex where John Barker was an overseer. In 1892, when the Barkers' daughter Annie graduated from Lawrence High (in the same graduating class as Robert Frost), she and John T. Lord got engaged, and John Barker cut down the pear trees in his side yard and built "my" house, 173 Prospect Street—an eight-room Victorian "cottage"—for the couple to live in after their wedding. The marriage itself would not take place until a few years later, however, and so the house was rented out to a music teacher and his family while Annie earned a degree at Salem Normal School (now Salem State College).

Annie wasn't John's only daughter, but the older one, Mary, who had earned a nursing degree in Boston, went back to England to work for a time. (She never married.) Her younger brother, Arthur, returned to England, too. Through a Prospect Hill neighbor, he had been offered a clerk's job by the Walk-About Shoe Company in their home offices, in London. In 1897, when Arthur decided to take the position, the United

States was again in a financial depression. The stock market had crashed in June 1893, and the slump had continued throughout Arthur's years at Lawrence High. The textile industry was one of the hardest hit. In 1894, the Wilson-Gorman Tariff Act, a reform pushed by free-trade Democrats, had lifted the duties on imported woolens; as a result, cheap foreign cloth, especially from England, began to crowd the American market. In Lawrence, as the protectionists had predicted, the new law translated into layoffs, contract cancellations, and reduced profits. Though his father and brother-in-law had made careers in the mills, Arthur must have believed that for him they offered an uncertain future.

Twenty-year-old Rose Edith Dawson, from Jackson Terrace, followed Arthur across the Atlantic. Rose had been in the same high school class as he; her family had attended the same United Methodist Church as the Barkers; and they also had come to Lawrence from the English textile mill district— Huddersfield, specifically (where the riots against mechanization had occurred). Now Rose's parents would briefly return to Europe to arrange and attend the young couple's simple wedding, as well as to accompany their daughter on a tour of France, Germany, and Holland beforehand.

Arthur and Rose moved into an apartment at 12 Sinclair Mansions in London's West Kensington Park. Their first daughter, Dorothy, was born at home in 1901, the year Queen Victoria died. The coronation parade for King Edward VII passed right by the Walk-About store at 140 Cheapside, where Arthur, with his slicked hair parted down the middle and his glasses pinched onto his nose, sat on a high stool to do his figuring. Their second daughter, Marion, was born at Sinclair Mansions, too, on November 23, 1902. I have seen photos of the family, posed in West Kensington Park and in front of St. Paul's, with Big Ben in the background; Rose, wearing cinch-waisted walking suits and stylish hats, is wheeling her daughters in a wicker baby carriage. All the Barkers look happy in these snapshots; in fact, they look like tourists, and as it turned out, in effect they were. In August 1903, the Arthur Barkers returned to Lawrence.

Probably they had heard from their families that the slump was over, the city was booming again, and that more mills were being built by a new corporation, the American Woolen Company. What they couldn't have known, because no one did, was that one man and his immediate family would grow very rich as a result of this sudden, manic expansion—far richer than any of the Essex Company members ever got from textiles—and that others, many thousands of others, would grow more and more desperate, their distress culminating in the great strike of 1912. In the meantime, the Barkers arrived home on the SS *Mayflower* (so, in a manner of speaking, these twentieth-century English, too, came over on the *Mayflower*) and rented one half of a duplex down near the mills.

What happened next couldn't have been more ordinary—more American, some would say. They settled into middle-class life. Arthur got a job, not in the mills, but doing the books for a Lawrence fire engine–manufacturing company, and Rose bore her third and last child, another daughter, Janice. She also joined the Lawrence Woman's Club (membership was limited to one hundred—someone had to die or drop out for a space to open up), where she drank tea and ate cakes, enjoyed concerts by sopranos and harpists, and listened to the lectures of archaeologists and swamis and, once, Julia Ward Howe. ("Is Polite Society Polite?" was the name of the lecture Mrs. Howe delivered; the suffragist who wrote "The Battle Hymn of the Republic" had been asked to speak on anything but suffrage.)

Then, in 1909, Annie and John Lord moved out of our house, and the Arthur Barkers moved in. No doubt because of the boom, Lord had received a major promotion and with it the use of an elegant brick residence across from the common. It was 1909, the year the Ayer Mill, the last of the huge mills, was built—the same year that seventy-two-year-old John Barker decided to buy his first car, which Arthur and brave Rose learned to drive, though John himself never did. It was a Cadillac, open like a carriage, with running boards and a hand crank. The whole family, standing in front of this black hulk of a vehicle, is pictured in a photo. All the Barker females now, not just Rose, are wearing big fashionable hats. Marion's has a prominent feather. In other photos, Dorothy and Marion are wearing identical dresses, made of Anderson gingham— fabric imported from Scotland even as miles of gingham were being produced down in the mills of Lawrence. Rose and her mother made those dresses in the kitchen of the Prospect Street house. Grandmother Dawson would come over in the morning and spend the day, working at a big, cluttered table, cutting and sewing and fitting, and all three Barker daughters would help. There are no photos showing these domestic scenes—perhaps because the camera had no flash equipment—but there are lots more of the girls standing outdoors. There they are as adolescents, after a snowstorm, one of them wearing a raccoon stole; and again, in spring, with Rose, in front of the vine trellis, squinting into the sun.

WINTER 1992. Photos may lie, but for several mornings now Miss Marion Barker has sat with me on the sofa in her apartment, supplying the captions for her family's pictures and affirming that theirs was indeed a happy life. And it is easy to believe this woman in her sensible woolen suit, straight-backed even as she pushes past ninety, whose daily breakfast is, religiously, oatmeal (accent on the second syllable); who has never had an alcoholic drink in her life; who rides her stationary exercise bicycle in her bedroom for half an hour every day; who would like me to call her Marion, but it simply isn't possible (it would be like referring to Queen Elizabeth as Betty); and who still drives her 1984 navy blue Ford Crown Victoria wherever she pleases. (While sweeping the rubber back-door mat at the house in Lawrence—a mat that spells BARKER to this day—I spied her driving by on the afternoon of her ninetieth birthday.)

Of her driving, Miss Barker says, "I'm not one to be afraid. I go all over Lawrence. I know the shortcuts and I still use them. I might lock my car doors at night, but I'm not afraid." Where she usually drives is to church or one meeting or another, including, until recently, meetings of the Lawrence Woman's Club, which disbanded in 1989, just three years short of its one hundredth birthday, after many of its aging members died. Miss Barker, whose grandmother, mother, and great-aunt had been LWC members, and who served as its president once in the forties and again in its final years, was distressed but also peevish at its demise: "Why don't young people join these organizations?" she asked me rhetorically. "They're too busy making money. Why do they have to have everything *now*? Their parents didn't have two cars and all the rest until they'd been married twenty-five or thirty years."

No, she is not afraid to speak her mind; not afraid of anything or anyone. Still, she moved out of Lawrence and into an Andover condominium in 1979, exactly one hundred years after her family settled in Lawrence. She is not afraid, but there was a burglary, and one of her Oriental rugs was stolen—rolled up and walked right out of the downstairs parlor. She is not afraid, but relatives were afraid for her. Besides, the house had grown too big. She was living alone. And so she sold it to Freddy Colvito's grandson and his wife, John and Diane Vaccarro (who resold it to us four years later, using the profits to help buy a place in Andover). Miss Barker's new home is in a building called Bradford House, namesake of her grandfather's English hometown—a coincidence she hadn't noticed until I pointed it out to her.

Bob and I met Miss Barker on Thanksgiving 1985. We were interested in the history of 173 Prospect Street, and so we asked the Vaccarros how to get in touch with her; when we learned she would be alone for the holiday, we had her over for the traditional dinner. As it turned out, our new friend would tell us not only about the house but a lot of the history of the city, since she and her family had been such active members of the community for so long. A graduate of Mount Holyoke (class of 1922), Miss Barker also taught biology at Lawrence High for close to half a century. She taught Tom Troy, the oiler boy who became a Lawrence firefighter; she taught her dentist, her eye doctor, and her county commissioner. Wherever she goes, she runs into former students. On the day I accompanied her to a doctor's office, the receptionist held up the insurance form—a poor Xerox, difficult for anyone to decipher, much less an elderly person—and suggested that she read it aloud to Miss Barker: "If you trust me." Miss Barker, her clear-eyed gaze steady and disapproving, took the form from the woman's hand and read it herself, every word. After Miss Barker had gone into the treatment room, the receptionist, Frieda Franks (LHS, class of 1966), muttered with as much admiration as chagrin: "She's just the way she was when she made me cut up that frog."

When Miss Barker emerged from treatment, she announced with satisfaction that the technician was a former student of hers, too.

SPRING 1992. I accompany Miss Barker again, this time to her monthly meeting of the Lawrence Garden Club—another throwback to that lost era in the city's history, when it still had a sizable middle class. It is held in the basement rec room—

cinder-block walls and fluorescent lighting—of the United Presbyterian Church, just a few blocks down from my house on Prospect Street. These forty or so women—most of them getting on in years, and many of whom live in the suburbs but return, like Miss Barker, nostalgically—are all wearing ladies' lunch attire: a fur piece or two, jewelry, and beauty-parlor perms. Their name tags say Miss or Mrs., followed by their surname; their first names are typed below that. And Miss Barker, in an emerald-green woolen suit and matching costume jewelry, probably looks much the way she used to look in the mornings toward the end of her career, when she'd leave our house on her way to teach school. Actually, all her former students, whether they had her in the thirties or the sixties, say she looks exactly the same as always.

Sweets—Miss Barker's date-nut bread among them—are served in tiny paper muffin cups while two members pour the tea and coffee from a formal service, each sitting at one end of a long, draped table. Ever proper, they also administer the cream and sugar. After the socializing and the business meeting, John Gould, a writer who teaches English at Phillips Academy, presents a slide lecture—photos of some of over 250 wildflowers and wild orchids he has spotted in Andover and other parts of New England. One of the orchids had come up three years in a row in the same tranquil spot on the Phillips Academy campus.

Impressive. But, as the pictures flash before us in the dark (to the tune of not a few of these senior ladies' snores), I can't help but wonder: Has John Gould spotted any of these specimens in Lawrence? If he has, he doesn't mention them, though many of those plants must have flourished here once, especially down by the river.

Walking home that day, I cross the intersection of Prospect and East Haverhill streets, where Perrotta's, a pharmacy, has a big sign above the front door: WE DISTRIBUTE FOOD STAMPS;

it is also where at election time the local politicians and large motley crowds of their supporters brandish their opposing placards. My route also takes me past a low brick building, with plywood covering its windows. Built in 1912, it has a peculiarly Lawrencian history. Originally, it was the local headquarters of an old German fraternal order, Harugari-halle; later, in the forties, it was a hangout for World War II veterans, called the Dugout; after that, it was a fruit-cocktail factory, called Flavor-Fresh, owned by the Gangi family; and later still—presently, in fact—it became a Latino Pentecostal Church.

Some would pronounce it seedy and drive (not walk) past as quickly as they could. (Some, like former mayor Buckley's frightened friends, wouldn't even drive past, I guess.) But that day, and other days before and since, it has struck me as something just as American, and just as resilient, as a native plant reincarnated three years in a row on the grounds of a fancy prep school in Andover.

Maybe more so.

Maybe even something to have a slide lecture about.

Still, I wouldn't be honest if I didn't say I also lament the loss for Lawrence of those ladies, those flowers. How many times have I thought to myself, If Lawrence still had those ladies and flowers, and the leisure that they represent, how different the city would be? How many times have I wished that Lawrence could have the ladies and flowers, and the layers of its successive generations of immigrants, too? Is it really too starry-eyed to wish for play as well as work? *Bread* and *roses* . . . ? The "nitty-gritty" *and* a viable tax base?

Certainly it would have been much more difficult for Bob and me to decide to leave if Lawrence had both.

"I wonder what Lawrence would be like now if we all had stayed," a Lawrence schoolteacher, who lives in Andover, wondered aloud one day while I was listening. She said virtually all the teachers at her school were former Lawrencians or the sons and daughters of Lawrencians.

"It makes me so mad to hear them all sitting around the lunch table talking about Lawrence's problems," said another teacher, who does live in the city. " 'What's happened to this place? Why is it like this?' they sit around and ask. You left, that's what happened," this teacher said she feels like saying, but doesn't.

Brain drain are the words she might well have mumbled under her breath. It has plagued Third World countries; in these last couple of decades, it's been plaguing Lawrence. Perhaps it always has.

TRANSFORMING THE CITY in my mind's eye, street by street, house by house, trimming bushes, picking up trash, removing asbestos shingles, pulling off siding, painting peeling porches and clapboards—that's what I used to do lots of nights, lying in bed in Lawrence when I couldn't sleep. I could see what that city might have been, what it might yet become if . . .

If, if, if . . .

Some nights, I would get up and sit in my study at 173 Prospect Street, which Miss Barker, at least in my presence, refers to as "the" house, not "my" house or "your" house—in deference to me, but also to the past, I suppose— and find myself thinking of Miss Barker's mother, who kept that house before Miss Barker did, before I did. She got rid of dust by putting wet newspapers down everywhere, then sweeping them out the door and into trash receptacles. I wonder what she would think of the central vacuuming system that has been installed. She died when she was just past forty. Her picture, taken with the women of her LHS class of 1897, on the occasion of their fifteenth annual reunion, the year of the great strike, hung on the parlor wall downstairs for nearly all the ten years we lived there. It's a copy we had made of one of Miss Barker's photos, because the house is also in the picture, looking smart, as smart as it still looks today. Rose looks smart, too, wearing a lacy high-collared blouse and long skirt, but she seems much older than thirty-two, as do all the other overworked ladies in the picture.

Being even a middle-class housewife and mother in those years was a physical trial.

When the Barkers lived in the house, my study—a small room in the rear, without heat—was used as a bedroom by one of the Barker girls. When I lived there, most of its square footage was taken up by an old mill supervisor's desk, no doubt similar to the ones at which Miss Barker's paternal grandfather, John Barker, and her uncle, John T. Lord, once must have worked, entering tiny figures in the small ledgers of the day. (I have seen John Barker's numerals in one labeled "Time Book," dated 1879–81, and measuring only about three by five; it is preserved in the North Andover textile museum, though Miss Barker said she didn't know who could have donated it.) Made of heavy golden oak, my desk had lots of big, heavy drawers, which were hard to open, and a green linoleum top, surely added more recently. Bob brought it home for me from the old Pacific Mills one Friday night shortly after we moved to Lawrence. He hauled it up the stairs with the help of a couple of guys from the factory. We shared beer with them in thanks. His employees were as surprised as any Andoverite that the president of Akko lived in Lawrence. Later, Bob would promote to supervisor one of those who helped us with the desk; later still, the worker would claim that the pressure, the anxiety, was too much for him, and he would ask to go back to being an underling again. There is something to be said for taking orders instead of giving them, I guess.

On many occasions, while sitting at that desk, I stared out

the window, the same window Miss Barker must have looked out innumerable times. She told me she remembers a horse looking back at her through the window of the barn on the property across the way. The horse is gone, and the barn has only three sides; the fourth blew down in a windstorm, revealing piles of junk accumulated over decades. Skip, who owned the barn and lived in the house alongside it with his wheelchair-bound mother, couldn't afford to demolish it. And so it remained. It and its rusty old tools. Birds' nests. Beehives. Feral cats. Mice. Raccoons, too. Three big raccoons once had a noisy fight on the roof: during mating season, there was one raccoon too many. Janis Moore, who was Lawrence's animal-control officer from 1986 to 1994, told me that she has seen unusually large litters of raccoons, skunks, and possums in the city. Before I finally learned my lesson, my dog was sprayed by a skunk four times in three years in the fenced parking lot where I used to let her run after dark. One morning, Janis saw a pale pink mother possum with thirteen babies on her back (the usual is five or six); the abandoned buildings make great homes, and there is an ample supply of garbage around for food, and a water supply in Lawrence's three rivers. So these creatures breed well, probably better than they do in the suburban wilds.

Janis had another observation to make about the stray dogs she used to pick up in the streets: "All purebred dogs, mind you. What are they? Abandoned? They're toys. Windup toys. They've got a lot of excess money around here. And they're spending it, some of it, on dogs. Where do they come from? Who is it that can afford not to come and bail out their six-hundred-dollar dog? Think about it."

While rescuing a cat at a house on one of the more crime-ravaged streets of the mill district, Janis once fell through a second-story window (she took her job seriously); she landed in the middle of a drug deal.

Out that same window in my study, where I used to sit all day and many nights, I could also see another neighbor's old barn, its original slate roof intact. It is missing something of value, though. A woman who rented an apartment in the house told me that one night about fifteen years ago, she heard a helicopter hovering overhead; it was hovering so low, she thought it might land. She looked out the window but couldn't see anything; then the noise was gone. A few days later, she noticed that the barn's weather vane was missing, apparently plucked off by someone hanging out the helicopter door. I have read about this sort of piracy in antiques magazines. The old weather vane was probably sold for a lot of money; it is probably sitting in somebody's country house right now, its comfortable owners unaware that it was once atop a barn in a gritty old mill city called Lawrence.

CHAPTER 6

The Houses That
Billy Wood Built

[W]HO] IS the most typical American?"
In his uncompleted, unpublished memoirs, deposited in the library of the North Andover textile museum after his death in 1972, Cornelius Ayer Wood, Billy Wood's second son, answers his own question this way:

> You find them in the Middle West, not so much along the seacoasts, where there is an intermixture of peoples from all over the world. I suggest if you really want to see a true-blooded American, look at my wife. Muriel is descended from numerous colonial deputy governors; and ever since then her family has married self-respecting, good quality Americans, but, unlike the case of the Coolidge family who boast descent from Hiawatha, no Indians, and no Italians, unlike the case of the distinguished Cabot family, who are originally Italians with the name Caboto. Muriel's ancestry includes the Keiths of Scotland, and an admiral of the Royal British Navy, Admiral Pringle, who is buried in Westminster Abby [sic].

"I personally have not checked into my ancestry," adds Cornelius, "and am willing to accept as gospel anything good about it, and to reject the rest."

He had ample reason not to delve too deeply; he knew that what he would discover wouldn't please him. How could it please anyone with views like his to learn what others had discovered before him—that one set of his grandparents was of "foreign" heritage?

William Jason Wood was Billy Wood's father's name. It's Colonial vintage all right, and no doubt star-spangled enough to suit grandson Cornelius. But it's almost certainly not the name he was given at birth on Pico, one of the islands of the Portuguese Azores, in 1827. Edward G. Roddy, author of *Mills, Mansions, and Mergers: The Life of William M. Wood,* published by the textile museum in 1982, reports that Boston-area journalists of the 1920s speculated that Wood's father's name was more likely Jacinto (Jason could be the anglicized version, they reasoned), Madeira (which means "wood" in Portuguese), or Silva (Latin for the same). One reporter positively identified him as Manuel Silva in his account, but no other source corroborates this.

Nor is it known exactly how William Wood got to America; there is no record of his entry. What is certain is that American whaling ships in the early decades of the nineteenth century regularly stopped in the Azores for supplies; and that many young men signed on as crew members, and never went home again. Billy Wood's father could easily have been one of them. At any rate, he was certainly living humbly when he rented a fisherman's cottage on Pease's Point Way in Edgartown, Martha's Vineyard, in the mid-1850s. Cornelius Wood himself, in a moment's candor in his memoirs, describes his grandfather as "a sailor, kicked around, browbeaten, and underpaid." It also has been determined that the young immigrant found his way from the Vineyard to New Bedford, Captain Ahab's home port, and survived as so many others did in those rough seafaring towns—by working on land or sea as he was needed: as a fisherman, a ship's steward, a night watchman, a shipyard worker, a day laborer.

Sometimes the young Portuguese was employed as a steward on the steamer *Eagle's Wing*, which sailed between the Vineyard and New Bedford. His wife, Billy Wood's mother, worked as a scrubwoman on the same ship, down on her knees with a brush. Her name—her real name—was Amelia Christiana Madison, but she was three-quarters Portuguese and only one-quarter English. And she, too, was born on Pico of humble origins.

I refer to her as "wife," but there is no marriage certificate—at least not one that Billy's painstaking biographer could locate, and no record of how she happened to come to America either; perhaps the mariner sent for her after he got settled. It is known that she bore ten children, only six of whom survived to adulthood, and that one of them—the second child and first-born son—was William Wood (he added the Madison himself later, in his teen years).

Nor is there any record that either of Billy Wood's parents ever applied for U.S. citizenship. Nonetheless, in 1900, when the census taker came around, his mother, then living in a house her son had built for her in the town of Woburn, Massachusetts, claimed that state as the place of her birth. (She also said that her parents had been born in England.) The same year, three of Wood's siblings reported that both their parents had been born in Massachusetts. Billy Wood himself told the census taker that his father had been born in Scotland.

I wonder if Wood was wishfully thinking of steel magnate Andrew Carnegie's lineage when he told that lie. He certainly shared with Carnegie the self-made man's love of hard work. Indeed, to Billy Wood, work was a pleasure; it was also, apparently, his obsession, his demon lover.

In the days of Wood's youth, going into textiles, at least the management end of it, held something of the romance that the shipping business had once held for a previous generation. The industry's scale and specialized vocabulary put many in awe of it and of the men who weren't afraid to command the huge factories full of the new, complex machinery and the thousands of workers jackspooling, burling, mulespinning, slubbing, gigging, napping, teaseling, winding, doffing, quilling, and carding. It was also a risky business—a glamorous gamble in which it was quite possible for the bold to make a great deal of money, or lose their shirts. Billy Wood did both.

Nobody knows whether Wood had romantic images of textile conquests in mind from the outset. He may have started in the trade at age twelve because that was the only job he could get in 1870—the year his father died of consumption and he was forced to quit school and help support his mother and siblings. He had not been a scholar, in any event. Of fifty-four in his class, Edward Roddy tells us, Wood ranked second from the bottom. "That he 'excelled in Greek and kept a diary in German,' as some of his obituaries reported, would appear to be the fancy of overeager journalists," Roddy writes. "There is no record of his enrollment in either Greek or German language classes." It didn't matter. He landed a job as an office boy for four dollars a week in the headquarters of the Wamsutta Cotton Mills of New Bedford. From the first day of that first job, and for the next nearly two decades, he spent himself in toil, mostly in New Bedford, but also in nearby Fall River and in Philadelphia. Then, in 1886, he decided to take a job in Lawrence.

Picture him at age twenty-eight, walking hurriedly from his Jackson Street apartment to his new job in the mills. The dark eyes under the heavy eyebrows are intense in every photo I've ever seen of him—intense and a little uneasy, always assessing. It is shortly after Christmas, and his heavy brush mustache is surely coated with icy condensation from his breath.

But he must have been pleased with his new situation. At eighteen hundred dollars a year, his salary would be four hundred dollars more than the pay he had earned at the job he had left in Fall River. He would have more responsibility, too, as head of the entire cotton manufacturing department at the Washington Mills. Best of all, he would be working for one of the richest men in New England: the white-bearded patrician Frederick Ayer, of Lowell.

Like the men of the Essex Company, Ayer was the antithesis of the self-made man: born into money, he had made still more money in business. Along with his brother James, he had amassed a fortune selling cough syrup, ague cure, hair restorer, and other patent medicines of dubious worth. The J. C. Ayer Company also published the *Ayer Almanac*. Sixteen million copies, filled with ads for Ayer products, were sold in twenty-one languages every year. Its humble slogan: "Second only to the Bible in circulation—is Ayer's Almanac."

Looking to invest their increasing riches in new ventures, the brothers decided upon textiles, first in Lowell in the 1870s, where they purchased controlling interest in several cotton mills and consolidated them, and later, in the 1880s, in Lawrence, where they rescued the Washington Mills from bankruptcy.

But just because the Ayers had succeeded in selling medicine didn't mean that they could manage textile mills. Money continued to drain away from the Washington Mills, the place was reorganized once again, and young Billy Wood, being one of the newest hires, was laid off.

Wood was shocked and despondent; he was also, obviously, gutsy—not one to take setbacks without a fight—and convinced the Ayer brothers to hire him back as a salesman. This was an unorthodox idea: textiles were not customarily sold by traveling salesmen in those days. Nonetheless, Wood left on the train that same evening. In a year's time, he had sold

$2 million worth of woolen yarn, and the Washington Mills were saved.

A phenomenal raise and a promotion were his just rewards. His new annual salary was $25,000—a vast sum for the era; his new job was management not only of selling but of the mills themselves. He also claimed another prize. In late 1888, in a life development worthy of a character in a plotty novel, he married Ellen Wheaton Ayer, boss Frederick's very rich, very eligible twenty-nine-year-old daughter.

If only we knew more. There is no reliable record of how this man, who very often worked sixteen-hour days and slept on a cot in his office, found time for a courtship. And why was the marriage allowed? She was a Radcliffe graduate (her brothers were Harvard men) who had also attended a French finishing school for young ladies, and her ancestors had settled in Connecticut in the 1700s, while he, despite his recent success in business, was an elementary school dropout who did not even approach being one of those "good quality Americans," as his son would later define it. "It is well known that Wood's wife wasn't fond of the Portuguese connection," Roddy states in an article he wrote about Wood's clouded ethnic heritage for *The Journal of the American Portuguese Society*.

They named their firstborn Rosalind, after the disguised heroine—the young woman dressed as a man—in *As You Like It* (ironically appropriate for the daughter of a man who had something of a forged identity himself). And when the Woods decided to buy a country house in Andover to supplement their five-story mansion in Boston's Back Bay, they named it Arden, after the forest depicted in the same play—the idyllic pastoral setting, "the golden world"—even as Wood prepared to make Lawrence a far more cramped and dangerously overcrowded city than it already was.

In all the accounts that I have read, Wood is given credit for these Shakespearean choices. I beg to differ. Surely his wife had more to do with them. She, not he, must have studied the plays in school and seen them performed. Supposedly, Wood was fond of classical music and Italian operas, too, but I wonder when he could have found the time to cultivate such tastes.

More likely, these were interests he thought he should have—part of his self-creation as a well-bred Yankee, a cultured American: a member of the New York Yacht Club, the Union League, the Metropolitan Club of New York City, the Algonquin Club of Boston, and the Brookline Country Club; a man who would also build mansions in Palm Beach and on Cuttyhunk Island, off the coast of Martha's Vineyard, his birthplace—perhaps to gaze at it across Buzzards Bay and marvel at how far he'd come.

Not far enough for some in Cuttyhunk, apparently: as the story goes, he was denied membership in the Cuttyhunk Club on his first try; later, like the nouveau riche hero *exemplaire* that he was, Wood "showed" them by buying the club itself.

THREE MORE CHILDREN, including Cornelius, were born in the early 1890s at Arden. (Cornelius's son, Cornelius Ayer Wood, Jr., lives there still, a curmudgeonish sort, to judge from the letters he has sent me—a retired Episcopal priest, of all things, who, in spite of our correspondence, avoided meeting with me to discuss his famous grandfather.)

Most of the estate's original sixty acres are hidden or have been sold and developed, but the main house can almost be seen from Miss Barker's condominium, which is across the street. (The fifties-style "Bauhaus" where Bob grew up is within walking distance through the woods. As a boy, Bob says, he always wanted to get a closer look at Arden, although he never succeeded. A caretaker always materialized to chase him away.) The twenty-room mansion is notable for its very tall, very wide, redbrick chimneys and its whimsical Carpenter Gothic decoration all along the eaves—"icicles," the Wood children called it, according to Cornelius's memoirs. It is not the most magnificent mansion, as mansions go—there are far, far grander ones in Greenwich—but, then, it wasn't the only house owned by the Wood family, and in its heyday it bustled with live-in servants who were paid a dollar a day and governesses who taught the children until they were old enough to attend boarding schools here and abroad. There were formal gardens, barns, stables, a tennis court, a pond for swimming and skating; several miles of roadway; a clubhouse for dances, live theater performances, and other celebrations; dogs, cats, rabbits, ducks, Hereford calves, ponies, and donkeys for the children to play with. The remnants of an old Victorian-style greenhouse, the glass gone, can almost be seen from Miss Barker's condo, too.

"Dad never was able to do things on a small scale," wrote Billy's memoirist son, who relates this example: as a child Cornelius once wished aloud for "a hen or a goose or a duck—so I can chase it." Billy Wood responded by building three henhouses and buying 2,500 Plymouth Rocks.

I suppose he couldn't help himself. He was used to commandeering huge numbers of livestock. At the turn of the century, experts estimated that the wool clipped from 12 million sheep from all over the world was being used annually in the mills of Lawrence. Ten years later, in the Wood Mill alone, the operatives would process into cloth the wool from 100,000 sheep (or 1 million pounds) *a week*.

But what sort of man was this, who wasn't afraid of such dimensions? Edward Roddy's biography is Wood's only published life chronicle, and it wisely doesn't attempt to be a psychological profile. Reliable personal information about Wood is simply not available, the son's memoirs notwithstanding. "Were I to select an adjective to describe William M. Wood,"

Cornelius wrote, "I believe most people would agree on 'generous' as the word. Others would suggest brilliant, broad minded, far sighted, industrious and kindly! He could not bear to cause suffering in others."

Journalists' accounts are no better for being cynical, though. The words they liked to use back then to describe him are, unhelpfully, the same ones they often invoked to describe other industrialists of the era: "shrewd," "impulsive," "domineering." *Fortune* magazine is more specific when it calls him "the swarthy Mr. Wood," but that is surely an ethnic dig. His face was round, this account goes on to tell us, and his hair was "sleek" (read: "oily"). He was also described as "short" and "impolite," with a penchant for spats and other dandyish clothing and a need to surround himself with "yes men."

Maybe the *Andover Townsman* came closest to the truth when it called Wood, simply, a "rare business genius." Wood did know how to make money—at least for a while. "He has a rightful place in the record of big things done by big men," gushed the *Townsman*, whose editors in September 1914 could not have known that within ten years Wood's "big things" would be his undoing.

By the mid-1890s, Wood and his father-in-law had come to own far more than just the Washington Mills. Because of the financial panic of the late 1890s—the same that sent Arthur Barker back to England—they had been able to pick up seven more mills at bargain prices. In 1899, the merger of these mills took place, and the American Woolen Company was born, with Ayer as president and Wood as treasurer.

Soon, construction of the gargantuan Wood Mill would begin, dwarfing all the mills that had previously dwarfed the mills of Lowell. The Ayer would go up next, crowned with a massive clock tower with four translucent moon-colored faces, their diameter only six inches smaller than the faces of Big Ben. It is, or was, not only the largest mill clock tower in the world but also the largest illuminated clock in the United States. Later, of course, it was the world's largest *broken* mill clock. But before it went dark in the fifties, this creation of the famed New England clockmaking firm of E. Howard tolled the hours for decades, telling the people of Lawrence when it was time to work.

Wood later called those workers "ignorant," "violent" plebeians who had "nothing to lose but everything to gain by coming to this country." In a speech before a group of Boston real-estate agents, he even went so far as to say that these laborers upon whom he depended were "sometimes so unskilled that even at the lowest wages [they were] not worth having." It's an amazingly callous attitude, but if Wood's opinions had been otherwise, he wouldn't have built his mills the way he did in the first place.

Many people still alive today have bitter memories of those factories, especially the Wood, and the work they did inside them. A woman named Lillian Donahue lasted only five weeks at the Wood: "I said to myself, I'm not going to spend my life in this place!" She went back to one of the older, smaller mills, lucky to find a place for an experienced jackspooler there.

Even many of those with a "good" job (like Lillian) and a deeply ingrained "mill temperament"—the docile nature that kept workers in dead-end mill jobs for a lifetime—didn't cope well at the Wood. For one thing, though electric lights were in use, people complained about the dim lighting. "It had big windows, yes," said a contemporary of Lillian's named Sam, "but the mill was so big, you would get all your light along the aisles. Go into the middle, where the frames are, where these ladies, the twisters and weavers, are, and the lumination was terrible; it was dark."

Technical problems weren't the only ones faced by workers inside that monstrosity, the Wood. Worse were psychological disabilities—acute loss of identity and feelings of expendability. These terms weren't used then and aren't used now by the workers when they describe their former workplace, however. They use only one word as if with one voice: *jail.* An article in *Fortune* magazine about the demise of the American Woolen Company in 1954 is illustrated by a photo of the Wood by Walker Evans; the caption reads: "Since the city of Lawrence already has a glut of such space in other closed mills, what to do with Wood is a puzzle. One gloomy suggestion: a state prison."

That's as far as the idea got. After half the U-shaped building was torn down in the 1960s, it was bought and rented out to various companies. The current tenant is a Bull Information Systems computer factory; it employs five hundred, where, in peak times, upwards of ten thousand used to work three shifts.

What may have contributed most to this feeling of being jailed was the size of management at the Wood. A huge, heavily hierarchical staff—a profusion of overseers, second hands (as overseers of the second rank were called), and section hands (third in command), many of them with official or unofficial assistants—was required to police the sixteen miles of aisles lined with 230,000 spindles and 1,470 looms. Those who ran around tending spindles or looms all day envied the supervisors—yearning for a job like theirs, "where you could sit and be the head of something or other"—even as they sneered at them. Like bored workers everywhere, they also learned to outsmart them. Jackspooler Lillian remembers how they signaled that a boss was coming by making a circle with their hand around their head; the gesture signified a hat: "The bosses," Lillian explains, "used to walk around wearing straw hats and act like they were King Kong." A mill operative named Bessie is vociferous about the bosses, too: "Ah, they all stink," she says, though she admits that there was one who was "nice" to her. "He said to me once, 'You know, I'd give a million dollars to have a smile.' I said, 'Oh, that's very easy.' He said, 'Yes, but when you're an overseer, you can't smile.' He was the only one that was good."

IF ONLY Wood, like Andrew Carnegie and other fabulously wealthy industrialists of the age, had left behind a legacy of philanthropy in addition to his mills . . . a specialized school or library, a museum or a public park. Lawrence could have used (and could use today) any or all of the above. But the city got nothing of the sort from Wood even as he built his monuments to himself in Andover, including the two hundred "dream houses" of Shawsheen Village for his middle managers. (By the end, of course, his corporate castle was crumbling, though how big a personal fortune he had accrued isn't known. Whatever the amount, it was dispersed to Wood family members, some of whom do award grants through a foundation, though certainly not on the scale of the foundations named Carnegie or Ford—not, that is, on the scale that Billy Wood used to do things.)

If only, having failed to provide his workers' city with "roses," Wood had at least seen to their "bread." As it was, however, he failed utterly to devise a plan to house the thousands who began pouring into Lawrence in search of employment, such as it was, in the mills. Long gone were the days of wholesome boardinghouses. While Wood's two flagship mills were being constructed and ambitious additions were being made to several older ones, the housing for the workers was left to chance—or rather, to other businessmen, who hoped to make their own fortunes. Of course, that was how it was done in America's industrial cities. Once again, however, Lawrence's situation was worse than most, because of matters of proportion and size. Remember, we are talking about the textile headquarters of the world, employing in 1914 some forty thousand workers and managers—crammed into a landmass of less than four square miles.

During the frenzied time of the new mill construction, not even the sacred hilltops were spared, as some residents, unable to resist the dollars they were being offered, sold chunks of their property to eager builders who squeezed houses into the front, back, and side yards of existing homes. Mail carriers who follow the warrenlike paths of the Prospect Hill route today tell me they loathe the assignment for that reason. Miss Barker remembers her parents and grandparents grumbling about the new three-deckers suddenly appearing smack up against the sidewalk, when most of the other houses on the street were tastefully set back.

But whatever was happening on the plush heights of Prospect, Clover, and Tower hills (growing less plush by the day), it could not compare with the scramble downtown, closer to the mills. Though they at least followed streets and alleyways in a straight line, new houses in the valley weren't meant for one, two, or even three families; they were four- and six- and twelve-unit tenements, one shoehorned in next to the other, or one behind the other, their designs often reversed or otherwise arranged on the lot like pieces of a cutout pattern laid upon fabric, so that no inch of land would be "wasted." A paintbrush couldn't fit between some of those nested buildings. Were they lowered in by block and tackle from above? Men who were boys then recall walking along the flat rooftops, jumping from one to another, traveling a mile or more without ever needing to touch the ground.

The Report of the Lawrence Survey (1911)—"a social inquiry" commissioned by a local charitable fund in the year before the great strike—found the "nearness" of Lawrence houses appalling. "Huddling people together is a disease," the authors wrote. "It generates profits that are a poison, intoxicating the whole community."

They went on: "Some of the new houses would not be bad houses in open fields, but are thoroughly bad for the center of Lawrence, because of their relationship to other houses. Some builders plan a house which is suitable enough for a good-sized lot. Then they use this plan over and over again, regardless of the size of the lot they are building on. This frequently turns a good house into a bad house."

Nor was it just greedy landlords who were building such homes; often the immigrants themselves swung the hammers. These amateurs must have been resourceful and proud, but *wretched* is the word the *Survey* authors use repeatedly to describe their creations. In their opinion:

> One of the worst [was] a new rear building constructed by [a] recent immigrant whose family lives in a small house in the front of the lot. His aged mother sleeps in a windowless room; his wife and daughter are kept hard at work in the kitchen cooking for boarders. He was planning to erect soon a second wretched tenement at the front of the lot. Such hard-working but ignorant and unskilled laborers have no sense of civic responsibility, and not the slightest ability to design a house for that most difficult of sites, the narrow city lot. Their right to own their own house is one thing, their right to go into the business of providing and maintaining homes for other people, under no control, is quite a different matter.

The *Survey* authors concluded that Lawrence's housing was one of its most egregious problems. (In 1990, a team of volunteer architects and city planners came to Lawrence to give the city a free consultation, and it reached the same conclusion, even though many of the densest clusters were knocked down years ago, during the urban-renewal craze of the sixties and seventies.) Nor is the density its only major defect. In the most blighted neighborhoods of Washington, D.C., when I lived there, I never saw such tumbledown places as these, because even though the poor here and there are comparably poor, D.C.'s row housing is made of brick, fired in the kilns of neighboring Maryland; in Lawrence, it is wood, and soft wood at that—spruce and pine. And as every child who knows "The Three Little Pigs" knows, frame houses are not so difficult to blow down.

If the houses do not simply crumble, often they burn. "The sticks are all laid for a most superb bonfire," wrote the authors of the *Survey*. Accidental fire. Arson, too. (A city in decline presents certain enticements for the unscrupulous.) But with or without the help of accelerants, Lawrence houses are engulfed immediately, for not only are they wood; they are virtually all of balloon-frame construction, which means that, unlike more modern, platform-frame houses, they lack fire-stops. (Older, Colonial-vintage wooden homes, framed with logs, have fire-stops, too.) In such houses, flames have a straight shot up through hollow, uninsulated walls, so a fire on the first floor will be in the attic in no time.

In my ten years in Lawrence, I saw no fewer than six multifamilies burn within sight of my front porch—my clothes and hair stinking from the smoke, my eyes stinging, my nostrils resisting the stench of charred, wet debris afterward. One of the fires, an easy hop across my former street, was set by a jilted lover; he threw gasoline into the house's unlocked front entryway. It was 5:00 a.m., and the woman he wanted to hurt lay sleeping in an attic apartment with her five-year-old son. Holding hands, they jumped onto an adjacent garage roof as the smoke and heat licked their feet. One advantage of huddled buildings, I suppose, is that they afford escape routes: the landing shattered bones, but their lives were saved.

When the firefighters left several hours later, their Red Cross coffee cups flung down atop the ruins, I went over to the property and had a look around. I stepped over mattresses, couches, dishes, children's toys—the remains of several families' possessions laid out for all to see. Then I heard the sound of rushing water. That was strange: I was, after all, in the middle of the city. I ventured to the rear of the lot and looked over the precipice that marked its boundary; I could smell the water now, more potent than the soggy, smoky aftermath of the fire. Then I saw it: at the bottom of the crevasse, hidden by a tangled jungle of weeds and sumac, was the Spicket River.

I'd lived there six and a half years by then and didn't know that the Spicket, one of Lawrence's raisons d'être, was so close. I needed a house to be downed by a fire to reveal the truth.

I went back home and got Bob and made him take a look. "Haven't you always wanted to live near water?" I asked him defiantly as we stepped around beer cans and tires, the fender of a car, several pieces of blackened house framing, even a pile of shattered green glass, like a modern sculpture, on our way to the river's dangerous edge. "Well." I gestured toward it. Subject of a Robert Frost poem. Used as a dump by my neighbors. Trash was caught in the tree branches that made it twist this way and that. "There it is."

THE BURNED-OUT HOUSE stood for over two years, a dangerous mess; but the owners, like those of the abandoned triple-decker next to it, simply walked away. So, too, did the bank that might have claimed it. Finally, the city got enough from the state to pay a wrecking crew to demolish it—along with some two hundred other burned-out houses across the city. Tearing them down cost ten thousand dollars each. I guess these houses that look so perishable are not so easy to get rid of after all.

It's a crime—the way this housing got built in the first place, and the way it has ended up. Built for money not love, and in such feverish haste, it's housing that, like the Irishmen's shanties, looked temporary from the start, as if nobody (not even Billy Wood himself?) really was expecting these workers to stay.

———

"Greenwich, Connecticut!" she sneered: No sociopath could emerge from there. "Were you a debutante too?"

—SUSANNA KAYSEN,
Girl, Interrupted

When I tell people where I was born, I often add the phrase, "But I was poor." Of course, I exaggerate for effect. Growing up in Greenwich, I sometimes did feel "underprivileged," especially since our backyard ended at the border of an exclusive area called Millbrook—a private association of faux Tudor houses, graced with its own country club (to which we certainly did not belong) and guarded by its own police force. But our house, on the other side of the fence (literally), wasn't "huddled" by any means. I never overheard our neighbors' conversations there. All we ever heard was "Fore!" from the Millbrook golf course.

My parents often debate whether to sell that house my father built and live in Florida year-round. They're most inclined when they get their local tax bill, which tripled in 1994; but they say they couldn't bear to cut ties with their well-heeled hometown forever, and who can blame them? Besides, where would they go during the summer months, when Florida's weather is unpleasant? "We don't want to be gypsies," my father says. "Visit Janet, visit me," I suggest, now with more confidence that they would pay me an extended visit since I no longer live in Lawrence, where, in the summertime when the windows were open, the noise of barking dogs and car alarms and sirens kept them awake.

Whenever they complained, however, I gently scolded them, saying they should consider themselves lucky that their parents didn't hear Billy Wood's call to Lawrence; or heard it, and didn't heed it. They should be thankful, I tell them, that they ended up where they did.

I don't mean to imply that, by living in Greenwich, my family escaped hard work—or even hard luck. Nor did they escape hard feelings. I remember how, as a child, riding in the car on backcountry roads of Greenwich on a Sunday afternoon, I used to gape at the mansions we passed, and dream. Occasionally, we—my family and I—used to have a look inside them, if an estate sale was going on: a family's possessions tagged to be sold right there on the premises, out of the dozens of rooms. Chintz-covered couches and chaise longues, a polished dining table as big as a swimming pool, a grand piano draped in a Spanish scarf, cases of dusty books, highboys and lowboys and china in stacks—a rich family's life was laid out for everybody to see, even people as lowly as I thought us to be.

On one of those outings, my father told me to remember that nobody ever came completely honorably by the shovelfuls of money it took to run such households. I guess that was my father's equivalent of the advice Nick Carraway says he got from *his* father in *The Great Gatsby*. And just like Nick, when I got out into the real world, I discovered for my skeptical self how much of what my father had said was useful and true.

My mother admits she once asked a friend to snap her picture in the pillared doorway of a grand Greenwich manor, pretending it was her family's home and not the house of strangers, who surely would have shooed her off their property if they had discovered her. But that was in Mom's adolescence, a dreamy time by definition. Soon enough, she grew

up and married Dad, and they, like legions of other children
of immigrants, were content to aspire to the much more modest goal of middle-class life, and in relatively short order, they
achieved it.

It's also true that, like many people who have risen in the
world, my mother reinvented her family's history. She never
went so far as to deny her roots completely, as Billy Wood did,
but I remember her telling me more than once that she was
descended from kings and queens who'd lost all their money,
jewels included, in a skirmish—or something—back in Italy.
Yes, she was descended from them and so, therefore, was I. I
know she meant it as a soothing fairy tale, but at least for a
while I believed it. Even now I can picture the palace that figured in that fantasy. It looks a lot like those backcountry
Greenwich estates I used to glimpse through the parted curtains of trees.

As we've seen, however, Billy Wood did more than
reinvent his past as a soothing salve for his psyche, and that is
why I have cast him (not the Essex Company) as the chief villain in my story of Lawrence's rise and fall: for isn't there an
extra hot place in hell for those who would disavow their own
kind even as they ruthlessly exploit them? Just because the
man embodies that other American dream, the rags-to-riches
one in the Horatio Alger tales (as my parents embody the
middle-class one), doesn't make what he did to Lawrence—
and to Lawrencians—any less ignoble. Nor does it make the
sorry state of the city today any easier to bear.

And I do lay a lot of the blame for Lawrence's predica-
ment upon Wood, for his legacy of mammoth mill complexes,
more gigantic than any built anywhere before—not to mention
the tenements built simultaneously to house his workers—has
generated many of the most intractable problems the city currently faces.

More to the point, Wood's architectural bequest killed any

hope that Lawrence would continue to be the kind of place where the poor could rationally pursue the middle-class dream *within the city limits*. After Wood was done with Lawrence, the life we still believe it is the right of all Americans to pursue, no matter where they live, would have to be pursued, for the most part, elsewhere.

CHAPTER 7

Bread and Roses, Bread and Wine

B ESIDES THE mill smokestacks, church steeples—Catholic ones, like the masts of so many tall ships in a crowded harbor—are the other prominent feature of the Lawrence skyline. There is a church, or more than one, for every Catholic ethnic group that settled in the city, starting with the Irish ("that priest-ridden Godforsaken race," says my Lawrence friend and former neighbor Jay Dowd, an Irish-American high school English teacher, quoting Joyce). In giving directions to a lost soul, it is not a good idea to use a church for a landmark. Doing so will only serve to get him more lost still. On Holy Thursday of Easter Week, it used to be the custom for Catholics to make a seven-church pilgrimage. Lawrencians could do it on foot, with ease: St. Mary's (the largest church, and Irish); St. Laurence O'Toole's (also Irish, named after the twelfth-century archbishop of Dublin); Holy Rosary (it used to be St. Laurence's, but when the Italians started arriving, the Irish turned the church over to them and built a new St. Laurence's a few blocks away); St. Patrick's, St. Augustine's, and Immaculate Conception (three more Irish); St. Anne's and Sacred Heart (both built by the French-Canadians); Assumption (for the minority of Germans who were not Protestants);

St. Anthony's (for Catholic Syrians—now called Lebanese—who arrived in the late 1900s, along with the Italians); Holy Trinity (for the Poles); Sts. Peter and Paul (for the relatively few Portuguese who settled in Lawrence). Obviously, Holy Thursday would very likely be the only time a member of one ethnic group would darken the door of the church of another.

The Immigrant City is a melting pot, is it? Like the neighborhoods, the bakeries, and the newspapers, so, too, the parishes were ethnically distinct—ethnically "pure," if you will. You went to the place of worship belonging to your own people, or you went nowhere. A contemporary of Miss Barker, the late Alameda King, who was of Irish descent, told an interviewer for the Immigrant City Archives that she believed the Italians were given Holy Rosary "to keep them away from the Irish." Mrs. Stella, a neighbor of hers, was the only Italian she ever knew. As a girl, Alameda was not allowed to dance with Italians "no matter how nice they were." Definition of an intermarriage in Lawrence in those orthodox years? When a Neapolitan married a Sicilian.

Now the Catholic hierarchy in Lawrence, as in most inner cities, has been trying without much success to adjust to radically changing demographics and the resulting slide in church membership. Between 1990 and 1993 alone, attendance at Mass in Lawrence declined by 10 percent; the number of christenings and weddings dropped by 25 percent; even the number of funerals fell by 6 percent. One would expect the Latinos, who come from predominantly Catholic countries, to be flocking to the parishes, but they don't. The majority apparently prefer the more colorful, less structured liturgy of the evangelical churches that have proliferated in Lawrence. I've been told they also feel less like intruders at the out-of-the-mainstream places of worship. But even if Latinos in great numbers did want to practice Catholicism, these new immigrants are poor and would be hard-pressed to support the church buildings and clergy the way the Boston archdiocese would like them to be supported, and so the parishes would still be in trouble.

ALTHOUGH THEY MAY still attend Mass, many Lawrence Catholics, like Catholics everywhere, have also grown increasingly distant from their faith, disillusioned by scandals and by dogma that has remained unresponsive to contemporary social issues and needs. Hang that, a Lawrence friend claims she said to herself when, one Saturday in the mid-sixties, she told her priest in confession at a Lawrence church that her husband wanted her to use birth control, since they already had three children, and the priest replied, "You tell your husband to go to the neighbor if he has to, but that he shouldn't sin with you."

In the old days, a parish priest in Lawrence could probably have gotten away with an instruction like that. Back then, the Catholic Church loomed as large as its steeples in the lives of all its congregations. Weddings, christenings, funerals—religion was central to every family's most momentous occasions. Those blessed buildings were much more than places to pray. Not only spiritual life but also social life was centered in the parishes. Not to be a part of one was to be a pariah.

It's well known that large Catholic families assured a continual renewal of the ranks of the faithful. The hierarchy of the most powerful institution in this city (after the mills, that is) was self-perpetuating, too. For the tradition in Lawrence was that one, or even more than one, per family would enter religious life. Sometimes meeting that challenge presented a hardship. The mill wages of sons and daughters were often needed to support a financially stretched household. On the other hand, the opportunity to take the cloth or the veil meant a job outside the mills (most likely outside Lawrence, too, for that matter)—perhaps the only such opportunity that many a Lawrencian of the city's textile era was apt to get.

Some of Lawrence's most gifted youth made religious vows in the decades between the city's founding and the mid-1960s. But while that was highly efficacious for the church, it was, like the later loss of the middle class, a brain drain for the city.

NOSTALGIA RUNS deep in Lawrence for heaven and hell (in my own soul, too, I'll admit it); for the days when men tipped their hats and women crossed themselves as they passed the stately steepled edifices (if their houses weren't regal, by God, the Almighty's would be); when, as one still-devout resident put it, there were "priests and nuns crawling all over the place." In those years, when Catholic orthodoxy was in the ascendancy, when heaven and hell seemed closer to Lawrence than the Andovers, nobody—except maybe Satan himself?— could have imagined the current decline of the church, any more than one could have seen the coming decline and fall of the mills.

Certainly Irish-born Father James T. O'Reilly never imagined it. The most glorified parish pastor this city has ever known, he reigned in Lawrence as surely as any mayor ever did—perhaps more surely—not only over spiritual life but over political life, as well. In fact, the two—politics and religion—which have traditionally been confused in Lawrence, were virtually indistinguishable from each other during the time that O'Reilly held sway. A shepherd who followed his flock (and across an ocean at that), instead of the usual way round, he ruled not only the members of his own parish—St. Mary's—but all the Irish Catholics in Lawrence between 1886 and 1925, his tenure uncannily coinciding exactly with that of Billy Wood.

"Father O'Reilly was the kingpin, the big boss, the boss man," says James Garvey, born in Lawrence in 1917, whose Irish grandfather worked on the Great Stone Dam; whose father served on Lawrence's common council in that year of James's birth and later ran unsuccessfully for mayor; and whose wife's father served earlier, in 1913–1914—one of the youngest men to do so (he was twenty). Garvey himself, after retiring as a state tax auditor, twice ran for city council (and twice lost). On the wall of the living room of the Garveys' well-appointed Clover Hill apartment, which this middle-class couple left in 1994 for the New Hampshire suburbs, oil paintings of the two family politicians hung for decades.

"Father O'Reilly was at my wife's house every Sunday," Garvey told me as we sat across from these portraits, chatting about the idiosyncratic ways of the clergy and of the Catholic Church. "Free meals. No good minister or good rabbi ever buys a meal if he doesn't have to. He calls on some of the faithful. My father's mother was very friendly with Father O'Reilly, too, because my grandmother knew how to make tea. Whiskey is the main ingredient. Irish tea," adds Garvey, who also describes this Sunday-morning scene:

"My mother and my sisters went to St. Augustine's. My father and I would walk down to St. Mary's. In the back of the church, near the baptismal font, in the last three pews, would be my father, and [lawyer and local historian] Maurice Dorgan, and a lot of the other political lights of the city. And politics was discussed from the time you stood up to bless yourself to start Mass until the time you left. All politics. And sometimes it was louder than what was coming from the altar."

Politics issued from the altar, too; Lawrence priests weren't shy about commenting on issues or even suggesting a slate of proper candidates on the eve of an election. A friend of mine remembers that even at the Children's Mass the priest told her to make sure her parents voted for certain candidates.

And to whom did the parishes steer their votes? In the decades right after Lawrence's founding, there wasn't much choice. Lawrence politics was an appendage of the mills. That's why Charles Storrow, the Essex Company investor, was elected the first mayor, and maybe even why Miss Barker's grandfather John, the Pacific Mills overseer, was an obvious choice for school committee: a member from 1891 to 1898, years during which he debated such Victorian-age quandaries as whether to excuse from "physical culture" female high school students who were "trussed up in corsets." ("If they can't exercise in corsets, make them take them off," one committee man, not John Barker, proposed.) John Rodman Rollins, a neighbor of the Barkers, was another mill man who got elected or appointed to several offices over the course of a long dual career. At various times between 1857 and 1892, he was a school-committee member, superintendent of schools, and mayor. He was also an accountant for the Pacific Mills and a bookkeeper and paymaster for the Essex Company. A school on Prospect Hill—a big brick Victorian period piece that is one of the oldest schools in Massachusetts still in use as a school (which may or may not be a point of pride, depending on your perspective)—is named for him.

The most electable local politician in those days, then, was not only for the mills but of them. After all, a loyal mill employee would have the backing of the mill owners as well as a natural constituency in his fellow workers, especially those who answered directly to him. It went without saying that these men would be Protestant and of either native American birth or English. Then, in 1882, the Irish elected their first mayor, John Breen, an undertaker born in Tipperary (his fifth-generation descendants still operate a funeral home in Lawrence today). But though Breen wasn't a mill employee, he certainly did not win the seat without the approval of the mill owners. Besides, by this time, many Irish were mill bosses.

Many others, like Patrick Sweeney, worked outside the mills, their small businesses surviving or, if they were lucky like Sweeney, thriving. They had begun to identify with their former oppressors, rather than with the currently oppressed—the newly arrived Italians, Poles, Syrians, and French-Canadians—who had taken their places at the noisy machines, and many of the mill owner's wishes had become the smart Irishman's wishes, too.

What the mill owners wanted, of course, was a ready supply of cheap and willing workers. And when the Yankees passed on their political power and this singular wish to the Irish, the churches understood it well. Indeed, the churches could help satisfy the need in a very practical way. For wherever there were Catholic steeples, there were also Catholic schools; and in Lawrence, that was the crucial component.

The schools, staffed by unpaid nuns and brothers, made mill work possible for every adult member of many a Lawrencian mill family during the Wood era. For example, the Venerini Sisters, an Italian order, came to Holy Rosary to minister to the Italians, who had begun to outnumber every other new ethnic group in Lawrence. (Many of these non-English speakers landed in Boston, not Ellis Island, and came directly to the city from there.) The Sisters arrived in 1909, the year the Ayer Mill went up, and cared for Italian children from bell-time to bell-time while mothers and fathers worked. They didn't call it day care at the time, but that's what it was—before school, after school, or both, depending on a family's circumstances. Adults who were children in the teens and 1920s still recall being walked by their parents at dawn to the cold convent, then waiting in the hallway while the nuns finished their morning prayers and chores. The nuns then walked them down to Holy Rosary as the school bell rang.

Nuns were also responsible for teaching the immigrant children bilingually. Some people tend to forget, when they speak disparagingly of today's bilingual programs, that most of these parish schools conducted classes in a native tongue for at least a few hours a week. Teaching pupils English was their main goal, however. English lessons for workers' children pleased the mills, not because these future mill workers needed English to do their jobs, but because the mill owners believed that, along with the language, they would absorb "American" values and thus be less susceptible to radical labor organizers.

ITALIAN-BORN Father Mariano Milanese was Holy Rosary's pastor during Billy Wood's reign. He was a priest nearly as powerful as St. Mary's Father O'Reilly, except that the Irish always had the upper hand, in church as in city politics. (The Irish had not only gotten there first; they continued to outnumber the other ethnic groups.)

If O'Reilly was the "boss man," Milanese is said to have been the "ladies' man." He is also described as a crook and a gambler, who not only bet on racehorses but owned them; who could get you a mill job but demanded your first paycheck for thanks; who would alter an underage youngster's birth certificate so he or she could go to work early in the mills, if the parents' finances required it. Or the church's: it was mill wages, after all, that built the steeples of Lawrence. Every one.

Indeed, the name Milanese can scarcely be uttered without the word *money*, in one form or another, coming along right after it. "Father Milanese once had a fire in the church," James Garvey told me, "and the insurance adjuster came out from Boston, and when he got up there, Milanese took him into the kitchen. They had a big potbellied stove, and the adjuster stripped down to his shirt, it was so hot in the goddamned room, and they stayed there about half an hour, and then, quick as a flash, Milanese grabbed him by the arm and took him into the church and sat him down in the pew. The roof was open, and he had him on the inside so he couldn't get out, and he kept him there, and the adjuster said, 'The longer I stayed, the more I agreed to.' And he said that when they got back inside, Milanese took off his cassock and had two sweaters and a coat on underneath. And the adjuster said, 'So much for priests.' "

Garvey's story and the others may be apocryphal, but they illustrate a fundamental truth: that these priests wielded power enough to have inspired such legends. This is especially true of the tales generated by the priests' roles in the 1912 strike. Both Father O'Reilly and Father Milanese naturally backed management, Milanese supposedly receiving a fifty-thousand-dollar bonus for his support. Some Lawrencians assert that their parents never attended church again as a result of the betrayal. ("My mother had us baptized when my father was visiting relatives in Italy," a woman in her seventies claims.) Garvey's father, being a middle-class Irish businessman and removed from the mill hands' world, didn't actively support the mill workers, but he had a falling out with Father O'Reilly over the strike all the same. Ostensibly, it was an argument over a building downtown called Lexington Hall:

"My father built that building, and he had stores downstairs and they had a hall where they had prizefights, but during this thing [the strike], the IWW hired a couple of places, and Father O'Reilly told my father he didn't think Dad should take that money; it wasn't good money, and my father told him that he would give up that money as soon as at the High Mass at ten o'clock, [Father O'Reilly] wouldn't collect from the people who owned the barrooms, because that wasn't good money. And although they were civil to each other, there was never a great deal of friendship after that."

MEMORIES OF the great strike still stir intense feelings in many Lawrencians—and ex-Lawrencians, too. At my friend's used-book store in Andover, I met a man with an Irish surname who told me that his father had owned a shop on Essex Street in Lawrence in 1912 and that the strikers marched right past its windows. The strikers' signs read NO GOD, NO COUNTRY, this man told me angrily, as if he had been there himself, though he wasn't born until nine years later. (Actually, the IWW slogan was "No God, No Master.") "They were Reds, you know," he added with a challenge in his voice. A hearing aid was curled in his ear; he was wearing a coat and tie, overdressed for an informal lecture at a bookstore on a Sunday afternoon. But he could get up an awful lot of Irish when he talked about Bread and Roses (he himself, of course, would never refer to the strike that way).

Radical labor union activity of the sort that eventually erupted in Lawrence was common in the United States in the couple of decades just before World War I. "Industrial democracy," by which workers, employers, and consumers would cooperatively determine work conditions, wages, and even the products to be made, was believed by many organizers to be not only desirable but inevitable: the "tendency of our times," as one magazine writer put it. Between 1890 and 1894 alone, there were approximately 14,000 strikes and lockouts involving about 4 million U.S. workers. It was also common for these actions to be forcibly, unpleasantly, sometimes morbidly halted, as in the bloody confrontation between locked-out workers and the Pinkertons at Carnegie Steel's Homestead Steelworks in 1892.

Carnegie, the steel king, is fondly remembered today as the philanthropist who donated the money for more than 2,500 public libraries in the United States and in Canada. It is not well known that labor unions protested these gifts. Dee Garrison's 1979 book, *Apostles of Culture: The Public Librarian and American Society 1876–1920*, offers these facts: "When Carnegie donated one of his first libraries to Pittsburgh in 1892, local labor organizations petitioned the city council to return the money, on the grounds that it was tainted by the way in which it was earned. Workers often charged that Carnegie wished only to glorify himself by his philanthropy. Especially after the violence of the Homestead strike, organized labor and the left frequently opposed the erection of Carnegie libraries, as in Detroit in 1901 and Indianapolis in 1903. This worker opposition . . . was not scattered, but was general and consistent."

(Lawrence Public Library isn't a Carnegie library, incidentally. It was established in 1872, with money from the White Fund, the same private local charity that sponsored *The Report of the Lawrence Survey*, the 1911 housing exposé. Daniel Appleton White, the fund's namesake, owned one of the large tracts of farmland that occupied most of Lawrence long before the mills were built.)

Reading Garrison's book made this bibliophile reassess her own long-standing reverence for Carnegie's largesse. Reading elsewhere that the wife of another magnate of the era wore a diamond tiara "as big as a coal scuttle" to a dinner party, and seeing a photo of a squad of Vanderbilt servants who *themselves* had servants, I found my sympathies for the striking workers of the day renewed.

Other research made me realize that many striking Lawrencians had a shaky grasp of radical labor's vision; some were even oblivious to its aims, or downright confused by them. Laura Gaetano, who was seventeen in 1912, recorded this on tape at the textile museum in the early eighties: "Yes, I was there. We were on strike with the rest of them. It was lots of fun. We were in the parade and made our own skirts."

Her words reminded me, again, of Chaplin's *Modern Times*, of the scene in which the little tramp picks up a flag that has fallen from the tailgate of a passing truck; he waves it vigorously, trying to get the driver's attention, then starts after him down the street just as a parade of strikers rounds the corner—and so, suddenly, unwittingly, joins the demonstration.

Being unaware of one's place in history doesn't make that history any less decisive, however.

————

The posters were very beautiful. But the man in charge told him they were not right. We don't want art, the man said. We want something to stir the anger. We want to keep the fires stoked. Tateh had drawn pickets, stark figures with their feet in snow. He had drawn families huddled in their tenements.

—E. L. DOCTOROW,
Ragtime

The Industrial Workers of the World, founded in Chicago in 1905—the year construction began on the Wood Mill—had not yet led a strike in New England before Bread and Roses occurred, nor were they much of a presence in Lawrence at the time. Out of more than forty thousand workers (half the population of 85,000 over age fourteen worked in the mills), only about three hundred belonged to the IWW's Local 20. (The United Textile Workers of America claimed a membership of several times that number, but it organized only skilled workers. The Wobblies, by contrast, wanted to organize entire industries. Also, unlike the UTWA, they refused to believe that immigrants and women were "unorganizable.")

So no large union organization ignited the protest that

erupted on the morning of January 12, 1912. Indeed, for me, that is one of the most impressive facts about Bread and Roses: that it was instigated by a small group of the workers themselves, not orchestrated by the big-time labor organizers whose names eventually came to be associated with it.

Though the housing hardships, the huddling and scraping—the eating of molasses, not meat—contributed to the workers' discontent, pay was the immediate cause of the strike: short pay. On New Year's Day, a new state law had gone into effect, capping at fifty-four the number of hours women and children were allowed to work per week, down from fifty-six. The mills couldn't operate, however, without their female and child laborers working along with the men. So Wood and the other mill owners in Lawrence decided the prudent thing to do was to cut hours—and pay—all around. They were within their rights, but the only thing the workers understood was that their weekly pittance (six dollars on average) now lacked the extra thirty-two pennies that was the equivalent of four very necessary loaves of bread.

All over Lawrence that morning, there must have been grumbling, anger, questions, and tears. That night, the members of IWW Local 20 met and hammered out their strategy; they also sent a telegram to the IWW headquarters in New York, asking for assistance. On the morning of the twelfth, a Friday, at a predetermined signal, five hundred workers at the Washington Mills, most of them Italians, sabotaged their equipment. They slashed power belts, jammed gears with tools, then ran up and down the aisles, urging others to follow their example—at least to come with them out into the snowy streets and leave their machines running, thus ruining the cloth.

This initial group then stormed the Wood Mill, a few blocks away, shouting at their astonished fellow workers to do what they had done; from there, the growing crowd crossed the road and burst into the Ayer Mill to gather still more mill hands to the cause. By this time, workers in the Kundhardt Mill and the Duck Mill could see from their windows the astounding thing that was happening in the streets below.

By midmorning, upwards of twelve thousand mill workers of all nationalities had left their machines and joined the rowdy, giddy, angry protest. A riot was declared. The strike had begun.

At least publicly, Wood and the other mill owners remained calm. They had decided to sit tight; let the hysteria subside. "I believe that as soon as our employees understand the real issue, and where the responsibility actually rests, they will see that their action at Lawrence was hasty and ill-advised," Wood told reporters in a prepared statement that afternoon. "There is no cause for striking and when the employees find that justice is not on their side the strike cannot possibly be long-lived."

But the strikers' passions didn't ebb. The following day, while half the city's labor force stayed home—many of them pressured to do so by the strike's organizers—another several thousand workers attempted to charge the entrance of one of the mills, only to be rebuffed by blasts of icy water pumped through fire hoses trained on them by local police. The strikers responded by throwing chunks of ice from the canal through mill windows.

Mayor John Scanlon was green—he had been in office only two weeks—and scared. On the third day, when the strikers attempted to storm city hall, he called in the militia.

They came with their horses, their bayonets, and their live rounds. A child's common memory: watching from tenement windows as the soldiers marched below; rode past in open cars or stamped their feet to keep warm; yawned with the cold and with boredom. Thousands of workers continued to parade in the streets daily.

By this time, the IWW organizers had arrived, including luminaries William "Big Bill" Haywood, Elizabeth Gurley Flynn, and Joseph Ettor. In the past, efforts to unionize Lawrence had failed because organizers, like those for the UTWA, had tried to do it according to craft or mill or employer. The Wobblies had another idea, simple but brilliant, and it worked. They organized their strikes by ethnic group—by language—so that the striking workers could speak to one another. (They broke their locals down into ethnic branches, too.) It was the way the mills themselves had organized them—not to mention the churches.

History is unclear about how many Lawrence mill workers actually joined the IWW either while the strike was in progress or afterward; figures supplied by the Wobblies themselves are probably inflated. Donald B. Cole estimates in *Immigrant City* that only four hundred enrolled, bringing the total in the city to a mere seven hundred, while membership in the UTWA increased to seventeen thousand within the year (though many did not remain members). Nonetheless, from the moment they appeared on the scene, the IWW leadership seized control of the strike, dictating its direction and dynamics. They took it upon themselves, for example, to hugely amplify the workers' demands. It was no longer just a matter of restoring the two-hour pay cut. Now it was a strike for a 15 percent wage increase on fifty-four hours; double pay for overtime; abolition of premium and bonus systems (which pressured workers into trying to reach sometimes impossible production goals); affiliation by all employees with the IWW; and a promise that all workers be allowed to return to their places in the mills regardless of any part they might have played in the strike.

The big-name Wobblies, their audacious demands, the singing, and the speeches in six languages—English, Italian, French, German, Flemish, and Syrian—made for colorful newspaper copy, and also attracted the pens of muckraking journalists like Lincoln Steffens and Mary Heaton Vorse, who wrote for respected news weeklies like *Harper's* as well as for the socialist press. The national attention in turn brought money to the cause from other trade unions, socialists, and ethnic organizations across the country. It also brought public opinion into the fray.

Lawrencians who opposed the striking workers were outraged, as well as embarrassed by the attention. Miss Barker, age nine, was instructed by her grammar school teacher to write a letter to a student in "a faraway city," stressing something positive about Lawrence, to counteract the bad press. (She chose to write about the city's state-of-the-art water filtration system.) One of Miss Barker's contemporaries, born in Lawrence in 1900, says her teachers refused to acknowledge the strike at all: "Never a discussion. If anyone mentioned it, the subject was quickly changed. Or they decided it was time to open all the windows and take physical education, although it wasn't called that at the time—it was called exercises."

Four wintry weeks passed. The "singing strikers," as they were dubbed, continued to raise their voices. Then two people were killed. One of them, a Syrian man, was bayoneted in the back while playing his French horn in one of the protest parade bands. The other, an Italian woman, who, according to strike lore, wasn't even marching that day, was shot through the heart.

After the deaths, many parents decided to send their children away. The IWW organizers arranged for them to stay with the families of socialist sympathizers in New York City; Philadelphia; Hoboken, New Jersey; Bridgeport, Connecticut; and Barre, Vermont. Margaret Sanger, who had not yet become famous as the leader of the birth-control movement, helped arrange the children's exodus.

On Saturday, February 10, 1912, the first contingent departed from the Lawrence train station, carrying headline-grabbing signs: A LITTLE CHILD SHALL LEAD THEM; WE CAME FROM LAWRENCE TO FIND A HOME; and SOMEDAY WE SHALL REMEMBER EXILE. The newspapers played the story up big, the large photos conveying the impression (belied by the fine print) that every household in the city was being forced to surrender its youngsters. (It's unclear how many children were actually involved: estimates range from two hundred to four hundred.) Hating the bad publicity, the mill owners tried to stop the children's flight; they ordered the police to prevent subsequent groups from boarding their trains and to arrest their parents on charges of neglect. The arrests were quickly ruled illegal, however, and the departures continued; all the mill owners had succeeded in doing was garner still more bad press.

Ten-year-old Ernest Calderone was one who journeyed to Barre, Vermont, where many of the stonecutters in the marble quarries were socialists. His father had come to Lawrence in 1889 or 1890 from Caserta, near Naples, with an understanding of machines, and at the time of the strike he was a fixer, one of the men who kept the machines running, and well paid by mill standards. Still, Ernest, who himself grew up to be a section hand in the Wood Mill, was amazed by the treats that awaited him in Barre: "They brought us to a hall, and put us up on a stage, and took us one by one, like if anybody wanted this boy or girl. They bought me a suit, they bought me a sled, they bought me shorts, they bought me ties."

Another detail of Ernest's experience reveals just how fully the IWW understood the important role that skillful manipulation of the media was playing in this battle. He says the organizer who put him on the train ripped his hand-embroidered shirt at the shoulder—a child of downtrodden workers shouldn't be as nicely dressed as this one was.

Meanwhile, back in Lawrence, a clumsy plot to plant dynamite in various locations around the city (a cemetery was one) and blame it on the Wobblies and their anarchistic ways failed when authorities arrested Ernest Pittman, the Andover contractor who had built the Wood Mill, along with John Breen (the son of former mayor Breen), who directed the family funeral parlor and served on the school committee. (Breen was convicted and fined five hundred dollars; Pittman confessed—drunkenly, it's been said—that Wood himself was involved, then committed suicide; Billy Wood was eventually indicted, too, but acquitted.)

Then, in mid-March, as the state's attorney general, the U.S. attorney's office, a U.S. congressional committee (before which Margaret Sanger, among others, appeared), and the Federal Bureau of Labor initiated investigations of working and living conditions in Lawrence, Wood and the other mill owners capitulated. The strike ended, the children came home, and a sweet victory was declared.

IF YOU CONSIDER it solely from the standpoint of the issue that started the rebellion—low pay—Bread and Roses was one of the most successful (as well as largest) strikes in U.S. labor history. Locally, wages went up to a minimum of $7.25 per week, and throughout New England, mill owners who hoped to avert similar troubles gave some 200,000 other textile workers 5 to 7 percent increases. But though the owners agreed to them during the negotiations, the Wobblies' other demands—overtime pay, for example—were never actually met. Moreover, some strikers did lose their jobs, and those who had been arrested during the disturbances, even for minor offenses like loitering, were given stiff jail terms by a local judge named Mahoney. Not only that but three out-of-town IWW organi-

zers—Joseph Ettor, Arturo Giovannitti, and Joseph Caruso—
were indicted for murder, the state claiming that the instigators
of the strike were to blame for the deaths of the Syrian man
and the Italian woman. In the end, the three were acquitted,
but the start of their trial—in Salem, Massachusetts, in late
September—sparked a sympathy strike in Lawrence.

This time, the workers who staged the strike were the
hard-core radical fringe. The others had had enough; they had
won their pay raise, after all, and were eager to make up the
wages they'd lost. There had also been grumbling among ethnic groups over uneven distribution of the strike relief funds.
But something else besides lack of momentum or interethnic
feuding prevented mill hands from joining the ranks again:
this second protest had distinctly anarchistic overtones (not
just philosophical underpinnings). Some paraders trampled the
American flag. Prominent, too, were signs saying NO GOD, NO
MASTER (the slogan misquoted by the angry man at the Andover bookstore). Most immigrants would have no part of this:
they wanted to become Americans perhaps more than they
wanted anything else.

The Wobblies quickly lost favor in Lawrence after the September demonstration, and a few weeks later, on Columbus
Day, a reported 32,000 men, women, and children marched in
a counterparade—organized and led by Father O'Reilly. Irish,
English, and native-born Lawrencians were the backbone of
this event, each of them waving a tiny American flag, their
purchase most likely financed by Billy Wood and the other
mill owners. The theme was a calculated reversal, too: "For
God and Country." In the common today, at the base of the
flagpole, you'll see a plaque commemorating the occasion. "As
a perpetual reminder of October 12, 1912," it says. Not there
or anywhere else in the city will you find a plaque that says a
word about the other events of that year.

"[FATHER O'REILLY] stopped them from doing all the radical things. There was a big parade, walking up and down, up and down. They [the Church] broke the IWW." The voice—and the skewed interpretation—belongs to Winifred Leonard, firefighter Tom Troy's aunt, who worked in the mills at the time of the strike and in 1977, at age eighty, recorded her recollections on tape for one of her grandnieces.

Jay Dowd, my Joyce-quoting friend and former neighbor, also recollects that O'Reilly "stopped them," but he calls it strikebreaking. It was Jay who told me about another parade, which took place fifty years after the strike, in September 1962, when he was eleven. He marched in his Boy Scout uniform along with the rest of Troop 16. At the head of the parade, the enormous American flag seemed to cover the sky.

Only years later, when he was an adult, did Jay learn about Bread and Roses (he says it was never once mentioned in the Lawrence parochial schools he attended or at home by his parents)—and that the 1962 parade had been staged to commemorate not the fiftieth anniversary of the famous labor victory, but the breaking of radical labor's hold on the city by the sainted Father O'Reilly.

The irony seems to be lost on former mayor Buckley. Proudly, he loaned me a treasured memento of the 1962 spectacle. It is an album of large black-and-white glossy photos of row upon row of Catholic-school boys parading in uniform jackets and ties, followed by grids of the girls in their plaid skirts, white gloves, and saddle shoes. Children dressed up as nuns, priests, even saints, follow them. Columns of altar boys in white bucks and cassocks take up the rear. (From these images, you wouldn't know that Lawrence had a public-school system at all.)

Paging through the album, I see John Buckley himself, with a shiny black top hat on his proud Irish pate and his long high-jumper's legs, striding ahead. And there is young Ted

Kennedy (about to assume the U.S. Senate seat recently occupied by his brother John). Next come huge floats decorated with paper flowers. A Mass is being said on one of them; St. Francis and his birds and other animals make a tableau on another. The backdrop to them all is Essex Street, its buildings festooned with patriotic bunting, spectators five and six deep on the sidewalk, hands clapping, waiting for more.

The parade goes on and on and on in a city whose favorite leisure pastime, or one of them, used to be watching parades and religious processions. But now here, finally, are two of the highlights of the day. Rolling along on its own float is a larger-than-life photo of Father O'Reilly himself, like a cult figure to be worshiped. A bespectacled man. Grayish. A vague Irish face. He could be any Irish priest, after all. Then, in two open cars, waving, come several old men, a half dozen of them, ghostly pale, wearing hats that appear too large for their heads. They are retired policemen who served alongside the state militia in 1912. Perhaps they are the same men who sprayed strikers with frigid water from fire hoses that day by the canal. Now here they are being cheered by a crowd that surely must include relatives of some of their victims.

If the odd reversal weren't bad enough, with the villains and the heroes so clearly switching places, far odder is a city that doesn't ensure that its own part in a significant historical moment is remembered by its young. The neglect is especially unfortunate, since the strike was significant even beyond its role in labor history, producing another far-reaching result unanticipated by its leaders. That is, what appeared to have been a solid victory for immigrants was actually quite the opposite, because the strike marked the beginning of a final and successful push for passage of a series of repressive immigration laws. A group called the Immigration Restriction League, dominated by Boston Brahmins—Henry Cabot Lodge, among them—had urged restrictions on the immigration of Southern and Eastern Europeans for years. (The door had earlier been shut against the Chinese and Japanese by a sequence of injunctions that began with the Chinese Exclusion Act of 1882.) Now, those hot-blooded foreigners had virtually shut down a world-famous city; clearly, they were a danger to the American way of life. Unquestionably, it was in the nation's interest to keep them out. And so the laws were passed. In 1917, a literacy requirement prohibited the entry of "illiterates" over the age of sixteen—that is, anyone who couldn't read or write in English or some other language twenty to twenty-five words of the U.S. Constitution. Four years later, the sweeping changes of the quota system would go into effect, limiting the number of immigrants of any nationality to 3 percent of the number of foreign-born persons of that nationality already resident in the United States; supposedly, this was to allow time for those already here to assimilate.

Locally, too, the strike created an unexpected backlash beyond Father O'Reilly's counterparade, a reaction that led to more problems for the city than the strike actually solved. For the truth is that, for years thereafter, businesses looking to relocate shunned Lawrence, because its workers had a national reputation as rabble-rousers. " 'Oh, Lawrence. That's a bad union city,' " John Buckley says he heard more times than he can count, in the fifties and beyond, when he was trying to entice new industries into the empty mills.

AFTER THE MILLS failed, many of them were torn down, some of their brickwork falling into the north and south canals; I know a man who has built a fine chimney in the suburbs with bricks from those demolitions—bricks that he fished out of the murky water. As the mills go, so go the churches: as of this writing, the Archdiocese of Boston has torn down two. In a matter of days, they topple—structures that took years and many thousands of parishioners' dollars to build. And I know some people who have salvaged bricks from those, as a holy remembrance.

St. Laurence O'Toole's, Jay Dowd's boyhood parish, where he served as a freckle-faced altar boy, fell to the wrecker's ball in 1980, when it was not quite seventy years old. The land was sold to a developer, but nothing has yet been done with the plot. The big, weedy, consecrated triangle at the bottom of Prospect Hill, where three streets converge, seems destined for the foreseeable future to serve only to anger Jay when he drives by.

In 1991, Immaculate Conception was demolished; supposedly, it needed only a new roof, for a cost of $150,000. Unraisable? Aside from its religious significance, the brick Victorian-style Gothic church, with its buttresses and pointed arched windows and doorways, was an important piece of historical architecture—and publicized as such in the 1970s by the Massachusetts Historical Commission, which recommended making it the focal point of the urban-renewed neighborhood that surrounded it. Apparently, this didn't faze the archdiocese, or the state.

Like the demise of the mills, the Catholic Church's abandonment of Lawrence began in the fifties, as it followed its flock to the suburbs. Much of the money the archdiocese might have used to bolster a Lawrence that was foundering as the mills closed was instead funneled into two new institutions—Holy Family Hospital in Methuen and Merrimack College in North Andover, both of which thrive today. Boundary lines were not so clearly drawn between the city and the suburbs in those days, it's true, and people say it didn't seem like abandonment back then. But I can't help thinking that Lawrence would be in far better shape today if it had those two substantial institutions inside the city's limits, not outside them. (I "can't help thinking" a lot of things, it seems . . .)

How does all this make Lawrencian Catholics feel? I ask, but they evade the question. On the other hand, Marist Brother Tom Pettite, an iconoclastic former local activist for the homeless (who has also ministered to lepers on the streets of India with Mother Teresa), doesn't mind being blunt. "The Church [in Lawrence] is in a crisis state right now," he told me, sitting in his flowing white robes behind his desk in one of the shelters he founded. "It's having trouble maintaining its buildings, its structures. But we don't need buildings to be a church. The people are the church."

People—declining numbers, dwindling collections—are precisely the problem, however.

THERE STILL IS a Catholic presence in Lawrence. First Communion suits for boys are still advertised in the *Eagle-Tribune* every spring. Abortions are not performed at Lawrence General Hospital as a matter of policy set, albeit not without controversy, by the Department of Obstetrics and Gynecology. And though St. Augustine's School on Tower Hill has lowered its tuition in order to attract and retain a shrinking student body, St. Mary's High School for girls is still considered a selective local school, its every green window shade pulled down precisely halfway—exactly as was done at my St. Mary's, in Greenwich, and, I realize to my horror, exactly as I used to keep the old green shades at my house in Lawrence (a measure of residual orthodoxy?).

Beyond that, Division 8 of the Ancient Order of Hibernians, named for Reverend James T. O'Reilly, still maintains a busy headquarters downtown, just off the north canal. To be eligible to join, the bylaws state, one must be of Irish birth or descent and a practicing Catholic. One of the bridges I drive over nearly every day is named for Father O'Reilly, too.

How long will it be before his name is forgotten?

"There's nothing deader than a dead priest," says Tom Troy, a practicing Catholic whose seven children—all named for saints—have gone on to become a lawyer, a plumber, a mason, a teacher, an editor, a graphic designer, and the assistant director for Adult Services at the Lawrence Public Library.

The librarian, Margaret—the only one of the Troy children who still lives in Lawrence, on Prospect Hill—often helps me find the research materials I need; but, thirty years after she marched in the 1962 parade, wearing her blue plaid St. Rita's School uniform, I was the one who told her what it was all about.

"If they [the clergy] took a fool's advice they would confine their attention to religion," the father of Stephen Dedalus huffs in *A Portrait of the Artist as a Young Man*.

"Politics *is* religion," comes the reply.

CHAPTER 8

Epitaphs

Nothing fails like success.

—LINCOLN STEFFENS,
Autobiography

ORLD WAR I was a windfall for Billy Wood. It also heralded his doom.

In 1908, Teddy Roosevelt had changed the color of the U.S. Army's uniforms from the navy blue of Civil War days to the olive and khaki that endure today; just a few years later, Wood's American Woolen Company beat out J. P. Stevens and other industry rivals to nab the government order to make the cloth for the millions of new uniforms and blankets that the doughboys required. The initial contract, for more than $50 million, was reported at the time to represent the largest single government appropriation for textiles in American history. Before the war's end, AWC would receive another government contract for just over that amount—a total of $102 million in all. Given this boon, it is hardly surprising that by the end of 1918, AWC had some fifty mills in operation not only in Lawrence but throughout New England; how else could such an unprecedented demand be met?

In his memoirs, published in 1923, Frederick Ayer, Wood's

father-in-law and business partner, pronounced the company "a perfect success." But Ayer's memoirs were posthumous. He had died in 1918, with the Great War still in progress; by 1923, it was already clear that he'd spoken too soon.

During that final war year, Alice Sweeney, granddaughter of Patrick, worked in Washington, D.C. Feeling patriotic perhaps, the Vassar graduate had taken a clerical job routing purchase orders, including those for textiles. One may imagine her delight as the familiar names of the Lawrence mills passed across her desk—and picture her dismay when, at war's end, the cancellations of those orders began.

Billy Wood didn't seem to notice. Why should he have? Profits in 1919 held steady, more than $15 million (double the rate for 1916); for AWC's eighteen thousand shareholders, dividends on both preferred and common stock were up 25 percent over the previous year. The continued growth was due not only to increased domestic sales (the war had been lucrative for other U.S. companies besides AWC, and their employees had money to spend) but also to sales in Europe, where war-damaged mills were still shut down.

So for a while, the good times rolled on, and the only change was in the color of the dye in the vats, from olive and khaki to civilian blue. In fact, as one of the company's ads proudly proclaimed, 70 percent of all AWC products were now dyed blue. It's a peculiar boast, unless you understand that pumping out a standardized product was what had made AWC, and many other American companies of the era, so successful. As Wood's biographer, Edward Roddy, remarked, blue serge was the textile industry's Model T. (It's easy to imagine that every fellow behind the wheel of one of Ford's motorcars was wearing a blue serge suit.) In the end, though, AWC's ability to produce huge quantities of a uniform product would turn out to be its only ability. Like an ocean liner steaming along, it couldn't easily change directions, and its sheer bulk, once its greatest asset, would be its undoing.

But not yet. Shortly after Armistice Day, Wood began to build his model corporate suburb, Shawsheen Village. It's unclear why he took on such an ambitious extracurricular project—his vision may have been inspired by more than paternalism; *hubris* may be the more accurate word—but it is certain that he personally tended to every last detail of the construction, from the window boxes (supplied with flowers by AWC) to the underground trash receptacles. He even chose the type and number of shrubs and trees to be planted on the properties. He also, of course, gave the streets of Shawsheen Village names that would win the approval of "self-respecting, good quality Americans" (the phrase Cornelius used in his memoirs to characterize people, like his wife, with Colonial ancestry): Argyle, Arundel, Balmoral, Burnham, Carisbrook, Carlisle, Dunbarton, and York on the White Shawsheen side, and Kensington, William, and Windsor on the Red side.

"Move those houses and eliminate the street," he reportedly told his private secretary, George M. Wallace, after returning home from a trip to Europe and finding that a certain block had deviated from his specifications. "Mark that," he allegedly ordered an underling on a trip to Valley Forge, and subsequently a small fieldstone building that is supposed to resemble one at the winter headquarters of George Washington's Continental army went up in Shawsheen. (To this day, it sits, functionless, at the edge of what is now a town of Andover soccer field; historians say it looks nothing like any building ever built at Valley Forge.)

Who knows if these anecdotes are true? If they are, early photographs taken from the air—the tiny houses all in neat rows, suggesting so literally engineering by God—must have especially pleased a man who had only to point at something to make it appear or disappear. Apparently, however, not all of Shawsheen Village's residents, who were able to rent the new houses from AWC quite reasonably, shared Wood's enthusiasm for his dream suburb. "When Wood directed the relocation of the executive and managerial staff from Boston to Shawsheen Village in the spring of 1923," Edward Roddy reports, "there were scattered grumblings and a few flat refusals to comply." In his memoirs, Cornelius Wood writes that no sooner had the new residents been settled than there was "a great clamor to get out." Maybe the Bostonians simply missed Boston, but many who had moved there from Lawrence weren't happy, either. While they no doubt appreciated their slate-tiled roofs, decorative cornices, and columned porticoes, the double-hung, many-paned windows, fireplace mantelpieces, and linen closets—not to mention the golf course, tennis courts, bowling green, swimming and skating pond, post office, retail stores, and kindergarten—the fact that, as it turned out, their paterfamilias intended to regulate their lives at home almost as closely as he regulated life at the mills probably did not sit so well. Housewives, for example, were discouraged—if not prohibited—from hanging laundry outdoors (just as my cleaning-lady friend's former tenant is barred from doing so at her condo in Haverhill); the Shawsheen Village Laundry was the place to take dirty clothes. Nor were garages part of the architecture: Wood thought they were "unsightly," and he required car owners to use the large central Shawsheen Village Garage.

And how many of the social and sporting activities that took place on evenings and weekends in the Village—Saturday-night dances at the outdoor pavilion was one—were actually command performances? As Cornelius Wood wrote in his memoirs, observing what most of us already know, coworkers "did not like seeing in off hours the people they had worked with all day."

Since Billy Wood's own Andover home, Arden, was just a stone's throw from the new neighborhood, maybe AWC's managers also felt a bit "underprivileged," even in the midst of their middle-class dream (as I did in Greenwich, driving by those mansions on Sundays). Not only did Arden loom; another lavish house went up on Wood's property during the postwar years. After all, his annual earnings from AWC had increased nearly tenfold, from $100,000 in 1914 to $978,725 in salary and commissions (excluding stock dividends) four years later, with "any and all income taxes, State and Federal," paid by the company. (The 1918 levy amounted to a whopping $681,169—large incomes were taxed heavily during the war— but if government officials thought Wood was profiteering, they didn't say so, at least not yet; excessive wartime earnings wouldn't become an issue until a few years later.)

Situated next door to Arden, the new residence was dubbed a "cottage," though it is certainly as palatial as Arden—three stories high, and with two belowground levels, which workers blasted out of rock. Designed in the Spanish Colonial Revival style, the house has siding of white stucco and a green tile roof; Wood named it for another *As You Like It* character, Rosalind's lover, Orlando.

No longer a private home, Orlando Cottage is now a private club "for business and professional men and their guests." I happen to be the acquaintance of one of the members, so I have had a look inside, and a guided tour by the club's manager, Bob Finney, who grew up in White Shawsheen and says that he and his boyhood friends used to play inside the house when it was empty for a time in the forties. (You may have glimpsed Orlando Cottage yourself if you saw the 1992 movie *School Ties*: the country club scene was filmed there.) Imagine room after dark oak–paneled room with hand-carved wood-work—the heads of Shakespearean characters border the doorways—and contrasting hand-molded plaster ceilings. Picture as well two wide staircases with hand-carved banisters, fireplaces of rare Italian marble, silver light fixtures from Tiffany's, and a dining room so large that it now serves as the club's restaurant, capable of seating eighty.

Who would live in Orlando Cottage? While it was being planned and built, three of Wood's four children had married. When it was completed, in late 1916, Wood gave the house to his firstborn son, William Madison Wood, Jr. Blond-haired and blue-eyed, he had been a football star at St. George's School in Newport, Rhode Island; had graduated from Harvard with the class of 1915; joined AWC directly; and was already the father of Doris Anne by the time he moved in. William Madison III was born in 1917 (according to Bob Finney, William recalls staring up at the painted cherubs that ring the ceiling of what used to be his nursery and today is a women's rest room). In 1918, upon the death of Grandfather Ayer, William Junior was awarded a vice presidency as well as a place on the company's board of directors.

In fairness, he earned his keep. It was he who had gone to Washington, at his father's request, and landed the unprecedented $50 million government contract, and he who, in 1917, instigated the establishment of an AWC Labor Relations Department. Biographer Roddy notes that William Wood, Jr., worked with the unions to increase worker pay by as much as 30 percent in some cases and decrease hours from fifty-four to forty-eight per week by 1918; what he doesn't mention is that during the war a stable labor situation was a national necessity, worth almost any price. (Afterward, of course, AWC crumbled, and with it all those jobs.) Not only that but Wood *père* continued to grace the enemies lists of radical labor unionists: when U.S. Post Office officials in New York intercepted thirty-eight identically wrapped letter bombs in late 1919, they found them to be addressed to such pillars of the establishment as John D. Rockefeller, J. P. Morgan, and . . . William Madison Wood.

Within a year of becoming an AWC vice president, young Wood resigned his position and went into the woolen merchandizing business with a partner. We can only speculate about what precipitated his departure; we do know that soon after he left the company, the U.S. government accused William Wood, Sr., of war profiteering, for having made so much money on the orders his son had secured.

At the trial in U.S. District Court in New York on June 11, 1920, Wood was acquitted, his attorney having successfully argued that while the law forbade excessive profit making on wearing apparel, the cloth from which it was made did not, technically speaking, constitute apparel. Still, this fanatically patriotic man, who so badly wanted to be a "most typical American" that he denied his foreign-born parents, must have been crushed by the indictment, inconsolable even by the banner emblazoned with the words A MAN WITHOUT A STAIN UPON HIS HONOR, supposedly fashioned by the workers on the day of the acquittal and hung from the Wood Mill windows (or, in other versions of the story, carried by workers from Lawrence to Arden) in time for Wood's homecoming.

Would things have been different for the mills and for Lawrence if father and son had been reconciled? Perhaps. But on the afternoon of August 15, 1922, William Wood, Jr., driving his Rolls-Royce from the town of Reading to Andover, crashed and was killed.

Wood was shattered. In his memoirs, second son Cornelius refers to his father's "new unreasonable-ness." He also alludes to "eccentricities," even "hallucinations," which eventually made it impossible for Wood to carry on. For a while, subordinates covered for him, but by then, the company was failing, too: in 1923, as the flamboyant era of the flapper began and suits of blue serge were starting to look hayseedish, profits at AWC were only $6.6 million; 1924 saw a deficit of $7 million.

Nineteen twenty-four was also the year that Wood's physical health started to deteriorate: in the spring, he suffered a stroke; he had another that summer. Finally, mercifully, he resigned—though he continued to draw a salary of $1 million, with all taxes still paid by the company.

Suddenly without work for the first time since he had joined the labor force at age twelve, Wood put all his remaining energies into his latest building project—yet another home, this one at Palm Beach, designed by Addison Mizner, famed architect to the moneyed of Florida. Called The Towers and boasting twenty servants' rooms alone, it looks in photos like a huge sand castle, bedecked with silver palms.

But the house didn't please him (perhaps nothing could anymore), and Wood sold the place at a substantial loss in 1925. By this time, he was frequently doing and saying irrational things, including, at one point, dropping son Cornelius from his will (he was later reinstated). In the winter of 1926, the Woods were staying at a hotel in Daytona, while, in the north, AWC's losses continued to mount. On February 2, Wood instructed his chauffeur to drive him to a deserted beach. While the chauffeur and a valet waited by the car, he walked alone up the beach, put the barrel of a .38-caliber revolver into his mouth, and fired.

AWC's CUMULATIVE net loss for the years 1924 through 1926 was nearly $30 million. And so, though the demise of the great mills of Lawrence officially dates from the fifties— thanks partly to the drama of Edward R. Murrow's documentary—the end wasn't sudden at all, but a long slow slide. In 1931, as AWC somehow managed to sputter along by selling off the mills it owned outside Lawrence as well as other holdings (including Shawsheen Village), *Fortune* got it right:

> The fundamental difficulty with the American Woolen Company was, and still is, the grandiose scale on which it was set up. . . . Indeed, the company is a perfect, if violent, epitome of American industrial history during the past forty years. The expanding of production units by men who had little realization of what they were bringing upon themselves, the overfinancing of corporations, and a miracle (a war) which temporarily justified everything, are all represented here in miniature.

Then, in 1941, a second "miracle" occurred. As the dye in the vats reverted to army drab, three shifts worked around the clock; the lights in the mill windows burned all night, and the noise never stopped. Other Lawrence businesses prospered, too. Many shops stayed open to accommodate workers' odd hours; grocery-store owners, often husband and wife, took turns sleeping in a bed in the back of the store. Beauty shops opened at seven on Saturday mornings so a girl just getting off the night shift could walk in, sit down in the chair, and get her hair done for the weekend.

But World War II was only a brief respite. Once again, when the bombs stopped falling over there, profits started falling over here.

And this time, there would be no recovery. Textile mills in the South had grown increasingly competitive and continued to do so through the forties: they were newer, and therefore more efficient; they paid lower wages to their workers (few if any were unionized); and they had no high fuel costs in the cold months.

Nor were they turning out the same old monochrome fabrics. They had gotten the message: the world was changing. Now not only flappers but "respectable" people wanted—and, in the post-war boom, could afford—fabrics other than blue serge. This middle class now constituted the majority of Americans, and their clothing would be less formal, less uniform, more diverse, following the example of the rich and the flamboyant, who have always embraced style. More practically speaking, central heating made wool less necessary, and the new synthetics—acetate, Orlon, Dacron, Dynel—were replacing king cotton.

A few businesspeople in the northern textile industry got the message, too; this was the time, remember, when my father-in-law, the textile chemist, moved to the Lawrence area to work at Malden Mills. Malden would stay in Lawrence and innovate, and it is still there, making specialty fabrics, like Polartec, for L. L. Bean, Eddie Bauer, and Patagonia. By delivering smaller quantities of more varied styles—and doing it quickly—Malden even managed to thrive during the recession of the early nineties. In fact, as reported in *The New York Times*, the company made some of its greatest strides during those years, which did such damage to the rest of the U.S. economy, especially New England's. While manufacturing in general in Massachusetts fell 32 percent, Malden saw growth, with Polartec sales alone more than tripling, from $60 million in 1988 to $191 million in 1994.

To accommodate the sales surge, Malden's labor force grew to 2,340, making it one of the largest employers in the city—a real Lawrence success story. It is significant, however, that at its peak, AWC employed more than four times that many *in the Wood Mill alone*, including the pariahs of today's economy: the unskilled. Malden employs few of those. "The business has gone from labor-intensive to semi-automated, capital-intensive," Malden's owner, Aaron Feuerstein, told the *Times*, while also revealing that his company exports 30 percent of its product (most other American textile companies export less than 10 percent). In textiles, then, as in other industries nationwide, the survivors who have shifted to "niche" production have also become ever more technologically advanced. So far in the "new-world economy," this seems to be the proven way for businesses to compete, not only with domestic rivals but with foreign companies, too. It does not bode well for Lawrence's legions of unskilled, unschooled workers.

ONE DETAIL of the demise of Lawrence the great mill city strikes me as curious. Why was it that the end, foreshadowed for decades, still took so many Lawrencians by surprise? Maybe they had heard rumors of the dissolution for so long that they had stopped believing it could happen. Accustomed to being laid off and rehired as business conditions fluctuated, they probably couldn't imagine that the cycles would end. Besides, the mills were so big, such a physical fact—and mill life so deeply ingrained—who would expect that either would become extinct?

Mary, a spinner: "In the Ayer Mill, they put in new motors on all the machines. Two or three months later, it was closed. We were shocked."

Nell, a jackspooler: "One girl was there forty years! Some of them never worked anywhere else. You should have seen them crying when the mills closed—all those who had been there thirty, forty years. I was there nineteen years and I was new!"

Blanche, a winder: "I would've stayed in the mills for as long as I could have, because I liked my job. I liked winding. It was nice; it was clean. It was good. It was hard, like everything else, but everyone was used to hard work."

In the days when Blanche, Nell, and Mary did mill work, "ladies" denied their ages. But when AWC announced that the mills were shutting down completely and that anyone sixty-five or older would receive one thousand dollars as severance pay, many who had previously pretended to be younger owned up. (The rest got little or nothing.)

The machinery and equipment of the Wood and Ayer mills was auctioned off from June 11 to 15, 1956, at what was described in the handbills that advertised it as "the world's largest auction." That's the American Woolen Company for you: hyperbolic to the last.

IN 1952, the arrival in Lawrence of Western Electric, now part of AT&T, was touted by newly elected Mayor Buckley and his supporters almost as if it were the second coming. When Buckley was a student at Georgetown in the 1930s, he had loved to boast about Lawrence. "Weaves three-quarters of the world's worsteds" was one statistic he used to quote for anybody who would listen to him talk about "the biggest little city in the world." There were "nine or ten things I used to say," he told me. Now, he hoped, there would be nine or ten more. Several other major companies, including Honeywell and Gillette, located in old mill buildings, too, thanks in part to Buckley's hustling. But none ever employed the numbers of Lawrencians that textiles had; and the pay wasn't as good. At one point, a study found, more than 72 percent of Lawrence's workers were receiving less pay in their new jobs—a statistic that, like the success of the early producers of specialty items, prefigures the national decline, both relative and absolute, of the blue-collar wage.

Lawrence was only a temporary location for most of these businesses, anyway. When they built their bigger, modern plants, they did so outside the city. Now people would drive to their jobs on the brand-new highways. Lawrence's streets were too narrow for traffic; mill workers had ridden the streetcar to work—it had stopped by every mill door—or else they had walked. (Miss Barker remembers awakening every weekday morning when she was a girl to the tramp of a thousand feet down Prospect Street.)

And so today we have AT&T of North Andover, not Lawrence, employing six thousand, only seven hundred of whom are Lawrencians (one—the director of public relations—is a Sweeney descendant, the great-great-grandson of Patrick, and he lives on Tower Hill). And we have the Raytheon missile systems division, of Andover—whose 3,600 employees produced the Patriot missiles for the Persian Gulf War—in a plant of 1.3 million square feet, exactly the size of the original Wood Mill, as it happens, though it doesn't seem nearly as monstrous, given its position in an open field "out there."

In another mood, these communities might have fought such an invasion of their open land. But many of their citizens had the education to understand that change was inevitable and even advantageous. Besides, they planned for traffic and parking from the start. Indeed, by passing new zoning ordinances, Andover actually courted the change and its attendant gains for the construction industry, local banks, and real estate. The whole town grew as the middle-class engineers and technicians and their families moved into their new houses—and what was supposed to have been a boon to Lawrence was actually one for the suburbs. So the gap between us increased.

ONE INDUSTRY that did come to stay in Lawrence after textiles—and died there in much the same way, though on a much smaller scale—was shoe manufacturing. The "shoe shops" reigned briefly in Lawrence, from the fifties to the seventies, employing former textile workers for much less pay. New Balance and Cardinal Shoe remain there today, but the industry never had the impact that textiles did, either on its employees or on the city itself. Lawrencians worked in those places resentfully and out of desperation.

Blanche: "The mills [mill workers] looked down on the shoe shops. We thought the shoe shops were something beneath us. We thought only the people without education went to the shoe shops. But once the mills closed, we gladly went to the shoe shops! Every one of us!"

Glad they may have been for the work—but while I've met many Lawrencians proud to have played a part in building the reputation of Lawrence textiles, I have yet to meet a proud former shoe-shop employee.

LUCILLE PIACENZO, my next-door neighbor in Lawrence, stitched shoes for fifteen years after the forty she'd already spent in the Wood Mill as a jackspooler. Finally, in 1975, at age seventy, she retired and now spent her days cooking; she wore no wool in an apartment overheated by the ever-lit stove, and nothing but slippers on her tired, arthritic feet, splayed by bunions and the sheer weight of her.

As for her husband, John, after the mills closed, he worked into his early eighties at a downtown bakery, stopping only when his weakened eyesight prevented him from driving to the place.

One day, I got a call from John. He had never called me before; it was always Lucille who picked up the phone. I hurried over.

Lucille was on the floor. At lunch, she had somehow fallen out of her chair. I saw smears of blood on the checkerboard squares of green and white linoleum. She'd split the skin of her knee. She was sitting up now, wearing a dazed look, but John hadn't been able to pull her to her feet. Instead, he'd covered her lap with a thin red blanket, and now he stood over her, his hands on his worried face.

I tried to pick her up myself, putting my hands under her arms. But she was heavy, and my back was weak. Anyway, she really didn't want to be helped, and she didn't want to go to the emergency room, either, because her hair was a mess.

"Lucille, you're vain!" I said, but it didn't help. Anyway, I knew that wasn't the real reason she wanted to avoid the hospital.

Eventually, John and I and a nephew of theirs, who had also been called and hurried over, picked her up, sat her back down in the kitchen chair that had toppled along with her, and got her cane. After a while, she tottered to John's bedroom (they had slept separately for years now); she would lie down in there, she announced, but demanded the special pillow from her room. And no, she would not go to the hospital, but she would have two spoonfuls of her favorite canned soup.

I never discovered whether Lucille had had a stroke or merely fallen. Anyway, she quickly recovered; though the pigment of the skin around her eyes was perhaps a shade or two darker than it had been before, and remained so, she was soon back at her stove in her slippers, stirring and tasting from the pot.

Next, it was John's turn to be ill. I would see him in the side yard picking weeds, looking pale, his usual old pants and sweaters suddenly grown baggy. He complained of having no appetite, and of an inner chill—of being unable to get warm even in the sweltering apartment in which Lucille wore her sleeveless housedresses all year round. He said it was because he'd spent all those years in the overheated bakery.

He would complain of other things, too—of the neighborhood going downhill, of the fresh kids, of the screeching of car tires on the street. It took him long minutes to cross that street to get the newspaper at Louie's Variety. Once, his fence was vandalized, pickets torn off and thrown here and there, all the way down the block. I collected them. He knew who had done it, but he was afraid to speak to the boy's father. He moved the piles of raked leaves away from the house, afraid someone would come into the yard and set a fire. A garage window was broken. Landlord Freddy complained that John wasn't keeping up the house. But he was tired, he was old; besides, he was only the tenant. For cryin' out loud, it wasn't even his house!

He went to the doctor, a series of doctors, who told him they could find nothing wrong. He didn't trust them.

One day, while we were standing together by the clothesline, he glanced furtively around, then looked me in the eye and asked, quite seriously, as if I were an authority, "Do I look healthy to you?"

"Well," I hedged, "you should eat more. You're not eating Lucille's good food. No wonder you're losing weight."

"Aw." He dismissed me with a gesture of his hand, then trudged with heavy steps, in loose shoes, into the house.

WHENEVER I WENT on a trip away from Lawrence in those years that I lived there, I wondered whether I would come home to loss. It's a city, after all, and one has to worry about the security of property. In the fall of 1987, I went to New Hampshire for a couple of weeks; when I returned, I learned of another kind of loss: John was dead.

"He cut his throat," said a neighbor almost gleefully, dragging her finger across her neck; a widow of about Lucille's age, she often walked past the house, carrying her red-haired poodle, which was named after her own dead husband.

I refused to believe it, but later Lucille told me John had indeed been a suicide. He had not cut his throat, but he had opened his wrists with kitchen knives, using three different ones before he got the job done. She had found a trail of blood. "Drip, drip, drip," as she described it, across the kitchen floor to his bedroom, at the other end of the apartment from hers.

Lucille showed me the note he had written: "THESE ARE MY THINGS." It referred to a shoe box of personal papers, not full.

She told me she had awakened early on the morning he died, hearing his moans. She had risen from her bed and followed the blood into his room.

"Why? Why?" she asked him. "Why?" But he couldn't explain. She says he did profess his love for her.

He was still alive when the police arrived. They asked her if she had done it. "Do I look like I could do a thing like that?" she asked them back, giving her cane a little shake, reprimanding them. The hospital wrote it up as a heart attack, because, they claimed, that's what it was in the end. The autopsy showed he was healthy otherwise.

John's bedroom had been the place where Lucille stored the cans of tomatoes for her sauce, as if she had canned them herself instead of buying them at the grocery store; now she couldn't make herself go in there to get them. Cardboard boxes were piled up against the closed door.

Otherwise, Lucille, the survivor, appeared to handle her widowhood well. She did begin to ask us for favors—to write her checks, for example. Her hands, like her feet, were arthritic; besides, she had never had a checking account before. She didn't know how to write a check. She asked us to pick her up a *TV Guide*, or her favorite tabloid. To cash her Social Security check. To fix a table leg. To replace a blown fuse. In return, she continued to cook us food.

Lucille stayed on, alone in the apartment, for a year, periodically asking me to write letters to the management of one of Lawrence's housing projects for the elderly on her behalf. Soon there was room for her, but she was afraid of elevators. Besides, she wanted to be on the first floor, and in a specific building at that—the one where her sister, Marie, lived. Finally, it worked out, and she moved out of the old John Barker house and into the big brick high-rise downtown called Essex Towers.

Then Marie died, and Lucille moved out of the city to Ohio, where her son (who long ago had escaped Lawrence) and her daughter-in-law and granddaughter live. She had no one in Lawrence now.

Occasionally, I hear from her. She calls me when I appear in her dreams. She wants to make sure I'm all right. Then she tells me more about herself, her hurts, her hopes, and I pronounce her stories "interesting," unsure what else to say or how to respond to her candor.

"Interesting?" She's annoyed, as if this comment proves everything she's ever suspected of me. "Honey, what can I tell you? That's my life."

PART III

TOMORROW LAND

CHAPTER 9

Immigrant City Reprise

I'm tired of living in an immigrant city. I don't want
this to be an immigrant city anymore.

> —Lawrencian at a public hearing
> about a proposed variance
> to expand a downtown rooming house,
> September 25, 1991

Carmen, a Dominican who works at the Akko factory:
"I'm going for my citizenship today. Does that mean
I'll wake up with blue eyes tomorrow?"

Richard, Akko's Italian-American plant manager: "No,
it means you'll wake up a Puerto Rican."

E VERY IMMIGRANT'S story is different; every immigrant's
story is the same.

"When they first came here, my father hated it. Nobody
understood him. He couldn't make them understand. He
wrote someone and asked to go back, because it was so bad.
He didn't get any support here. I think both he and my
mother were very lonely. It was very hard. He didn't want to
work at the mill. He hated it. And my mom would cry every
day, missing her parents. All of my relatives are still there.
They write letters."

What nationality do you think the speaker is? Italian? Lebanese? In what year do you think she is speaking? Eighteen seventy? Nineteen twenty? Actually, the year is 1992, and the speaker is the daughter of a Vietnamese couple. She is chatting with me in a quiet corner of the Lawrence Public Library, one day after her graduation as valedictorian of her class at Lawrence High. I'd been curious to meet the student who would claim that distinction one hundred years after Robert Frost, and so I arranged this encounter with demure Dung Nguyen, who is not permitted to date ("As an issue it never even came up—I knew it was forbidden, so I didn't even approach it"), but who will be off to Yale University in September on a full four-year scholarship.

Born in Vietnam in February 1974, Dung arrived in Lawrence with her father, mother, and older brother two Augusts later. The Nguyens were among a half dozen or so other Vietnamese refugee families whose resettlement in the city was sponsored by the International Institute of Greater Lawrence, a private, nonprofit agency that was one of the first immigrant social services in the United States when it was founded as a spin-off of the YWCA in 1913, the year after Bread and Roses. Two other early International Institutes were founded in New York and Pittsburgh in the early 1900s, their purpose the same as the one in Lawrence: to "Americanize" newcomers— to instill in them "American" values, along with the language and social customs—in an attempt to dissuade them from socialism, so that a thing like Bread and Roses might never happen— anywhere—again. Since the 1950s, independent branches of the International Institute have been established in some twenty other "gateway cities"—from Trenton, New Jersey, to Flint, Michigan, to Santa Rosa, California—for a more modern "American" purpose: to help relocate displaced persons, particularly those fleeing communism, for the U.S. Department of State.

Conceivably, then, the Nguyens might have ended up in any of the other locations served by the International Institute's umbrella group, the Immigration and Refugee Services of America, headquartered in Washington, D.C. (known at the time of the Nguyens' flight from Vietnam as the American Council for Nationalities Service and located in New York). Fate landed them in Lawrence, where, with a federal government allotment of $465 per person, the International Institute and its church volunteers rented an apartment for them, furnished it, bought food for their refrigerator, and offered them English lessons, medical screening, and other assistance.

The International Institute also found Dung's father a job—in the Everett Mill. He wasn't hired to weave textiles, of course—that business was long gone by the time the Nguyens arrived. Instead, he became a stitcher for Polo Ralph Lauren, which was renting space in the old mill complex for manufacturing and for a factory store. In Vietnam, Dung's father had been a secretary for a government official. He had expected to be at least a bookkeeper in the United States—in fact, he thought his sponsors had promised him that kind of position, so his disappointment was acute, and his sense of betrayal ultimately led him to write the Vietnamese authorities to ask if he could go back.

Were his letters ever answered? Was permission refused? I asked Dung, but she didn't know. In any case, he stuck it out at Polo and after eight years, having worked his way up to foreman and better wages, he finally saved enough to open a grocery store, which he stocked with the usual American quick pickup items as well as a variety of Asian delicacies, including kimchee (pickled cabbage) and braised cuttlefish. Viet-My, as it's called, is on South Union Street in south Lawrence, where many Southeast Asians have settled, next door to the Nguyens' impeccable duplex. "It's where O'Neil's market used to be," Dung points out, without a hint of irony. In fact, the faint painted-over letters of the old sign can still be seen beside the new one.

IT INTERESTS ME that Dung's father, who now toils in his store twelve hours a day seven days a week, tried to go home again, even to a ravaged country. It interests me, but it doesn't surprise me. The immigrant story is always a tale of yearning, of loss. My own grandparents never spoke of what they had left behind, but I remember Bob's grandfather, who was born in Russia in 1898 and emigrated here with his family in 1905, telling me how his older sister was sent back by American immigration officials, one of those hateful X's chalked on her coat, because she had tuberculosis. He never saw her again.

"You don't know how hard it is to leave your country," a Puerto Rican woman named Anna told me over tea at a downtown Lawrence lunch counter. She had left the island when she was a teenager, twenty-seven years ago, first following a trail of relatives to Philadelphia before settling in Lawrence, where the shoe shops had jobs for them all. When the shoe shops closed, she worked at a Lawrence wig factory.

During those years, Anna lived in the Hancock Courts, a housing project at the foot of Tower Hill; got married; and had children. Now she was a secretary for the manager of another city housing project and lived in a well-kept low-income apartment building at the foot of Prospect Hill. She was doing okay, she thought. Not bad at all. Her kids, born in Lawrence, have learned English and know Spanish, too, but—her smile faded—something wasn't right. "I wish I knew what was missing," she said, adding that she dreamed of returning to Puerto Rico someday to try to recover it, whatever it was. "I'm certainly not going to die here!" she insisted, then told me with disdain that Carmen, another Latina who was sitting silently with us, "has never even been to the island." Anna solemnly shook her head. "She hasn't even seen her own country."

Many don't just plan to return; they do it. "Where's so-and-so?" a Lawrence High School teacher might ask her class if a student is missing for a while. A frequent response: "Oh, he went back to Puerto Rico. He didn't like the winter."

Air travel has certainly made it more convenient for some to go back home, if only temporarily—but doing so may bring harsh criticism down upon the commuting exile's head (the ungrateful SOBs grab-and-go). These critics often forget, however, that many from earlier waves of immigrants retreated regularly, too; it just took them longer to get home. Think of Miss Barker's father, Arthur, who returned to his birthplace and came back, and Arthur's sister Mary, who crossed the Atlantic many times to nurse her various relatives' babies on either side of it. The paternal grandfather of England's present prime minister, John Major, settled in Pennsylvania in the 1860s, returned home to Britain in 1877, resettled in the United States, and finally returned to England for good a few years later.

Italians regularly returned to their homeland, especially when cold weather came. Or they'd go in the spring, to till the fields. Women often went home to give birth; they longed for the familiar customs, the company of relatives: they were afraid to have children here. Like many others, Lawrencian Joseph Vinceguerra's family intended to return permanently "once they accumulated money." They did return briefly—because their Common Street bakery went bankrupt after extending credit to so many during the great strike. Vinceguerra, who became a New Hampshire county judge and is now retired in Shawsheen Village, described the reverse trip (which would later be reversed again) in an account on tape at the Immigrant City Archives that uncannily echoes the stories immigrants tell of sailing into an American harbor for the first time:

"The whole family—it took us two weeks. We went tourist class. I enjoyed the stormy weather. We went on *La Patria.* People were getting sick. I could see people swaying. Real bad weather. Then, when we passed the Rock of Gibraltar, at the end of the Mediterranean—unbelievable, unbelievable! We landed in Palermo. We landed at night, and to me it was the most beautiful night picture—the lights, the harbor, and the serenity of the city."

Even the Puritans—some of them—went home. William R. Bagnall, writing in *The Textile Industries of the United States* (1893), notes that when, in 1640, the Puritans secured control of the Long Parliament and persecution of them ceased, "the tide . . . turned in the opposite direction, and, for nearly an equal period of twenty years, the number of emigrants to America did not more than equal the number of those who returned to their old homes and privileges in England."

GIVEN THE IMMUTABILITY of the typical immigrant tale, air miles notwithstanding, you'd think by now that Americans would know what to do about newcomers and their yearnings and their griefs. You'd think, too, that we would know what our reaction to strange new neighbors will be and what we should do about it. You'd think that people would especially know these things in Lawrence. But the city's latest immigrants are just as bewildered and disoriented as they've ever been, some coping with the stress of adjustment to a new country better than others, and most of the established residents are just as resistant as those who clashed with their forebears. It's almost as if the previous waves of immigration and assimilation never happened. And organizations like the International Institute are underfunded, their staffs overwhelmed.

(The executive director of the International Institute in Lawrence from 1970 through 1982 was my friend who now owns
the used-book store in Andover; he was so burned out by
those twelve years that he quit not only the job but also his career in social work.)

Why are today's old guard so unyielding? For one thing,
between the 1920s and the late 1950s, Lawrence ceased to be
the Immigrant City. (The United States in general stopped
welcoming immigrants in those years, except for a smattering
of refugees.) Instead, because of the slow but sure snuffing out
of the textile industry and the absence of any significant re-
placement, there was a continuous out-migration. Then,
around 1960, the first of the *new* newcomers arrived, initially
from postrevolutionary Cuba and from Puerto Rico (American
citizens since 1917, of course—another fact many Lawrencians
find easy to forget). Though the economic outlook in Lawrence was bleak, those who came in those years were fleeing
communism or revolution or living conditions and prospects
far more dismal than those they would find in their new home.
Later, after the 1965 revision of the immigration law, which
abolished the national-origins quota system, people from other
parts of the Caribbean, Central America, Latin America, and
Asia found their way to Lawrence, too—all of them unwittingly settling in a city whose residents were probably among
the least likely of Americans to accept them. These U.S.-born
Lawrencians were one or more generations removed from the
immigrant experience. They had only heard about the ordeal,
and, almost certainly, a prettied-up version of it at that. They
couldn't know firsthand what their strange new neighbors
were going through. Their dire economic situation, caused by
the textile companies' pullout, didn't help, either, as everybody
tried to compete for a dwindling number of jobs, with the immigrants willingly working for less.

Still, no matter how strong the feelings of resentment

against them (on the part, for example, of the former Lawrence neighbor of mine who, late to the store on Mother's Day
morning, could find for his wife "only two greeting cards left
and neither one of them in English"), they came, and they
have multiplied. The members of the expanded Department
of Obstetrics and Gynecology at Lawrence General Hospital
can tell you that as well as the statistics.

That the Latinos are now the largest subgroup in the city
would be apparent to even a casual visitor. In 1970, they num-
bered 2,325. (This initial influx is sometimes referred to as
"the writing on the wall," as in this comment from a
Lithuanian-American Lawrencian: "The Jews on Tower Hill
saw the writing on the wall in the early seventies, and they all
moved to Andover.") In 1980, the figure was 10,289; and in
1990, it was 29,237, or 41 percent of the city's population—
and this figure is deemed an undercount not only by local Latino leadership but by the conservative Greater Lawrence
Chamber of Commerce, too. According to them, the total
would be closer to 60 percent if illegal residents were tallied.

Whatever the accurate number, the Latinos have become
not only the most populous group but the dominant cultural
force in Lawrence—as well as the largest linguistic "minority" ever to live there. The history of the mills is virtually un-
known to many of them; the obituaries of the old winders,
weavers, and spinners, with French and Italian surnames, appear nightly in a newspaper that the Latinos do not read.
Many cannot read Spanish, either. Radio—Spanish-language
radio—is their medium. Programs broadcast from Boston and
Lowell and Lawrence, too, spill from tenement windows, especially on weekends, and sometimes it seems that every passing
car is thumping out Spanish words and music as their drivers,
hoping to be admired, tool slowly down the street. One of
those streets, named Butler, misheard by Latinos as Butter
Street, has been rechristened Montequilla.

Is it any wonder that the old-timers look around and ask in bewilderment, How did it happen? How is it that our city was chosen for this?

"The churches brought them in," I've heard more than one angry person mutter. "The churches like poor people. They're the backbone of the Church." These critics are next apt to mumble the name Father Lamond, then fire off an insult or two, as in "He turned his back on his own people and went after the scum." Or, more civilly, but no less resentfully: "The word got out that there was this priest in Lawrence who would take care of you. It went out on the ethnic telegraph after that. You know how that works."

Actually, I didn't know, so I went looking for Father John Joseph Lamond—a Lawrence boy, born in 1909, who offered himself to the Augustinians—Father O'Reilly's order—when he was only fourteen, had a long career, and retired in 1980 to a monastery on the campus of Merrimack College. I found him there.

A gruff-voiced, slow-moving, prideful octogenarian, he was seriously ill (though I never guessed it) on the three mornings in the spring of 1992 that I spent with him; he died not too long afterward. Collarless, he still wore a priest's black trousers and a black sweater. And he was, at first, not particularly pleasant, but salty and suspicious of "journalists." Yet he enjoyed his own stories very much and couldn't resist telling them, especially those that embraced aspects of the history of the city he obviously loved.

He gave Father O'Reilly credit for his father's existence—and, hence, his own. As he told it, his grandfather was a Protestant from Glasgow (Lamond is the name of a Scottish clan, with the accent on the first syllable, though most people pronounce it as if it were French), and he married an Irish Catholic. ("He was put out of his house for it, and she was put out of hers.") They had two children, but both died at birth. "And so my grandfather said, 'There's something wrong with this marriage,' and went to see Father O'Reilly at St. Mary's Church. And he took religious instructions from him and became a Catholic without telling anyone. And then he went home and had seven children who lived, and my father was one of them.'"

Father Lamond's parents both worked in the mills, then made their escape into the retail trade. His father sold insurance door-to-door; his mother worked at a well-known Essex Street department store, Sutherland's, in the lingerie department. The couple had five children; four of them took religious vows. It's an unusually high number even for Lawrence, but as Father Lamond himself admitted, the seminary or the convent was a good place to be during the Depression.

His own religious training began well before the crash, in 1923, when he was sent away to the Augustinian Academy on Staten Island in New York City. But even he didn't escape a stint of mill work: one summer during his seminary years, he got a job as a bobbin boy in the Washington Mills, changing the bobbins on machines operated mostly by non-English-speaking Italian women. Lamond knew Italian numbers and would recite them. "Smart boy! Smart boy!" the women would say.

He was ordained in 1935, and his first appointment set the route he would travel for the rest of his ministry. The young priest was sent to the Augustinian College in the Philippines, where he learned Spanish over the next four years. From there, he went to the Augustinian College in Cuba, then back to various Augustinian high schools in the United States, including one in Philadelphia with a growing Puerto Rican enrollment. In 1963, the Boston archdiocese "was clamoring for priests who spoke Spanish to come to Lawrence," and so he wound up at St. Mary's, his old parish church.

At the time, the Spanish-speaking population in Lawrence was only three to four hundred, he says. (In 1960, according to the U.S. Census, it was only twenty-eight.) Some worked in the shoe shops, where, for a few more years, jobs were easy to come by. ("Once I took a girl down to one of the shoe factories at ten o'clock in the morning," Father Lamond recalled. " 'Did she bring her lunch?' they asked me.") Others were hired as seasonal workers, harvesting Massachusetts apples and other crops—until, that is, the farmland disappeared, making way for the suburbs.

Even when the jobs started disappearing, the Latinos stayed: fewer opportunities and greater poverty awaited them back home. The Cubans—invited by the Augustinians, who were themselves fleeing from their about-to-be-confiscated college—couldn't return in any case.

The priests settled them in the Italian area around Holy Rosary Church. They said Mass for them and heard their confessions in Spanish in the church basement. They also established what was called the Spanish Center in a tenement on Orchard Street, in the Plains (the area that was once the Irish shanty village, then later an Italian stronghold). Actually, the place was a rooming house, said Father Lamond, who was its director; Latinos stayed in those temporary quarters until he and his staff could find them apartments. The Spanish Center offered English lessons and ran children's programs after school, on weekends, and during the summer. It also hosted a half-hour radio program on the same Lawrence station that serves up commercial Spanish radio today. Called "Spanish Information Time," it featured Father Lamond and his weekly guests giving encouragement, comfort, and advice.

One of Father Lamond's success stories is a Cuban immigrant who arrived in Florida in 1959 and found his way to Lawrence six years later. Today, a landlord of some renown, he makes his home on Prospect Hill, in a huge mustard-colored Victorian Gothic mansion. His name is Clemente Abascal, and he strengthened his bootstraps at the Spanish Center.

Father Lamond told the story this way: "He started out in a store on Newbury Street that wasn't much bigger than a motel room, where he sold costume jewelry. I don't think the store had a name. But there was another shop, near Branco's Florist, a place that sold appliances, and in no time at all Clemente had that. In the meantime, he started buying small apartments, fixing them up a little bit. And he put Hispanics in them. He would carry them for some time. He still does that today. A little while later, he bought a furniture store. That was called The Gold Key. Five stories. He ran that for a few years, then sold the upper floors to the bank next door. Today he's only concentrating on real estate, I think. But I'd rather have him tell you himself."

Alas, however, Clemente (he is often referred to by his first name only), who nonchalantly parks his silver Lincoln Continental in restricted parking spaces outside city hall without getting ticketed (the drivers of his Abascal Construction Company pickup trucks do, too), said through an assistant— who happened to be Father Lamond's cousin *and* a former Maryknoll missionary sister fluent in Spanish—that he didn't have time to speak with me.

THE SPANISH CENTER, with Father Lamond in charge, endured for fourteen years, from 1965 to 1979, helping to settle not only the Cubans but the Puerto Ricans, as well as the many Dominicans who followed the first two groups. (With the 1961 death of dictator Rafael Trujillo, who forbade emigration, the exodus of over 1 million Dominicans began; fifteen to twenty thousand eventually settled in Lawrence, quickly making them—not their occasionally rivalrous counterparts, the

Puerto Ricans—the most populous Latino group in the city to-day.) And so inevitably, Father Lamond's name is associated with the influx of them all; but I have a feeling that the priest didn't have much decision-making power during his tenure. When I asked him why, when it had been so successful, the Spanish Center closed, and also why the archdiocese never en-couraged the Latinos to establish their own parish—as all the other Catholic ethnic groups had done before them—he grew agitated, gestured for me to turn off my tape recorder, and said, "Well, that's a long story." He wouldn't elaborate, though, even off the record. Instead, he changed the subject.

It's not difficult to fill in the silence. In the seventies, as fewer and fewer parishioners could be found kneeling in the church pews on Sundays, the archdiocese must have known that there would soon be an empty church—or two. When the Latinos—about two hundred of them from Puerto Rico, the Dominican Republic, Cuba, Ecuador, Colombia, and Guate-mala—finally got their own church, it was not a new one; it's the old Assumption Church of the Germans, rechristened in 1994 Asunción de la Virgen Maria.

Still, if the archbishop thought the Latinos were to be the new Catholics of Lawrence, why wouldn't the Spanish Center have persisted and even expanded? The answer to that ques-tion is a sad commentary on our prejudices and, depending on your point of view, on the declining power of the Roman Cath-olic hierarchy. Because the truth is, no matter what the arch-bishop thought, the Latinos had become the scapegoats for all the social and economic problems that had begun to plague the city by then, and the Boston high clergy's advocacy of them had become decidedly unpopular. There are some who say that the local parishes' cold-shouldering of the Catholic Latinos is the reason so many in Lawrence have defected to the Protestant churches, or else started their own. The arch-diocese simply was not able to square the circle: faced with the challenge of trying to accommodate the old and the new, the hierarchy chose the old—and now, as I've already noted, is forced to knock down empty churches.

It's also tempting to speculate that Cold War politics—or the absence of such—played a role; that is to say, the archbishop might have been more strongly motivated to lobby for a heartier welcome for the Latinos if the majority had been fleeing from communism, as the Cubans were; instead, the Puerto Ricans and Dominicans were—and still are—only running from poverty.

And there is one other, crucial way in which these larger groups of Latinos differ from the Cubans: the color of their skin.

Until now, Lawrence has never had a large nonwhite population. (The dearth of industrial jobs in the city is one reason why few African-Americans found their way there when they migrated from the South after World War II.) Many of those who fled Castro were fair-skinned—"and very proud of their European heritage; some of them, if you listen to them, think they truly are conquistadores," says Jorge Santiago, executive director of Centro Panamericano, a social-service agency in Lawrence that specializes in helping Latinos. (On the other hand, most of the 125,000 Marielitos—that is, those who left Cuba in 1980 from the Port of Mariel—were very dark-skinned; and that includes the twenty who were resettled in Lawrence by the International Institute. They were still political refugees, however.) The Puerto Ricans and Dominicans, by contrast, are perceived by Lawrencians as black. Never mind that they may not consider themselves to be so. (In a poem called "From an Island You Cannot Name," Martín Espada, who was born of Puerto Rican descent in Brooklyn, writes: ". . . grabbing at the plastic / identification bracelet / marked Negro, / shouting 'I'm not! / Take it off! / I'm Other!' ") Nor does it seem to matter that American whites of Italian descent may be as dark or darker than many of them. Our country's problem with color becomes the newcomers' problem, too—one more thing with which they have to cope, and which may make it all the more difficult for them to finish the immigrant's journey: to climb the hilltops of this city, this country, into the middle class.

WINTER 1992. I make the acquaintance of a young Dominican woman whose parents emigrated to the United States in the early sixties and have achieved a tenuous middle-class existence in Lawrence. Lisette Anderson is her name, and she is an art student whose watercolors feature dark-skinned people—full-lipped, big-breasted, brown-toned women who don't always resemble earthly beings. Dreamlike settings, hyperbole, caricature—Lisette uses them all to get her message across. In one painting, interchangeable padlocks and credit cards dangle from the ears of some dolled-up Latinas. In another, called *Salon*, a young woman is sitting in a hairstylist's chair and crying big, cartoonish tears over what appears to be a botched permanent wave.

The text is not hard to read in Lisette's paintings—yet something subtle is being said beneath the shout—and I find myself listening to that whisper when I first see her works. They are hanging in a show downtown, part of a week-long celebration of the 148th anniversary of the Dominican Republic's independence. The all-Dominican exhibit is in the city's state-financed visitors' center, a refurbished mill boardinghouse on the north canal. I'm used to seeing Lawrence-inspired art that features artsy brick-mill scenes. Not at this show: there isn't a brick in sight—least of all in Lisette's works. And yet her paintings are very much about Lawrence. Lawrence today. That's what the whisper is saying—this is the real Lawrence, not those old mills—and that's why it interests me so. She agrees to meet me one noonday at the Dunkin' Donuts on Essex Street, across the square from city hall.

She is twenty-three, girlishly slim—not at all like the buxom women in her paintings. She is dressed in harmonizing colors—beige jeans, orange parka, a woven scarf of yellow, orange, and pink, and stylish brown leather boots. There are no earrings in her pierced ears, I notice. And there's no permanent wave in her Indian-straight black hair, which is pulled back into a high ponytail. "But that scene in the beauty-parlor painting really happened to me," she says. "The salon is down on Jackson Street."

Right now, she's working as a file clerk at a Haverhill hospital from 2:00 to 10:00 p.m., while trying to earn enough money to finish her BFA degree at the Massachusetts College of Art, in Boston. The paintings in the exhibit were old ones, she tells me; since she gave up her studio at school, she hasn't had a place to work; at the moment, she's set up in her parents' basement. Do I happen to know anybody who could sublet her some space in one of the mill buildings? Actually, I tell her, I very well may, thinking of Bob and of Akko in the old Pacific Mills, in view just across the canal.

Her speech has a barely perceptible Spanish cadence, though she was born in Lawrence in 1968 and has lived there all her life. And no matter what she's saying, she is animated, as if the words alone couldn't possibly convey all their meaning (in a multilingual place like Lawrence, they often don't). I ask about her Anglo name. She reminds me that a lot of African-Americans, after they were freed, made their way to the islands.

Many of Lisette's relatives are still in the Dominican Republic ("Everyone there wants to come here!"), and she herself has been to the island three times for visits. When they write, they address the envelope "Lawrence, Massachusetts,

New York." They think the whole United States is New York, says Lisette, who also has relatives in the South Bronx.

Manhattan is where Lisette's parents met, soon after they arrived there; so it was from that island, not directly from their own, that they came to Lawrence. Like many Latinos, they had heard that in Lawrence they might find a more affordable, quieter life than the one in Spanish Harlem, yet still be in a place where there were lots of other Latinos, speaking the language, cooking the food, dancing the dances. They'd heard there were jobs and apartments, too: if you were willing to work for low enough wages and to live in less than regal quarters, you could find employment and a rental, both in one day. The shiny passenger vans I see parked downtown, emblazoned with LAWRENCE–NEW YORK, attest to this connection between the big city and the little one, which persists today. The van drivers—or their passengers—are periodically suspected of carrying drugs. The accusation reminds me of similar ones leveled against the drivers of the jitneys that, from about 1910 through 1940, used to travel between Lawrence and the hinterlands of Methuen, carrying Italians to the little garden plots they rented seasonally. Local police suspected they were making wine out there and using the jitneys to smuggle it to town. (Even after Prohibition ended, making your own wine was prohibited; in any case, the drivers were probably innocent: the Italians made their wine in the basements of their apartment buildings right inside the city. They stamped and sang all night long, wearing special boots.)

The Andersons arrived in Lawrence shortly before the birth of Lisette, who is the oldest of their five children. Cesario Anderson worked "odd jobs" (Lisette's phrase), including one at Honeywell, the computer maker, which occupied the old Wood Mill for a number of years, before he found better-paying work as a machine operator at an aluminum-can factory in Lawrence, where he is still employed. Crown Cork and Seal, an international corporation, opened its plant in a newly built industrial park near the Andover line in 1969, where today it employs two hundred in the production of twelve-ounce beverage containers. Lisette's mother, Olga, worked in the shoe shops; today she is "a homemaker," says Lisette, and attends classes on the Lawrence campus of Northern Essex Community College, taking courses that she hopes will lead to a job as a substance-abuse counselor.

As Lisette and I stand chatting by the big glass windows of the doughnut shop, we keep getting interrupted by Lisette's friends, who catch sight of her and rush in to embrace her and exchange words in rapid Spanish. It's time for Lisette to go to work, anyway. We walk outside, and while we are making plans to chat more on another day, an older Latina greets her with a kiss and recounts the tale of her latest surgery. And it suddenly occurs to me that Essex Street, the place so many old-time Lawrencians avoid, citing "suspicious characters" who frighten them, is Lisette's main street now.

A WEEK LATER, I take Lisette and her sister Betty to meet Bob at Akko. He has said that he would be happy to give Lisette a place for a studio. The boom years of the eighties are over; in 1987, Akko had moved into a bigger space, expecting growth to continue. It didn't. In fact, the whole furniture industry has been in decline, beginning even before the stock market crash of October 1989. And so Akko has room to spare for the young artist—a large area in the rear, close to some big windows.

Up the factory steps Lisette, Betty, and I lug canvases, a box of art books, supplies of brushes and paints. I introduce the sisters to Bob, who helps arrange the space with tables, extra lights, and shelves, then shows them the rest of the factory.

Seeing the Akko products, Betty remembers that their aunt Alba once worked in an acrylic-furniture factory in Lawrence. It had to be this one, says Bob; there isn't another.

Lisette has to get to work. Betty is due at her job, too; she works part-time in addition to attending Northern Essex, like her mother. Lisette thanks Bob very much, then invites us to her house to meet the rest of her family on Saturday afternoon.

THE ANDERSONS LIVE on Hillside Avenue, near the summit of Tower Hill—Prospect Hill's twin on the other side of the city. I used to be able to see its tree line from my attic window in Lawrence, and I have a few friends over there. But I'd never been on Hillside Avenue before I met Lisette; curious, I decided to cruise the area before our meeting.

Like the rest of Tower Hill, it's a street of large, mostly well-kept Victorians, both single-family houses and duplexes, where middle-class Irish, including my friend the political pundit James Garvey, grew up in the twenties and thirties. I've heard Garvey boast that Hillside Avenue and its environs have produced more millionaires than any other section of Lawrence. Alex Rogers, whose family started the forerunner of the *Eagle-Tribune*, was one (the Rogers family, now of North Andover, still publishes the paper).

Lisette and her family have lived on Hillside Avenue since 1988, the year they finally escaped the three-family tenement that was their residence for their twenty previous years in Lawrence. Their old address is 54 Margin Street, just a few doors down and across the street from where my friend Charlene grew up in the thirties and forties, when it was inhabited solely by French-Canadians. Charlene remembers it as the proverbial nice, clean, friendly place where nobody ever locked a door. Today it's considered one of the worst streets in

Lawrence. Only a two- or three-minute drive from Lisette's new neighborhood, at the foot of Tower Hill, it's a desolate, drug- and crime-ridden stretch across from the public housing project called Hancock Courts. The place where the mild civil disturbance between Latinos and French-Canadians occurred in 1984, the one that was referred to as "the riot" in the national media during the slow news days of that August, it's the subject of a poem by Martín Espada: ". . . white adolescents / who chanted USA and flung stones / at the scattering of astonished immigrants, / ruddy faces slowing the car to shout spick / and wave beer cans." Burned-out, trash-filled ugliness prevails. Decrepit three-deckers (and the Andersons' old home is one of them) are built right up against one another—and the sidewalk. Charlene says her father painted their tenement gray every other year; she used to ask him to pick a brighter color, but he never would.

These days, nobody seems to paint the houses any color. Their worn siding looks as flimsy as cardboard. On some blocks, more buildings are boarded up than not. And I find myself wondering what I often hear other people (non-Lawrencians) wonder aloud: Why don't they just bomb the place and start over from scratch? Those who half-seriously propose this are usually talking about all of Lawrence; driving down Margin Street, I think it might not be a bad idea to bomb just this one part.

The worst thing is, there is absolutely no one around. (Maybe that's why I can so easily fantasize the efficacy of a precision bomb.) Two o'clock on a Saturday afternoon is too early for many, I suppose. Saturday nights on Margin Street, on the other hand, are notorious. So are all the other nights. For years, I have read news stories about the knifings, the holdups, the beatings, and worse. Lisette has told me that kids play on the sidewalks till all hours, even on weekdays. (She has also said that the street reminds her of her cousin's block in

New York City's South Bronx.) Flung over some telephone wires, a rubber baby doll is hanging from the crook of its elbow.

Hillside Avenue, then, is quite a step up. Lisette, however, didn't find it an entirely welcome change at first. The street was "too quiet" at night without the noise of the kids: she had trouble sleeping; so did her sisters. Nor were they used to so few streetlights; they found the darkness "scary." And they were "surrounded by white people," not many of whom had the welcome mat out.

AT THE APPOINTED TIME, Bob and I go up the path to the door of the Andersons' big beige duplex. It's a lovely house, without the usual vinyl or asbestos siding covering its original clapboards and fancy-cut shingles. Inside the gate, there is a side yard, with a picnic table. Everything is fussily neat. The family bought the place from a family named Bodner, who, according to Lisette, begged, "Please take care of it!" Apparently, they have.

Lisette isn't home—she's grocery shopping—but a third Anderson sister, Mayra, who is a student at Lawrence High School, lets us in and shows us through the French doors of the den into the spacious living room, decorated with patterned rugs and reproduction antique furniture; next, the dining room, with its silk calla lilies in the middle of the highly polished table and wood in the grate of the fireplace; finally, we reach the kitchen, which still sports the original painted wood cabinets and a little polychromed wall safe.

"With fake money inside! Fake!" Lisette's mother laughs in the same dramatic way as Lisette, swinging the door open for us to see the colored bills from a board game lying there. Olga laughs a bit wistfully, though, for she worries that they won't be able to stay on Tower Hill. They still own and rent out their

Margin Street tenement, but two of the three apartments are vacant, and it's "killing" them, she says.

A striking woman, fifty years old, wearing pearl earrings, a houndstooth blazer, and stonewashed jeans, Olga has just returned from showing one of those troublesome apartments. She says that since it's across the street from the Hancock projects, many people don't want to live there. Also, it has lead paint, and if the people have children younger than seven, she cannot rent to them. Olga and Cesario would like to refinance their mortgage on the Hillside Avenue house, but the bank won't let them, because they once missed a payment ("Once!"). A double bill one month and that is the end of the discussion with the banker. They would all very much hate to go back to Margin Street, says Olga, who worked hard for years saving for the down payment on this house. She spent eight years as a stitcher at one shoe factory, until it closed; then several more years at two other shoe shops, until they, too, closed. At the end of it all, in the late seventies, she recalls, she was earning only $1.85 an hour.

Lisette arrives home with the groceries and puts them away as Olga continues to talk with us about many other things besides her family's precarious finances, including the term papers that she is writing for her courses at Northern Essex (later, I will notice her name on the honor roll published in the *Eagle-Tribune*). She also thanks Bob profusely for making the studio space available to Lisette. Then she tells him that he reminds her of her father. Alba, her sister, who, it turns out, did once work for Bob at Akko, saw the same resemblance, Olga says. It's not a physical likeness, she admits. And I think, How interesting, and hopeful. Bob, white-skinned and of Jewish descent, can yet remind this black-skinned woman, who is ten years older than he, of her father. It's promising that she can see beyond color and age—a skill we all might do well to develop.

As for Lisette's father, I don't meet Cesario that day: he's gone suddenly to the Dominican Republic. His father has died in the night, at age 101. Mayra shows me her grandfather's photo in a family album—a straight-shouldered, proud-looking man, wearing glasses. In the album also are snapshots of many other relatives who stayed behind on the island, and of the Andersons themselves, taken on their trips down there to visit. Such a paradise of vivid tropical pinks and greens and blues! Here, too, is the otherworldliness that finds its way into Lisette's paintings. Surely the Dominican Republic is one of the most beautiful spots on earth—not the sort of place you leave on a whim. But then I remember: the beauty hides poverty. Even Lisette's relatives, whom she describes as middle-class, believe they would be better off if they left.

IN THE NEXT FEW WEEKS, Lisette worked only sporadically in her Akko studio, but she did manage to make a purple-and-gold papier-mâché vase; she also started a satirical watercolor of a Latino Elvis. She was apologetic—embarrassed that she wasn't using the space regularly; she was busy at work, and at church.

The Spanish Methodist Church, a simple clapboard building, about halfway between their old house and their new one, is a focal point of the Andersons' lives. Indeed, Lisette considers herself born again as of spring 1991; another of her sisters, Evelyn—also a Northern Essex student—says that she is born again, too. And once, when I asked Betty to name the person she most admires, she replied without a moment's hesitation, "The Lord."

"God is right there, right in front of you," Lisette tells me on another day at Dunkin' Donuts. (The flags of all the different countries of Lawrencians' origins snap in the wind along Essex Street. Put up with much fanfare a couple of years ago by the city council, they are small, hardly noticeable. All Lawrence could afford? I see that Ireland, Italy, and Cuba have the places of importance, closest to the entrance to the square leading to city hall.) "You don't have to go searching for Him."

Her remarks—and her devotion—call to mind something I heard a Latino social worker say at a lecture he gave in Lawrence to mental-health professionals on immigrant adjustment problems. In the same room in the visitors' center where, only a few weeks before, I had seen Lisette's paintings for the first time, Eduardo Ruiz had been speaking of spiritualism and its effects, both negative and positive, on the transplanted islanders: "Voices are heard! Visions are seen! You are a medium! This is a positive trait in the islands; here it can land you in a psychiatric hospital." The invisible world will take care of you, many Latinos believe, and the idea lends them strong emotional support; on the other hand, explained Ruiz, who is a Puerto Rican, such a set of beliefs can be emotionally crippling, breeding a stultifying passivity. (The southern Italian worldview, with its saints and witches, its curses and spells, is similarly hobbling.) For better or worse, however, among Latinos it's simply accepted that there's magic around.

Lisette and I aren't talking about magic at Dunkin' Donuts, though. (And the only counseling she and members of her family are apt to get will come from her pastor, not a social worker.) We are discussing her career plans. She doesn't have any beyond her schooling, and finds the notion alien; she also refuses to speculate about whether she'll still be living in Lawrence ten years from now. She will say that she'll never live apart from her family until after marriage. Of course. And no, she doesn't have a boyfriend. Any discussion of romance is foolish, it seems: in time, God will provide that, too. "God's in control," she tells me firmly but with the patience believers reserve for nonbelieving souls like I am. And by way of proof of

His providence, she announces that the Margin Street apartments have finally been rented out. "See what He did for us?" she says, grinning.

A year or so later, Lisette would go back to art college, finish her degree, and make plans to go on to graduate school in art therapy.

THE ANDERSONS have insisted for years that their children come home directly after school, and this still goes for Olga and Cesario's youngest—thirteen-year-old Alex. Unsupervised children, on the other hand, can be found on plenty of other streets besides Margin: I used to meet them on Prospect Street often, and, unlike the Andersons, they did not inspire much hope for the future.

One school day, I encountered a scrawny, squirmy little girl, no more than nine or ten. She was on her way to her nanny's, she said. "Do you think that if I took my Medicaid card to the hospital they would give me something for my throat?" she asked in a hoarse voice. I told her that her nanny might be able to give her something to make her feel better when she got there.

A few weeks later, she stopped me to show me her report card. She had all unsatisfactories in Conduct; all unsatisfactories or "needs improvement" in Behavior; in the academic subjects: straight D's.

She had a Latino surname.

On another day, not long afterward, I saw her standing in the middle of the street, daring cars to hit her.

LAWRENCE HAS FELT the impact of the new immigrants, all the different groups of them, most profoundly in its public schools. This is especially so because the new wave of immigrant children began to swell enrollments just as many of the city's parochial schools began to falter and close, forcing their students to move into the public system. In fact, one public-school administrator—in charge of discipline—goes so far as to blame the archdiocese for the magnitude of the present crisis, which includes one of the worst dropout rates in the state. Lawrence's Catholic schools were responsible for "the ruination of the city," he tells me one morning—the same morning on which he confiscates a knife from an eleven-year-old. More attention was paid to the parochial schools than to the public schools, which were "left to fend for themselves," he says hotly.

What exactly did he mean? This graduate of Lawrence High didn't explain. But when I repeated his words to others, they nodded in a knowing way, for there is a widespread feeling that the city's commitment to public education decreased proportionately as enrollments in parochial schools increased.

It is a difficult claim to prove. More supportable—and perhaps more to the point: for decades, the city leadership has consistently been drawn from the Catholic schools; indeed, it is difficult to name a recent city official who is not a graduate of a Catholic school. To name just three who are: former mayor Kevin Sullivan and the current superintendent of schools, James Scully, are graduates of Central Catholic; the current mayor, Mary Claire Kennedy, went to St. Mary's. (Under the city charter, the mayor doubles as the chairperson of the school committee.)

I've also heard the role of the Catholic school system in Lawrence defended, however (by another Central Catholic grad who was once the director of Lawrence's Department of Planning and Community Development): "If the Catholic schools hadn't educated so many, it would have been a tremendous burden on the city. I call it give-and-take."

Whatever the truth of the matter, the fact remains that Lawrence's public schools are failing their terrible test. Even if they weren't overcrowded, their teachers and administrators would be overwhelmed by the needs of their vast multilingual and multicultural school population. Thirty-three percent of students are in bilingual classes taught in eighteen languages: Arabic, Burmese, Chinese, Dutch, French, German, Greek, Hindi, Italian, Khmer, Korean, Laotian, Polish, Portuguese, Spanish, Thai, Turkish, and Vietnamese. But their needs are often much more urgent than expertise in English. Once, when Lawrence High teacher Terri Kelley tried to show a class a film that included a scene of turn-of-the-century immigrants disembarking at Ellis Island, she had to shut it off before the end: "Everybody was crying. Leaving one's homeland—that's their immediate experience. I've been getting students lately from Zaire," she adds. Why did they come? "I hate to ask. I never ask. Plenty of these kids are spooked by loud noises. You can look at their faces and see they've been through a lot. One of my current students was born in Lebanon during the civil turmoil sixteen years ago. His father dropped his mother off at the hospital in labor, then went to pick up his grandmother. Father and grandmother were both killed by gunfire and his mother died giving birth to him. He lived in Texas for a while. Now he's [living with relatives] here."

The advantages of such a diverse student body are often overlooked—or undervalued—by those who choose to avoid the Lawrence school system at all costs. A few years ago, a collaborative school was proposed—a place where Andover and Lawrence students would elect to go to school together. The idea was that Lawrence kids could benefit from rubbing shoulders with Andoverites, and the Andoverites would benefit by rubbing shoulders with "people of other cultures." It got nowhere. The Andoverites, who voted it down five to one, were adamant. If you want your kids to go to school with *them*, go live in Lawrence, the opposition told the Andover advocates of the plan—which didn't wash in Lawrence, either, for the most part. Many Lawrencians were indifferent or else they resented the paternalism. The whole debacle seemed to epitomize a huge, sad gulf of fearful ignorance on both sides.

Which is not to say that within the Lawrence school system different groups always get along. (Terri Kelley says a Vietnamese girl told her: "If you don't hate Koreans, you can't be my friend. You have to learn to be prejudiced correctly.") What can be said, however, is that the cultural-exchange opportunities at a school like Lawrence High make the staging of a Model United Nations Week a redundancy. One small proof: when that week comes along, annually in the spring, the teachers who are in charge of organizing it have no trouble finding kids who know the national anthem of just about any country you can name.

SPRING, 1992. I've decided to pay a visit to the Model UN, so I'm sitting in the auditorium, in the row marked "Bangladesh," which is empty for some reason. I guess the Bangladeshis haven't shown up yet. I notice only after a while that the kids are in native dress—it's not very different from everyday street clothing in Lawrence.

No one in the row of seats behind me is speaking English, so I cannot even eavesdrop. Onstage, the choir sings the national anthems of three countries other than ours: Germany's, Cape Verde's, and the Dominican Republic's. At the first few bars of this last one, there's cheering, whistling, loud talking, then scattered standing, somewhat defiant, and hissing, too. The specially appointed student security guards start roaming the aisles, trying to look mean. The girl behind me is softly singing the words in my ear. When it's over, "The

Star-Spangled Banner" strikes up; everybody stands in a thunder of exuberance to sing; afterward, there is the loudest cheering of all.

They may love America and each other, too, but do they love Lawrence? Living there, do they feel they've arrived? Or is Lawrence just another island off the mainland—like Ellis Island, not yet the real America?

I met a young Cambodian, Heng Meas, at that Model UN Day. That is, I tried to meet him after he asked a probing question at the assembly. But he thought I was a teacher, and so he brusquely put me off. A still gangly nineteen-year-old in a white dress shirt, preppy tie, and khaki pants, he is obviously not a typical Lawrence student. Later, I called him and we arranged to meet at the library, where I had earlier met his classmate Dung. This was a few days after he graduated fifth in his class and three months before he joined the class of 1996 at Amherst College, where he'll study on a full scholarship. Though Dung had delivered the valedictory, Heng had written and recited the class poem on that stiflingly hot June day at the Lawrence football stadium: "Crowds of diversity walk through the painted hall / Black, yellow, brown, white are colors of thee / Beautifully they march in moving harmony / Needing not a Mending Wall."

In addition to borrowing from Frost, Heng had also paid homage to Shakespeare with a phrase about dreams from Puck's last lines in A Midsummer Night's Dream. "I read the play on my own," he told me, happy that I, a kindred spirit, had recognized the allusion. "It wasn't assigned in school. I made my sister read it, too."

He slouches in his chair and speaks rapid-fire, as if he thinks time is running out, or that the oxygen in the room is. Considering his early years in prison—"I was three or four years old, in prison. It was a dreary moment, but I got past it," he tells me—I don't wonder that he feels an urgency about his life and about the world. I have the impression that more than anything he is still trying to catch up on lost time, that he doesn't want to miss anything ever again.

After prison, he tells me, he and his family wandered like nomads for seven years—staying in refugee camps in Thailand and the Philippines, where Heng learned his first English words: *Never mind.* ("I think I was trying to draw an apple that time, trying to say something about an apple: 'Never mind . . .' ") Later, in Massachusetts, the Meases moved from one cramped apartment to another, from one city to another—from Dorchester, to Allston, to Cambridge, to Malden—until finally they settled permanently in their own two-family house in Lawrence in 1986. Heng's father had a job at Hewlett-Packard in Andover; his mother soon found work assembling electronics at Wang, Digital, and other computer companies. Heng was far from settled, however; even with all that had come before, he wasn't prepared for Lawrence:

"I cried coming [home] from school for the first time. I told my parents I didn't like this place at all. It was tough. I didn't make many friends. There weren't many Oriental kids. There was all Spanish people. I was trying to learn English, and they were speaking Spanish. I went home and said, 'I don't want to stay here.' When you're young, it's sort of hard to take the name-calling. They think it's our fault that we came here. But my parents said we had to stay.

"So I was scheduled to go to Lawrence High; I didn't want it. I didn't like it—the concept of Lawrence." He applied to Phillips Academy and was rejected, and crushed, especially since one of his good friends got in. "I looked into trying to attend Andover High, North Andover, Methuen. Was there any way I could get away from Lawrence High? That's how bad my perception of it was. That summer, though, Phillips did give me a 'kind' scholarship for a four-week boarding program. What did I know? I was in eighth grade. I was too young and immature and had all the qualities of a young eighth grader.

"Then ninth grade began, and coming from Phillips, I had a lot of ego. More ego than confidence. I felt better than these students. But gradually my feelings changed. I went to Phillips again for the Urban Studies Program, and studied about Lawrence itself. It gave me a better impression. I learned how Lawrence got the way it is. How it is an abandoned city. I felt, after that, that Lawrence is Lawrence. So that gave me an air of superiority about Lawrence and about myself. But most students probably can't say what I am saying."

Later still, belatedly, Heng was offered a place in the ninth grade at Phillips. He didn't accept it. He didn't want to lose a year by having to repeat it. "I have to go to college, get a job, and take my parents' place pretty soon economically," he says. There was something else, too, though—another reason to refuse: "I was really disappointed that they didn't take me that first time," he admits. "But in the end, I was happy that they didn't. I told them that Lawrence is my place now."

WINTER 1992. I see a young woman who looks like Lisette, with her car hood up, at the corner of Prospect and Haverhill streets, not far from my house. I wonder for a moment whether it is Lisette. But it isn't. It's snowing. I walk past without asking what the trouble is—I'm on my morning dog walk—but decide I will offer to call someone for her on my way back. And I wonder, Is this really the way of it? Seeing people who look like people we already know, we are more compassionate, friendlier, than we otherwise might be? Is that what keeps us together, keeps us apart? I don't get a chance to make my offer, though. Her car is gone, slipping and sliding down the hill in the snow by the time I get back to that spot.

I HAVE two students from Lawrence in my class in the private school where I teach. One is of Korean descent; the other was born in Lebanon, where her uncle was kidnapped and killed during the fighting in 1983. Her father, kidnapped twice, still has a bullet in his head. They are two of the smartest kids in the class, but they are apart from the others, I can see. They sit like two small islands, apart even from each other.

ODD to think of my parents on a cruise that stopped in Puerto Rico, since, in my part of the world, so many have come from there. Dad describes San Juan as a "noisy, unpleasant city" in his letter, and he says he was "totally unimpressed." He must have gone through it with his eyes closed—he remembers little about it except that it has a deep-water harbor. He isn't a city person, anyway. Though he does appreciate Lawrence.

Unlike my mother. "Don't you find it depressing to see poor people all the time?" she once asked while visiting me in Lawrence.

"No, they're doing the best they can," I said. "Not everybody can be a preppy from Andover."

"That's right," said my father.

WHILE I AM visiting my parents at home in Greenwich, my mother takes me to her tennis round-robin at the public park. We are twelve women in all, and as I'm being introduced, I hear at least half a dozen foreign accents. Marika, Inger, Lisbet, Gerta, Shoshonna, and Decima are from Denmark, Sweden, England, Holland, Israel, and Austria—

immigrants of a different sort, from the better-heeled countries, for cosmopolitan Greenwich, which nobody would call "Immigrant City."

TERRI KELLEY tells me that she knows of a Vietnamese student who has changed his name to Patrick.

"I want to have an American name," he said.

"Patrick is an Irish name, you know," Terri told him.

"Yes, that, too," said Patrick.

CHAPTER 10

Trash

WORK IS what used to bring people to Lawrence. It's not what brings them now. With the local unemployment rate at 16 percent, the city doesn't have many employment opportunities to offer. Even the industries that are still located in Lawrence disproportionately hire the usually better-educated, better-skilled suburbanites. Gone are the days when a job meant bending your back instead of pushing the right button; when, in a noisy textile mill, gestures were the universal language. I've heard a man whose parents worked in the mills remark, "The mill owners cut out their tongues and said, 'Give us your hands.' That's all they wanted." It turned out to be quite a lot; but today it isn't enough. At the Wood Mill, where the current occupant is Bull Information Systems, Inc., the multinational computer maker, only fifty-nine of five hundred employees live in the city. I didn't have the heart to ask which jobs those Lawrencians held.

Meanwhile, the irony in the fact that the regional field office of the Massachusetts Department of Public Welfare currently occupies the first floor of the old Everett Mill is lost on few of the new immigrants' harshest local critics. Where rows of textile workers used to toil for hourly wages, there is now a honeycomb of little blue cubicles for the privacy of caseworker and client. On the day I visited, as I was leaving I glanced back at the heavy wooden door that was closing behind me. Stenciled on it in red was a leftover designation: WEAVING. Because of what one worker, a quality-control reviewer, called "taxpayers' emotions," a nonresident parking ban was established in the neighborhood surrounding the new office, which is in the old Italian district—where, in fact, many Italians still live. There is resentment, admitted the worker, who, like many of his 115 coworkers, rents a parking space for fifteen dollars a month several blocks away. (Before the field office moved to its present, roomier location, its address—1 Mill Street—was even more ironic: the two-story brick building on the north canal had been the payroll office of the American Woolen Company.)

Considering their own personal histories, how could working or retired Lawrencians *not* be bitter about the benefits programs and their recipients? Never mind that these critics, or members of their families, may have received food, clothing, and coal from the government during the Depression. That was temporary, and shameful—as it should be, they're the first to tell you. They cannot understand a world where it is often easier to get on welfare than it is to get a job; a system that makes it the smarter choice for someone to draw benefits than to work at the minimum wage; rules that allow an illegal alien to apply for benefits but not for employment. They drive past the welfare office every day, as I used to do, and see the cars double-parked, the young men waiting outside, the young women and their children piling in and out of taxicabs. They probably don't know the exact numbers—and I expect it's better that they don't—but Jacquelyn Hunt, an operations manager for the Massachusetts Department of Public Welfare and previously director of the field office in Lawrence from January 1988 to October 1992, told me that it had been her job to issue monthly nearly $3 million to 5,300 Lawrence households (multiply by 2.8 for the number of people). That was the cash allotment for Aid to Families with Dependent Children alone, and it didn't include grants to those same households for food stamps and medical assistance—and it made AFDC the city's largest "employer" by far, in many cases the only one the recipients had ever had. Over 40 percent of them had never held a job, and most had little hope of getting one that could support them and their dependents. Seventy percent did not have a high school diploma. Five percent (246 heads of household in that city) said they had had no schooling at all.

Despite these grim statistics, local critics are unmoved. What's especially galling to them—especially in a Catholic city like this one—is the welfare department's unwillingness to disseminate morals along with money. In June 1992, Jacquelyn Hunt told me this sad, illustrative tale:

"A man calls up this morning and says, 'I want to report a fraud.' It turns out that he is a landlord who rents to one of our clients who is a drug addict and who may be selling drugs, and he wants her out of the building. So he says, 'Well, her boyfriend lives there.' But people don't understand that, number one, just because someone's selling drugs doesn't mean I can throw them off welfare, because they may still be income-asset eligible, and, number two, the boyfriend living in the home is not the father of the child and has nothing to do with the fact that the child is needy and needs care, and I can't throw her off because she chooses to live with a boyfriend, a girlfriend, or anybody. If he's paying the rent, it may affect how much her budget is, but she's still probably going to be eligible. It's amazing. People really can't understand why, if somebody isn't paying their rent or is destroying the apartment or is doing something wrong, we can't automatically take away their money. 'She didn't pay the rent last month,' they'll say. 'Why are you giving her a check again? She's probably not going to pay it next month, either.' And you have to say, 'Well, the law doesn't allow me.' "

State and federal laws, imposed upon a tiny locality like Lawrence, make the ugly jargon verb *impacted* a necessary contemporary coinage, and these local critics understand that only too well. But do they also understand that the system is more insidious than that? Do they realize that it supports a whole *other* group of people, most of whom live outside Lawrence? And I don't merely mean the social workers at the city's myriad social-service agencies—a group I've heard a homeless man on National Public Radio generically refer to as "the poverty-industrial complex," and which the critics in question do indeed vociferously protest against every chance they get. When Merrimack Valley Legal Services defended a convicted Lawrence drug dealer and fraudulent welfare recipient whom the city was trying to evict from public housing, their angry voices were heard down in Washington. The U.S. House of Representatives, inspired partly by that case, voted to bar Legal Services from representing drug dealers in certain instances. (The measure, tied to another law package, died in the Senate.) And the critics were mildly appeased.

But are they aware of the less obvious but no less direct connection between welfare and abandoned buildings? Between subsidized tenants, who have made low-income rentals a high-profit investment game, and neighborhood blight? What do they have to say about the checks that landlords receive from the government once or twice a month, depending on the programs for which their tenants are eligible? The *Eagle-Tribune* has reported that Lawrence property owners received $4.8 million in rental subsidies for welfare families in 1992 alone (and as you'll learn below, that wasn't even a very good year). Nobody talks about *their* dependency, *their* habit, which has become just as destructive to the community as the welfare habit itself.

THE IDEA of treating housing as a source of income rather than shelter has had a long history in Lawrence. In the thirties, when thousands were unemployed, many multifamily houses were by necessity cut up into even smaller and more numerous units than they'd initially been meant for, since families needed the dollars that extra rentals could bring. A building code was on the books, as always, but it was easy to ignore in the face of all the hard-luck stories.

Single-family houses were divided, too; in fact, it happened, in a minor way, to the John Barker house, next door to ours in Lawrence. In 1939, nurse Mary was the only family member left living there, and it was decided that she would move into 173 Prospect Street with Miss Barker, her niece, and Arthur, her brother, and that 175 Prospect Street would be sold. The money would be useful. Miss Barker had her teaching job, but Arthur had been laid off by the feed company where he had been working as a bookkeeper for years. Mr. and Mrs. Alfio Colvito—that is to say, Freddy Colvito and his wife, who were living on Union Street, above a fish market and barroom—offered the asking price, ten thousand dollars, in cash.

It's unclear whether the house was already divided by then, with the bottom half rented out for income. Miss Barker recalls nothing of the sort. But Ann Vaccarro, Freddy's eldest daughter, who was in the sixth grade when the house was purchased, swears that it already had an upstairs and a downstairs apartment and that, just like the Barkers before them, they rented the first floor to a succession of families until 1960, when John and Lucille Piacenzo moved in and started paying ten dollars a week.

However the division occurred, at least it wasn't a more radical one. It's not uncommon to hear of Victorians in Lawrence that have been divided into half a dozen apartments, with windows blocked up, doors leading nowhere, hallways like fun-house corridors. There is a twenty-room turn-of-the-century mansion on the common that was cut up into eleven apartments, according to the superintendent who spoke with me one day during a break from his saxophone practice on the porch. The yard was neat by Lawrence standards, which means no trash, but no shrubs, either. At least from the outside, however, the place looked to be held together with wire and glue and the chipped brown paint that covered it.

Luckily for our house, the Arthur Barkers could afford to keep it intact. The Colvito house, on the other hand, was not only divided but, in the fifties, also had its front yard dug up by Freddy and replaced with a handy but ugly three-stall garage, also for renting out (we were happy to rent one of those stalls from him). An enclosed sunporch—a Florida room, with glass jalousies—was added to the front face of the second floor, like a box on stilts. Though completely out of character for the house (a "remuddling," *The Old House Journal* would call it), the renovation provided an extra room when the Colvitos needed one. And no matter what its aesthetics, at least until aging Freddy moved in with daughter Ann, the house was maintained as well as Miss Barker's, if not better, with a border garden of lilies, iris, red and white roses, and chrysanthemums coming up, all in turn, and a picket fence regularly whitewashed by Freddy himself.

Maybe the Colvitos kept up the house so well to show Arthur Barker that he had been wrong to worry about whether they were good enough for his house. Ann claims that Arthur "checked out" Freddy for six months before he finally took his money and welcomed the Colvitos to Prospect Hill at a time when Italians had only just begun to achieve hilltop status. Probably, though, the biggest reason for them to keep up the property was the simplest: they were the ones who lived there.

Having the landlord on the premises was a common feature of virtually all rental property in Lawrence in those years. As a tenant, you didn't send your rent to a post office box in the suburbs. In fact, you might have placed it in the hand of your own mother. Tom Troy, the firefighter, told me: "We lived in a three-decker, on the first floor. My grandmother lived on the second floor. And my uncle and aunt lived on the third floor. We had a battery radio in our apartment and speakers on the second and third floors—one radio for the whole house. It was just like a car battery that had to be re-charged every week. And we had one telephone for everybody, and if there was a call for the third floor, three raps on the pipe. Second floor was two raps. Nobody went in or out of the house that my mother didn't know about."

Today, one is hard-pressed to name more than a handful of "on-the-grounds" landlords in Lawrence; and one that I could name but won't is a well-known city character. He swims in the canals in all sorts of weather; occasionally wears streaks of red war paint across his nose and cheeks, and (I've seen this once) drives his car around with one bare leg sticking out the window. Does that mean that to live in one of your own rental units today in Immigrant City you have to be crazy? Whatever the state of his mental health, his buildings—three-families, four's, and six's in one of the rougher sections downtown—are meticulously kept, by both him and his tenants.

A typical list of "nuisance properties" from the local paper, on the other hand, shows no owners in Lawrence. Instead, the roll call features a list of people with addresses in Windham, New Hampshire; Salem, New Hampshire; Chester, New Hampshire; Palm Beach, Florida; and Norristown, Pennsylvania. Are these absentee owners holdover investors from the real estate boom years of the eighties? In 1986 and 1987 especially, when Lawrence thought that Emerson College was going to relocate there—and advertised itself as a soon-to-be college town—investors (or is *speculators* a better word?) were

buying up everything they possibly could and squeezing condominiums into the spaces between the buildings. I remember
well hearing stories at suburban cocktail parties of financial
killings made in Lawrence, but though our own tax assessment
had increased nearly 400 percent—from $34,000 in 1984 to
$130,000 in 1988—we were not tempted to join the specula-
tors' ranks. We had bought a home, our first, not "a property."
(In 1994, of course, when we were ready to sell, the assessment had plummeted again, to $59,000.)

LIKE THE on-the-grounds landlord, the caring tenant is a
rarity, too, many complain. They long for those erstwhile
household saints, now vanished, who, in everybody's favorite illustration of their fastidious ways, scrubbed the front steps
leading up to their rented lintels. Sam DeAngelo, born in
Lawrence in 1948, offers his late Italian grandmother as the
consummate example. She washed her stairs every Friday afternoon, he says. "She used what they called *giavelle* water—
diluted Clorox. Down on her knees! It's true! I mean, I was
there!"

Not only fastidious but steadfast: she lived in the same
apartment from the time she was married until the day she
went into a nursing home.

Today that sort of constancy is unheard of, says DeAngelo,
and he should know. He is himself a landlord now, not on-the-
grounds, but absentee, though he's considered to be "one of
the clean ones."

He made his first real estate purchase in Lawrence in
1977: the tenement next door to the one he'd lived in as the
infant son of parents who both worked in the Ayer Mill until
it closed. He would have bought that one, he said, but it no
longer existed; it had been torn down for a parking lot. As of
now, in Lawrence—and in Methuen, where he lives—he owns

a total of one hundred units, and he says he can count on one hand those tenants who work and do not pay him with some sort of subsidy: "They're either on Section Eight, which is a federal subsidy, or Seven-oh-seven, which is a state program, or on welfare—AFDC, usually," he told me as we sat in his pleasant pink-walled office on Broadway in Methuen, just over the Lawrence line. "And what happens is, I cannot discriminate against these people—and I hate to say 'these people,' but I will say 'these people.' Anyway, even if I wanted to, I'd be out of business if I tried, because that's the clientele. That's the clientele we're all renting to. With the Eight and the Seven-oh-seven, I get the money paid directly to me, and with the AFDC, I can request what are called 'direct vendor payments.' "

It sounds easy enough, a gravy train, even. But is it? On Fulton Street one afternoon, I saw the driver of a black Mercedes hop out of his car and roll the metal trash barrels back into a tenement yard. I assumed he was the landlord, and I wondered, Is it *that* lucrative to own slum real estate in Lawrence? For most, it isn't. "Did you ever see that movie *The Money Pit?*" DeAngelo asked me. "Well, that's what these buildings are like. And a lot of people find it overwhelming, and so they can't pay their mortgage, and certainly, if you can't pay your mortgage, you don't have enough money for repairs. And a lot of these people get into this business not knowing what they're going to face. That's when the abandonment begins."

And that's in the best of times, which is not where Lawrence is now. As DeAngelo explains it, "If you go back to the mid-eighties, we had almost nothing for a vacancy rate. Rents were escalating. People were going crazy. And we had a large influx of people from New York. And when you had an apartment that vacated, instead of crying about the fact that you had to put a lot of dollars in, you were almost happy, because you knew the rent could be increased. That's how fast things were changing. But in 1990, 1991, 1992, vacancy rates started climbing dramatically. I don't know where these people were going, but the vacancy rates were going nuts, and as a result the rents declined anywhere from fifteen to twenty-five percent. You might have been getting five fifty a month, five and a quarter for a two-bedroom deleaded unit, four rooms in total, in Lawrence. That is now down to four fifty, four and quarter. The decline in rents and increase in vacancies in turn fueled a lot of these vacant buildings. These people bought at the height of the market, so they were paying between thirty, thirty-five, and forty thousand dollars per unit. So like a three-decker would sell for a hundred and twenty thousand. Okay? Once they started having these dramatic vacancy rates and declines in rents, they couldn't keep up with insurance, the water, the sewer, the taxes. There was no revenue to keep their buildings going, and they started slipping on their mortgages. And these were people who really weren't equipped to deal with the vandalism and things that were occurring, because as soon as the building was vacant, the copper got stolen, and the building was just going down fast. And these people ended up walking away. They either said to the bank, 'I can't do it anymore,' and the bank foreclosed. Or they said, 'I just can't do it period,' and let things happen, whatever they were."

Not only landlords but also banks have been abandoning buildings in Lawrence lately—not the local banks, but out-of-town banks, for which, as DeAngelo puts it, "Lawrence is not a big part of their puzzle. So they say, 'Wait a minute. We have lead-paint liability, fires, code enforcement—we're not going to take over this building.' So they either abandon their mortgage in place, which means they never take ownership of the building and the building sits there and deteriorates and becomes a fire trap, or they say, 'We don't want this building, so we're not going to bid it back at the foreclosure, but we will foreclose on these buildings—we want to clean up our balance sheet and get the heck out of Lawrence—so we'll have an 'absolute' auction. No minimum, no reserve. We won't bid. Whatever it goes for, it's yours."

DeAngelo talked a long time that morning about the absurdities of the system in which he is, nonetheless, an apparently willing participant. In fact, he sounded a lot like the landlords who used to call up Jacquelyn Hunt at the welfare office (and who now, no doubt, call her successor) to complain about their tenants' morals. "When you were growing up, if you didn't do the things you were supposed to do, you probably got punished for it, right? You paid a price. There was a penalty involved. So you learned your way through life what you should do or shouldn't do. Now these people are actually rewarded for their misdeeds. If they aren't paying their rent and are being evicted, do you think anybody at welfare says, 'Well, wait a minute. What did you do with the money that we've been giving you? Why haven't you been paying your rent?' No. They're not allowed to. Isn't that ridiculous? They're getting something for nothing and we're not allowed to ask the question. And you know how they're rewarded? They're given an emergency voucher to rent another apartment if they get evicted. Or they're given an emergency voucher to pay their back rent so they can stay where they are. Or in some cases, they're placed at the head of the list for public housing."

DEANGELO WAS describing a federally funded program called Emergency Assistance. Designed to prevent the homelessness that often follows eviction, it entitles a welfare family to apply for three months' worth of "rental arrearage" per year (provided there is a dependent "child" under twenty living in the household); but many agree that the program has been abused by welfare recipients who see it as a way to pad their benefits. In 1992, 13,360 Massachusetts welfare families received an extra $15.1 million in Emergency Assistance.

It's a mess, all right. But I wish that people would remember that the users—and abusers—of this system did not create it. And anybody who thinks the typical welfare-dependent life is one of ease should become familiar with the teenage mothers who regularly move in and out of some of the sorriest buildings in my former neighborhood. I regularly saw listless groups of them walking by the house when I was out gardening in my front yard in Lawrence. They would trudge along in their flimsy shoes, toddlers in hand, clearly exhausted. Once, I watched from my parlor window as a trio of them mustered the energy to swoop down on a couple of broken chairs that I had left on the sidewalk for the trashmen.

These are not women living high on anybody's hog.

MAYBE I would feel better if in the same breath that people passed judgment on the absent morals of those on public assistance, they also discussed the ethics of neglectful landlords, and of the delinquent property owners—and banks—who leave their trash buildings behind.

June 1992. On the afternoon of my morning conversation with Sam DeAngelo, I happen upon a foreclosure auction half a block down the street from my own house. This particular building is not a triple-decker; it's a group of new condominiums. I had seen them being slapped together about five years before, when the speculative frenzy was at its peak. The lot was the side yard of a crumbling lime green tenement. One morning, bulldozers came and dug for the foundation. A few days later, the condos—four units, prefab—went up, far to the rear of the property line and set sideways to Prospect Street to fit, however awkwardly, on that inappropriate lot. Within the week, the rest of the lot, from the edge of the new building to the edge of the street, was blacktopped: that was the parking lot. A row of locked mailboxes and a bunch of metal trash barrels were the crowning touch.

It is in the litter-strewn parking lot that today's auction is to be held. As I walk up the street from my house, following arrows on telephone poles, I notice a brown Mercedes with Florida license plates cruising slowly down the street. I guess, correctly, that the driver is heading for the auction, too.

Property auctions have been going on all over the city for months, and this is not to be a large gathering—half a dozen people, mostly bank employees and the auctioneer's staff. The owners are nowhere in sight.

The auctioneer, leaning against his black Saab, is a congenial young man in his thirties, with the look of a banker about him: gray pinstriped suit, white shirt, red tie. The Saab has a sunroof, open, and its Massachusetts license plate reads SEA- SKI. He takes my name and phone number: "Will you be bidding today?"

"I don't think so," I say. "Anyway, I don't have my five thousand dollars." (Which is the deposit per unit required of bidders.)

He smiles cordially and goes with his clipboard to the man who drove up in the Mercedes. He is trim, bald, wearing jeans and sneakers, dark glasses with a chartreuse cord around his neck, and drinking out of a very large Coke-brand paper cup. His address is a post office box in the town of Amesbury, a few exits up the highway.

Others begin to arrive: three men and one woman. The woman is middle-aged, her makeup perfectly applied, and wearing a pumpkin-colored blouse with spangles and mirrors sewn into it. She is introduced by the Mercedes driver to one of the other men.

"Oh, you're the nicer brother," she says to him flirtatiously; then, turning to the Mercedes driver, she's strictly business: "Are you all out now?"

"I got out in '88," he replies, "but I just bought a package."

"This city is going down, down." The woman shakes her head. "Listen," she adds, "this is a true story." She motions them all to come closer to hear in confidence what she wants to tell them. When she has finished whispering her tale, which, I manage to hear, had something to do with a rooming house, she glances at the condos: "I had these up for seventy-nine thousand dollars per unit. We didn't have a call on them. He's a good builder," she says of the man who squeezed these places in sideways to the street. "He's a nice person." It sounds like an epitaph.

"Lawrence is over," one of the other men says.

"It's gone," another agrees.

"It's going to get worse," says the third. And the four of them stand in silence for a moment, as if paying their respects.

The auction is about to begin. The auctioneer puts on his sunglasses to read the legal notice aloud to the gathering.

"You gonna bid?" someone asks the one who has been called the nicer brother.

"No, my brother wouldn't give me a check. He's getting tough."

"I thought you were the moneyman." The woman teases him.

He shrugs.

The auctioneer has taken off his suit jacket. The sun is strong and yellow. He is wearing shiny black tassel loafers. He crosses his ankles, leaning up against his warm car.

He starts to read the legal notice rapidly, without inflection. "By virtue and in execution of the power of sale con-

tained in a certain mortgage given by . . ." Conversations re-
sume as he drones on about water bills of over three thousand
dollars, unpaid, and a tax bill of six hundred dollars and warns
that "if the buyer wishes to evict anybody, he must do so at his
own expense."

In the middle of the speech, a beat-up gold Impala pulls
up. Two mothers and five children are aboard. The mothers
are brown-skinned young women in stirrup pants. They saun-
ter into one of the condos, ignoring the gathering in their
parking lot. The children stay in the car, to tumble around and
honk the horn as the auctioneer goes on talking. Then one of
the children disembarks and starts hitting the row of mailboxes
with a silver plastic sword.

When the sun goes behind a cloud, the auctioneer
switches to reading glasses framed in tortoiseshell. He is starting to remind me of a priest saying Mass. "It's assessed at
sixty-eight thousand dollars," he says. "That's per unit, and
there're four of them."

When he finally concludes his soliloquy, I realize that everyone is waiting for the Mercedes driver to speak. He is,
apparently, the sole potential bidder.

"Mr. Lopez? Any questions?" the auctioneer asks him.

Mr. Lopez looks at the blacktop beneath his sneak-
ered feet.

"Fifty? Forty-five? Forty?" goes the auctioneer's solicitous
litany. "Give me a number," he suggests.

No response from Mr. Lopez.

"Maybe he wants to see the inside," someone says. "It's
clean," he is assured. But Mr. Lopez shakes his head and
smiles, as if to say he's not falling for that one, still looking at
the ground.

"Easy highway access," hums the auctioneer as a boy of six
or seven crosses his path, returning from the corner store with

a brown bag that he can barely carry. "An easy commute to Boston."

Finally, the mortgagee—that is, the bank (a local one)—in the guise of an excruciatingly well-dressed young man named Jose, says glumly, resignedly, "Forty thousand dollars," and the gathering swiftly disperses.

CHAPTER 11

Cronies

Italian-American teacher in the Lawrence public
schools to whom a new African-American teacher
complained about having been given an undesirable
teaching assignment: "Do you think it's because you're
black?"
   (Huffily) "Yes, I do."
   "Well, it's not. It's because you're not Irish."

F ALL 1991. I'm sitting scrunched together with other Lawrencians on a wooden pewlike bench in the city council
chambers downtown. It's a packed house this afternoon in the
small wood-paneled assembly room on the first floor of city
hall. The side walls of the room are decorated with the black-
and-white photographic portraits of several former mayors and
other elected officials (James Garvey, my friend the political
pundit, calls these panels "the walls of death"). During the
winter months, its windows are covered with sheets of clear
plastic, just as they would be in the home of any strapped family trying to save money on its fuel bill. In fact, as I sit hearing
about hardships, grudges, and stretched resources at this
emergency city council meeting, during which a bill mandating
unpaid two-week furloughs for all city employees will be approved, I think, This must be exactly what it's like to live in a

large, poor, worried household. No one even finds it amusing when the proceedings are briefly interrupted because City Clerk James McGravey must go perform a marriage in his office across the hall.

On this same fall afternoon, as one great big unhappy family, we receive more bad news. It's announced that the reason the current Lawrence mayor, Kevin Sullivan, isn't in attendance is that he stayed up till 2 A.M. with the school committee, only to be awakened a few hours later to find a stolen car parked on his front lawn. A message of sorts: the day before, the *Eagle-Tribune* had reported that car thefts were down a third in Lawrence—though they were up a third in Methuen. Somebody seems to want Mayor Sullivan to know that car thieves are still a force in Lawrence.

My reaction to this announcement surprises me. For all the world like a true Lawrencian, I find myself feeling smug about Methuen's misfortune, and uninterested in a more appropriate response—for example, that the two municipalities might work together to solve the shared problem. But no: Lawrencians prefer to wrangle with their problems alone, just as a shamed, proud household usually does. By the same token, the surrounding towns would rather Lawrence keep its problems to itself, though isolated regional efforts, like the Merrimack Valley Project, founded in 1989 by a Chicago-based organizer named Ken Galdston, have had some success, pushing, in particular, a regional fire department. (Perhaps the willingness of Andover, North Andover, and Methuen even to discuss such a thing is less of an achievement than it appears to be: the fire departments in those towns are repeatedly called upon to provide traditional mutual aid to Lawrence, anyway. In 1991, North Andover adopted a policy against sending engines to blazes of fewer than three alarms; Methuen followed suit in 1994.)

In the meantime, "Where do you live? Do you live here?"

are the questions asked most frequently by the onlooking members of the citizenry whenever someone steps up to the chamber's microphone to speak his or her piece to the councilors at their regular meetings. They're exactly the questions their progenitors must have asked unfamiliar people traversing the boundary lines of the old, ethnically segregated neighborhoods. "I say nobody but tax-paying Lawrencians should be allowed to speak" is an opinion often hotly expressed by those who resent the suburban addresses of the lawyers, architects, and other consultants who come to council meetings to represent various interests. For how could anyone really understand what the issue is if he or she hasn't experienced life here? And who are these outsiders to offer solutions when they don't have to live with the consequences? What are these people trying to put over on us now?

From Lawrence's point of view, these are good questions. The suburbs have drawn wealth from Lawrence for decades. What have they returned?

Usually, it's a real estate development of one kind or another that gets a Lawrencian's blood boiling—at least it was during the boom years of the eighties. Which isn't to say that all development detracts. Of course it doesn't. And Lawrence badly needs the extra tax revenues that new construction can bring. But while squeezing another building sideways onto a piece of property is perhaps the fastest way to increase the value of a particular lot, isn't it also a way to decrease the value of the lots east, west, north, and south of it? And if the building is packed with apartments to be rented to families with children, what about the burden placed on the school system and other social services?

Local psychologists say such overcrowding does damage not just to the city as a physical and social entity but to its inhabitants as human beings. They believe that Lawrencians—immigrants and their offspring, by definition—are psychically stunted by the cramped quarters in which they have always lived. They say that while closeness fosters cooperation and family strength, it also creates problems, such as overinvolvement and dependency. Close family (and neighborhood) networks, while providing all the traditional benefits of those extended social systems (built-in "day care," for example), can become dysfunctional, discouraging the autonomous and independent behavior that's required to "succeed."

If you're from a large immigrant family yourself, maybe you've experienced that well-meant but cloying intimacy so often depicted, with a bittersweet edge, in books and movies with ethnic themes. Or maybe you've witnessed one manifestation of it from afar: the grown sons and daughters who never marry, who never leave home. It used to be that one adult child of an immigrant parent would stay behind in the old household—to be translator, buffer, emissary to the outside, English-speaking world. Not uncommonly, this arrangement was accomplished through manipulation: a young person's confidence would be undermined so that he or she would "choose" to stay home. My own intimidating grandmother Schinto managed to keep *three* unmarried children—two daughters and a son—at her side, a married son in the apartment downstairs, and two other married children (my father was one) not more than a mile or two from the old stucco homestead.

Call it huddle fever—for it can be as limiting as a physical disease. Teachers at Lawrence High testify that they see another manifestation of the syndrome daily—a fear of doing something no one in the immediate household has ever done before—even amid the bravado and swagger for which inner-city students are famous. Is it a throwback to the days when venturing beyond one's own neighborhood could mean a black eye or worse? Even valedictorian Dung Nguyen admits she applied to Yale partly because she knew that other LHS graduates had gone there and so believed that it was "attainable."

(Incidentally, Dung's parents understood neither the ambitiousness of her application nor what an achievement her acceptance was until her father's native-born accountant, hearing the news, got excited by it. "Is it *that* important?" Dung's father asked his daughter. "Well, Dad," Dung told him, "George Bush went there." Dung says he understood better then.)

Teacher Terri Kelley, daughter of first-generation Italian-Americans, doesn't have to search for evidence of huddle fever in her students' lives; she recalls its effects on her own. "You don't read the *Boston Globe* if your parents read the *Eagle-Tribune*. It's an insult to your parents. When my uncle Sully became a doctor and moved to Methuen, all sorts of snide comments were made," says Kelley, whose own father, Uncle Sully's younger brother, had to drop out of law school during the Depression. They called Uncle Sully "the King" thereafter, Kelley told me. "They'd say things like 'Who does he think he is?' It was this 'uppity' thing, though it went along with affection." Kelley herself was accepted into the class of 1961 at both Radcliffe and Smith, but instead she attended Emmanuel College, a small Catholic women's institution in Boston, because, she says, her family convinced her that she "wasn't good enough" for the more selective schools. "It was good to excel, but not too much. We were taught to be so dependent on our family, upon 'our own kind.' We were told that we didn't even need friends. For years into adulthood, I was under the impression that if I ate something my family didn't cook, I could easily die. That keeps you close to home."

The family tie that can eventually become a noose is, then, a prime feature of the fever. It's more than a manifestation of the fear of rejection, more than a search for security in the familiar. It's a means to a sort of compromised survival. Shunned by the wider world or unable to see how they might fit into it, the feverish hunker down and do what they can for their own.

IN A WORKING-CLASS CITY, the biggest favor one can do for one's own—or anybody—is to employ them. Mulespinner Alphonse recalls the simple formula: "If a section hand liked you, he'd give you the good work." But Casparino Robito's ethnocentric take on mill hiring practices is probably more accurate: "You see, when you're an Italian, you can get a good job if you know an Italian that's got influence with some other guy. Whether he's Irish or whatever, he can get you that job. That's the way it was in them days. You know, we took care of ourselves, our people."

In the twenties, as opportunities for employment in the mills grew increasingly uncertain, people looked to city government for work—an especially desirable alternative because the local bureaucracy, unlike the mills, would never go out of business. And how were those jobs acquired? At city hall, too, personal preferences played a role in hiring, not only because it was customary in the mills whence many of these workers had come but because giving jobs to supporters has been a hallmark of democratic political life since time immemorial. In Lawrence (as in other cities), it was the Irish who were in power, and so it was they who moved their fellowmen into jobs in the police force and elsewhere in the expanding bureaucracy, while immigrants from other countries were only just starting to establish themselves.

Quite apart from any political leanings, then, a citizen had a sensible, single-minded, survivalist's reason to go out and campaign for his or her chosen candidate. To the victor went the spoils, and everybody who'd held a sign or delivered the umpteen votes of his or her many cousins had wrangled to collect a regular city paycheck after the swearing-in. As James Garvey describes it: "You're elected and take office, and the one hundred and fifty or one hundred and seventy-five or whoever who are working there are out, and you bring your own people in. Loyalty to the man is the only qualification.

You got to be a card-carrying member, lady. If not, you were out the door, McGinty. Unless you had a political saint [patron]. And that was . . . whoever. Those who had them stayed working during three or four or five consecutive administrations. Now, the political saint could have been anybody downtown—any one of the businessmen, or a lawyer, anybody." Anybody with political clout, that is.

The political-spoils system became even more entrenched during the Depression, when WPA funds allowed the city to put thousands to work—rebuilding roads, bridges, parks, playgrounds, the very sidewalks under everybody's feet, including stretches of cement in my own former neighborhood in Lawrence, in which I would periodically note the small commemorative metal plaques dated 1935, 1936, 1937. A friend of mine, Casey, told me that her father worked in a WPA bookbindery in Lawrence during those years. Later, he got a permanent government job, as a policeman, though it took a while to secure the slot: Casey's mother had supported loser after loser in the elections; finally, her man won, and her husband was in.

By then, of course, not only the Irish were participating in the system; the French, Italians, and Polish were now so numerous that a savvy politician's net had to be more widely cast. Freddy Colvito's daughter Ann sounded just like Irish-American Casey when she told me matter-of-factly how Italian-born Freddy got his city job in the thirties: "He followed politics, supported a couple of candidates who didn't win, until finally he supported one who did." He became a city laborer then and remained one until he retired. In fact, leaning up against his house for all the years that I lived next door was a remnant of that career: a laborer's shovel whose handle was burnished with LAWSD—the insignia of the Lawrence Sanitation Department.

THAT THESE coveted government jobs were awarded on a less than scientific basis is a fact that Walter Augustine Griffin, who lives on my old street in Lawrence, doesn't deny. Born in 1901, he was actually *Mayor* Griffin from 1933 to 1940. "Of course we had some influence as far as . . . well, you know, you helped people," ex-mayor Griffin stammered as we sat in his living room one morning, his spent cigar in the ashtray. "They came in to see you. But I mean, after all, if they weren't eligible, they didn't get it."

Griffin wasn't the only elected official empowered to give people jobs, of course. Under the city's aldermanic form of government, four biannually elected, full-time, fully paid aldermen (never an alderwoman) presided over the municipal departments—Engineering; Public Parks and Properties; Public Safety; and Public Health and Charities—and each acted as his own personnel director.

Father Lamond worked for the Parks Department during some of his summers off from studies at the seminary. This is how he got his temporary jobs: "In those days, you would go to one of the aldermen and say, 'My mother or my father or my uncle or everybody else, they all voted for you. Could you give me anything?' And he could usually give you a couple of weeks' work. You were lucky if you got three weeks. And the pay was pretty good. I remember one of my pays was thirty-three dollars, which was a lot of money back then."

Such solicitations naturally invited corruption. (Apparently, they also bred gall: "There was an alderman by the name of McNulty," Father Lamond told me, "and he was supposed to have the snow shoveled, but he said, 'Well, God put it there. Let God take it away.' ") In the mills, by all accounts, there had been plenty of bribery, and even more rumors of it. "Ah, the bosses all stunk," one former mill worker told me. "They didn't pick out who was good or who did their jobs [when they rehired people after layoffs]. I imagine they all brought them something, you know? That's my opinion."

"Some people who got far built a special relationship with the boss," another said. "They went out and cut his shrubs."

Lawrencians swear it was the same at city hall for decades. "You had to have a brain and a half like Marion not to [have had to] pay for your job in the twenties," my Tower Hill nonagenarian acquaintance, Elspeth Kepple, told me, referring to Miss Barker; she herself was passed over for a teaching job in those years, she added with disdain, leaving it to me to assume that it was because she had scruples. (She eventually got a job with the Methuen school system, which at the time was considered inferior to Lawrence's.)

When I asked Walter Griffin about these accusations, which I'd been hearing routinely, he defended one of his old cronies with touching fervor—as if the man's transgressions had occurred only last week: "I'm not going to name names, but . . . It wasn't anything illegal, but this one alderman just had a big heart. And anybody who asked him for a job, he gave one to. It was illegal in the sense that he was going over his budget. And in order for us not to get into trouble, I took the department off him and had it run by someone else. He was a good-hearted man—don't misunderstand. There was nothing crooked about him—but he couldn't say no."

That may be true, but rumors of job selling tainted Griffin's final years in office, and in 1941, two aldermen actually spent time in the city jail for corruption. It's the reason, Griffin claims, that he was ousted and never reelected, though he says he had nothing to do with the scam. "But," he adds, sounding as bitter as he must have been fifty years ago, "like everything else, someone gets painted with the brush that doesn't belong to him."

Civil-service reforms in the 1940s, designed to end political patronage at the local level and introduce a system of hiring and promotions based on test taking and merit, seem to have been only mildly successful in Lawrence, with many of the changes merely serving to make the practice of awarding jobs as political favors a subtler, more devious art. Tom Troy told me: "There was an old joke. If you wanted to be promoted in the fire department, you had to pass the examination, and then you had to pass political science. Political science could involve a lot of things. It could mean, in some cases going back years and years, people paid for it. People went to jail for it, years ago. Since I've been on the department, I don't know of any case like that. But I know of political pressure. You could campaign for somebody. You could rent a headquarters for him. You could buy tickets to an affair. And so you could end up with a good mark. And when time came for promotion, they would take the three top test takers and the aldermen would get together and promote one of them, as long as they gave an excuse as to why they didn't promote the other two. The excuse could be anything they wanted to put on the piece of paper. Usually, the excuses wouldn't be made public. If you were skipped, you didn't make too much of a noise, because there would be another promotion coming and you didn't want to get on the wrong side of the fence. I know a fellow who ended up as a captain. He was a lieutenant, and he was on the list, and he was skipped. And the next day, he went down to see the aldermen, thanked them for their consideration, and asked them to make sure he was considered the next time. He told them he wasn't the least bit upset. And the next time, he was promoted. And we had another fellow who went down and threatened to shoot an alderman because he was skipped. And he never was promoted from a lieutenant."

Troy himself, I should mention, rose through the ranks of the union instead of management, ending his career as vice president of the Fourth District Professional Firefighters of Massachusetts.

THE ALDERMEN COULDN'T give everybody jobs, of course— not even when there were three or four times as many city employees as the one thousand or so on the city payroll today (due, of course, to the fact that, as in the mills, there were many more unskilled and semiskilled jobs in those days). And so, I've been told time and again, if a job couldn't be managed in exchange for your vote on Election Day, you could always seek another kind of favor, and you would probably get it. "Would you be sure that my street is plowed in winter?" "Would you see that the park across the street from my house is cleaned up?" These were the sorts of bargains many Lawrencians struck with candidates who hoped to retain their fiefdoms at city hall. Never mind that a well-run municipality would remove the snow from every street and keep clean every piece of public property. Maybe Lawrence wasn't running so smoothly after all. How could it be if constituent service, not legislative prowess or long-range planning, was the stock-in-trade of its ideal, and perennially reelected, politicians? "You know the old story in politics," James Garvey told me. "What did you do for me lately? And I don't mean yesterday. I mean this morning. So the last thing that happens is the first thing. I mean, if I go over and kick you, fine, but if afterward I go over and give you a hug and a kiss and twenty-five dollars, which are you going to remember? You know? It's just that damn simple."

Even in the fifties, as the mills failed and Lawrence was desperately in need of a new collective direction, elected officials found it most politically advantageous not to proffer visions of the future of their "Forgotten City" (so-called by visiting U.S. presidential candidate Dwight D. Eisenhower), but to give "aid" through jobs and other favors, on a recklessly extravagant case-by-case basis, to its smallest and most expendable economic unit—the one most cherished and protected by feverish Lawrencians since the beginning—the family.

IN THE FALL of 1983, a year before Bob and I moved to Lawrence, the aldermanic system was abolished. Advocates for change had been campaigning for over a decade, but they couldn't muster the needed votes because so many Lawrencians who benefited from the old ways were against it; finally, as the city slid ever more deeply into its post-industrial-age decline, enough voters decided to support what by then seemed like a solution of last resort. And so Lawrence ceased to be the only city in Massachusetts to retain what had long been considered an outdated and problematic political arrangement—one which had been made fashionable by local-government reformers of the early 1900s (Lawrence had adopted it in the great strike year, 1912).

A charter change had been required to oust the aldermen. Taking their place, the revised charter mandated, would be two groups: one elected, one appointed. First, a nine-member neighborhood-based city council—chosen by the citizens—would sit weekly in the wood-paneled room at city hall where the aldermen used to make the laws that they themselves would enforce. Part-time, only nominally remunerated (one hundred dollars a week, plus health insurance), the councillors would also oversee hired department heads, who would work upstairs in the aldermen's former offices, doing their predecessors' management chores. The opposing, and often conflicting, tasks—legislation and implementation—would now be sensibly split.

And how would these department heads be hired? The mayor would make the recommendations, but the city council would have to approve them. Ideally, those hired would have credentials, expertise, management skills—all of which many aldermen had lacked. Increased professionalism was the hope, but it hasn't materialized in many quarters.

One problem is the residency law. The controversial ruling, a part of the new city charter, requires that those hired after 1986 be Lawrence residents or move into the city within two years. The policy was designed to ensure that employees would have a vested interest in the community they were being paid to serve; at the department-head level, it was also meant to lure back middle-class taxpayers. Instead, it has become a hindrance for many promising candidates who might otherwise take the jobs, while more than one have accepted posts, then, after the two-year grace period, moved on. Few current Lawrencians are qualified for the work, making the mayor's choices meager all around. With so many white-collar managers being laid off these days, you would think more of them would seek the positions—that they might be willing to make the sacrifice and move into the city; instead, it's the law that may change. (As I write this, a referendum is in the offing.)

Beyond those difficulties, even the most capable leadership would be stymied by the city's precarious finances. How much easier it all must have seemed when something James Garvey calls "the cycle" was in place—that is, local taxes went down during an election year, and up the next, when there were no political lives at stake. Currently, less than 40 percent of Lawrence's budget is locally generated. Not only does the tax base itself continue to shrink (between 1992 and 1994 alone, Lawrence lost $884 million in taxable property value, a portion of those properties actually destroyed, by fire), but the state law known as Proposition 2½—one of those measures passed by frustrated taxpayers in the late seventies and early eighties as part of a regressive national trend—has capped property tax-rate hikes at an annual 2.5 percent. In the years since the law's passage, generous state and federal programs have bailed Lawrence out of tight financial situations. In short, though a vocal portion of the populace complains of layabout welfare recipients, essentially the city is one, too. Except that now those funds are no longer readily forthcoming—both nation and state have been forced to curtail their largesse—and all of Lawrence is suffering a painful withdrawal as a result of it.

As for the old-time political favors, it's certainly harder to do one for somebody these days, everyone agrees, but, because of the way things have been going, it's also harder to get anything done at all.

FALL 1988. I'm upstairs at city hall, waiting in line at the Building Department. What a sad state of affairs. I worked in the Building Department in Greenwich for a few weeks over twenty years ago, so I know the first impression that a well-run department should give, and this disheveled rabbit warren isn't it. I was nineteen years old, home for the summer from college, and the position was, come to think of it, my own temporary patronage job; after all, I was hired by my father. This was at the peak of the corporate-office building boom in town, however, so there was plenty of work to do, and I well earned my five dollars an hour. I remember the office had just made its first foray into the age of technology, and though I was given an old manual typewriter to use, I was also taught to duplicate black-and-white transparencies of building permits and blueprints on state-of-the-art equipment.

The new machinery was costly, but the department did pay its way and then some, my father has told me. When he was hired as an inspector, in 1963, the place was losing money; by the time he retired, twenty-three years later, he was chief building inspector and the office, now fully computerized, was actually turning a profit, even after salaries and expenses: in 1986, their net was $700,000. And though the building boom was essentially over by the late 1970s, the department continued to subsidize many of the town's other municipal agencies.

Lawrence is quite a different scene. And while I know it isn't really fair to compare the two locales, with their radically different tax bases, I cannot help it as I'm ushered back to a makeshift cubicle by Inspector Lawrence Hester. Its walls—threadbare partitions—are supposed to make this area private, but they haven't been set up right, so we're in view of the people still waiting in line at the counter, all of them men in work clothes—plumbers, builders, electricians—and many of them looking impatient and angry.

Hester takes his seat and motions to a chair for me, but there are papers on it. Papers and rolled-up building plans are everywhere, in fact—on his desk, on the floor; he is a fairly big man and there just isn't enough room. Isn't that always the way of it in Lawrence? Huge—gargantuan—mill buildings sit empty, and Lawrencians huddle together in tiny spaces.

When I tell Mr. Hester what I'm here for, he looks apprehensive, but I'm not deterred. I'm a citizen with a complaint: a house across the street from me—one that burned over a year and a half ago, in February 1987—is finally being renovated, and that's great; but it seems, at least from the outside, that it's being divided into more apartments than it had before the fire. And since the street is now zoned R-2—that is, two-family maximum—the renovation may be in violation; and would the department please investigate?

Hester seems flustered; I wonder why. Is this an unusual inquiry? It wasn't unusual in Greenwich, where civic watchdogs are a part of every neighborhood. He takes me into an adjacent room, opens the drawer of an ancient metal three-by-five index-card file, and looks up the address: 168 Prospect Street. He pulls a card, which leads him to a larger metal file of permits; he selects one, studies it, and says that, while it's true the building was once a two-family, apparently a permit for four units was okayed. I ask to see the forms. They are signed at the bottom, but few of the blank spaces above are filled in; I also see that the building is owned by an infamous landlord and real estate developer (who will later get into trouble with the feds for taking a loan and then not building what he said he would build with it, and not paying back the loan, either).

It doesn't look like everything's in order here, I say, pointing to the places where information is missing. Hester looks worried, and after some hemming and hawing, he suggests I speak to his boss, Commissioner of Buildings J. Robert Quimby.

Bob Quimby's cubicle is the same size as Hester's, and right next to it, but neater and more private; I shake his hand. Hester was dressed more or less like the men at the counter—in corduroy jeans and a sweater; Quimby is wearing dress pants and a navy blue blazer. Before we speak, he takes a phone call, then makes a call himself, pushing the buttons with his car keys; bantering with somebody in the fire department, he schedules a walk through the scene of yet another suspected arson. When he's finished with the phone, he listens to me state my case.

He nods; he seems to know all about the building. He tells me that a former inspector, now deceased, "visualized" four apartments; that's why the specification is on the new permit.

He "visualized" them?

Yes, Quimby tells me, the man stood outside the building and visualized the number of apartments inside.

A man visualized something, and now he's dead?

Yes, this is a high-stress job, Quimby says; the man died of a heart attack.

But he didn't write it down after he visualized it.

Bob Quimby looks me in the eye; I'm forced to look away: I don't want to accuse anybody of being a liar. Besides, I cannot penetrate the logic, and so I cannot argue; it would be like trying to argue with the devil. Remember, too, I myself merely "visualized" a suspected violation.

I leave city hall with another idea and walk the few blocks to the fire department's headquarters. In a big black loose-leaf notebook on the front counter, I look up the report on the fire, but it's not clear from that, either, how many apartments the building had. It does say, though, that the fire was suspicious and an investigation was made. I ask about the results of it; the clerk tells me that a Lieutenant Ord will get back to me.

Later that afternoon, I get a call from Ord, who is quick to protest that he can't discuss the investigation. That's okay, I tell him; all I want to know is how many apartments the building had on the night of the fire. According to his information, he says, there were two apartments. Two? Two legal apartments. I thank him and hang up, elated because my hunch was correct—the landlord *is* trying to stretch his assets. My elation is short-lived, though, for I remember the reason for my complaint in the first place. Extra apartments mean extra cars on the street (the building has only one off-street parking spot); extra trash barrels in the tiny front yard (or merely extra trash stuffed into the inadequate barrels that this irresponsible landlord provides); and cramped tenants in the undersized apartments.

Oh, well. At least it was refreshing to meet a Lawrence city employee as efficient and as competent as Lieutenant Ord. Unfortunately, he is an exception, not the rule. And so is my favorite city worker of all time, Janis Moore.

THERE HAD BEEN five different Lawrence animal-control officers in the two years before Janis took the job in 1986. She resigned in 1994—forced out by political pressure, according to her. During her long tenure, however, she not only professionalized the pound but also organized a cleanup of county property behind it—a quiet, rustic pathway that runs along the river—for the first "dog park" on the East Coast (there are at least thirty on the West Coast). Now a place for leashed dogs and their owners to romp, the land used to be a quasi-extension of the city dump; Janis saw its possibilities and organized tours of it to convince potential volunteers to help out. I went on one of the so-called hikes—a thorough skeptic, I'll admit, as I stepped over old TVs and tires and other junked car parts half-buried by branches in the thick underbrush. The smell was acrid, foul. "And here's the beach," Janis announced when our group of half a dozen, our long sleeves and pants rubber-banded at their hemlines to keep out ticks, reached a strip of sandy silt at the river's edge. "The inmates come here and sunbathe," she added, referring to the residents of the minimum-security Essex County Alternative Correctional Facility next door. (Where else but Lawrence would a jail be built on prime riverfront property? Some people call this the "OIL factor"—"Only in Lawrence.") "See the deer tracks?" We looked where Janis was pointing; she was right: there were hoof marks in the sand.

Eventually, a small band of believers was assembled (aided by less-dedicated, onetime helpers like myself); and, treated to occasional sightings of white-tailed rabbits and the rustlings of other wildlife, they worked for several months alongside Janis and a band of inmates she borrowed from the jail to realize her unlikely dream.

For the dog park (which didn't cost the city, county, state, or federal government a cent) and other accomplishments,

Janis received statewide recognition and awards. She was sometimes hampered, however—on the job and at home, too—by the lack of professionalism among certain fellow city workers, as well as by the enduring traces of the old way of doing things in Lawrence.

She says she was down at city hall on other business when she saw the posting for the animal-control-officer opening and that she filled out the application to kill time. She'd been working in Florida—running tests on cattle—and was home visiting her Lawrence-born parents in Methuen. She had no experience as a "dog officer," but she did have an associate's degree in agriculture and large animals from Essex Agricultural and Technical Institute and a BA in vocational education and animal science from the University of Vermont. Soon she got a call: out of the two hundred who'd applied, she and forty-nine others had made the first cut and had to go for the physical.

She was the only one who passed the drug test, she claims. She said, "All right, I'll try it for two weeks."

SPRING 1992. I'm following Janis's dust down a road near the river—where mills were never built—past the jail and incinerator. It's midmorning. I'm driving my VW Golf, and she's speeding along in her big, old, beat-up city van, headed back to the pound after taking a vicious German shepherd to the Massachusetts Society for the Prevention of Cruelty to Animals, in Methuen, for euthanizing. She'd found it fastened to the entrance of the pound with a brand-new leash; its snapping teeth had made it difficult for her to unfasten the unhappy animal.

The situation was reminiscent of her first day on the job—a frigid one in December—when her way into the little white cinder-block building was barred by not one big dog but five: dead and frozen. She asked the guys at the incinerator what they thought she should do with them; they said, "Throw 'em in the river." Young (born 1956); strong (she plays amateur softball and volleyball); and not petite (she's nearly six feet tall), Janis wrestled the bodies into the van and took them to the MSPCA for cremation.

She unlocks the door today, and as we step inside, I notice that the pound is chilly, even for spring: it isn't insulated and there isn't much heat. The building was officially condemned at one point; at the moment, it's minimally up to code, but it still has no bathroom. (In 1994, it would be condemned again, and demolished.) Janis herself painted the kennel area a tranquil green and her office walls a bright yellow, fixed the hung ceiling, and scavenged houseplants from the incinerator.

There are only two dogs impounded here today—and a rooster named Reebok. Janis spotted the bird a few years ago running down the middle of West Street, in a rough section of the city, without a feather on its body and a Reebok shoelace around its leg. It has been living at the pound ever since. All its feathers have grown back—it's a colorful, preening bird— and Janis takes it with her when she's asked to speak at schools and places like Miss Barker's Lawrence Garden Club.

She goes into her office and listens to the messages on her answering machine, taking notes on a legal pad. She receives twenty thousand calls a year and logs every one. A sampling, which also happens to be a reading on small, densely packed Lawrence, with its many people, pets, and wild animals living in close proximity:

Stray cat foaming/violent/bit son
Abandoned dog locked in apartment
Bellevue Cemetery/another possum
Dead cat in house/someone came in and killed it
Raccoon in barrel

Someone left a beaten animal on porch/needs attention
Stray Chihuahua/owners moved
Young boxer in heat 2 a.m./ howling all night
It's a free country/you can't tell me what to do
Pair green parrots in backyard Pleasant Street
Kids with python, 14 Beacon Street, long story
Neighbor's dog snapped at him/wants that dog taken care of
Question: Do you have any idea what it's like
Sorry for being so bold/not yelling at you

When owners come to pick up their strays, they pay a fine. Janis told me that she collected between fourteen thousand and twenty thousand yearly, the top figure only three thousand less than her annual salary. Her total revenues, she says, didn't even include fees for dog licenses. Eight hundred were issued in 1991. "Of course we have way over that many dogs in a city of seventy thousand," says Janis. "Statistically, fifty-five percent of the population have pets."

Yes, she knows her statistics. And she did her homework (on her own time, she took a rappelling course—"so I can rappel into the river or out of buildings"). But she wasn't an exemplary city employee according to certain of her coworkers at the police department. She refused to join their union, for one thing; she wanted to be independent: she didn't want the union to assign her " 'a volunteer'—somebody's relative."

Her own father, mind you, worked for her part-time, but he and she were "in synch," as Janis puts it.

A retired surveyor—a dapper man with a white goatee and handlebar mustache and who wears suspenders and a jaunty cap—Guy Moore could often be found tending the kennel when Janis was out on call. Paid for twenty hours a week, he worked many more, says Janis: "I had him driving all over the city doing my stakeouts in the mornings. If we had a problem, dog barking or dog loose, I said, 'Dad, tomorrow, six a.m., go there, sit on the corner and watch.' And he'd come back and say, 'Yup,' or he'd come back with the dog."

She also took her father with her into the more notorious neighborhoods, not because she was afraid for herself, but because she feared for the van, which had its windows broken more than once while parked overnight. Nothing ever happened, but if she'd ever needed help, she says, she wouldn't have called the police; she would have called the street-department guys (though she did resent seeing them taking early-morning snoozes in their trucks).

Even if she had called the police, I wonder if they would have come to her aid. With a couple of them she had some serious disputes. For four years, she lived across the street from a certain officer and his dog—"the worst barking dog in the city"—and couldn't resolve the problem. "People say, when I knock on their door with a complaint about barking, 'Why didn't my neighbors come to me directly?' But it's like, 'Don't you understand how emotional this issue is? That's why I'm here. I'm the mediator.' But there was no one to mediate for me."

Eventually, irony of ironies, she moved to get away from the noise—to Methuen, flying in the face of the residency rule (which she says nobody mentioned when she took the position).

Her troubles with coworkers didn't end there. She became embroiled again the day she impounded a policeman's loose, unlicensed dog. When the officer showed up to claim it, she told him the fine was one hundred dollars; he refused to pay. Instead, one night when he was off duty, he took the pound's emergency keys, kept at the police station, and attempted to "rescue" the dog.

"But he forgot about the alarm system," says Janis. "Or he thought it went to the station." It didn't; it went to Janis's house—and she went over and caught him in the act. "I beeped the chief out of a meeting. It was about eight, eight-thirty in the evening. It was all hell after that."

In April 1994, Janis was injured on the job and was out for some weeks. When she returned, there were "difficulties" at city hall and down at the police department—problems she believes stemmed from the still-simmering Padellaro incident (Padellaro is the name of the officer whose dog she impounded). So in July, she tendered her resignation. As of this writing, she is hoping for a job with the World Society for the Protection of Animals, which has sent workers to places like Kuwait, Bosnia, and Rwanda to take care of animals injured and abandoned during the chaos of war; Janis figures her experiences in Lawrence make her the perfect candidate.

WHAT WILL FIX Lawrence's broken bureaucracy? Or, *who* will fix it? And how?

When the brand-new city council took office in January 1986, the first to be elected after the charter change—a young and somewhat diversified group (it even included two women)—Lawrence pinned all sorts of hopes on it, hopes that obviously didn't materialize. But did it fail because its nine members were only part-time—most of them with full-time jobs in addition to their city hall duties—and unable to devote the hours a thorough job would have required? Or was it because of their bitter differences with Kevin Sullivan, who was elected mayor along with them—at twenty-six, one of the youngest people ever to run a city of our size? Or was it because they were sidetracked—then sandbagged—by the Emerson College issue?

Some Lawrencians saw Emerson as a chance for new jobs, a new image—a new life—for Lawrence. Others saw it as a tax drain, a boondoggle, a prohibitively expensive pet of Mayor Sullivan's and his supporters. Though I was in favor of Emerson's move, I often pointed out to those who spoke of the college as a panacea that Worcester, Massachusetts, with *nine* colleges within its city limits, isn't doing all that much better than Lawrence. And look at New Haven, which a friend who teaches at Yale once characterized as "Lawrence with Harvard in the middle of it." Still, I continue to believe that Emerson would have been, if not a cure-all, then at least a tonic for Lawrence.

The councillor who represented my district during the time of the college controversy was Jay Dowd, my Joyce-quoting neighbor who so lamented the tearing down of St. Laurence O'Toole's in 1980. James Philip Dowd, Jr., is a third-generation Lawrencian, born in 1951, whose father was a Lawrence night-school teacher and whose mother worked at a local bank for over forty years. Coincidentally, Jay's paternal grandparents once lived in the burned-out building about which I complained to Chief Inspector Quimby. Jay's Grandmother Annie Dowd, when she was Annie McCabe, lived with her brother, John, in one of the Fulton Street houses right behind it. The man she married, Philip Dowd, emigrated to Lawrence as a nineteen-year-old from Ballybay, Ireland, in 1890, when those houses were still fairly new. Sidestepping mill work, he became a popular streetcar operator on the Lawrence line of the Eastern Massachusetts Street Railway Company. Jay has a photo of him in his busman's uniform—a double-breasted jacket, bow tie, and banded cap. He also has a photo of Annie's brother, a plumber, in *his* work clothes, formally posing with wrenches and a Bunsen burner, as van Gogh's mailman is formally posed, and looking just as pleased with himself. "Look," says Jay, "his hands are full of tools—all the tools of his trade."

Wasn't it unusual for workmen to pose in their work clothes in those days, instead of in their Sunday best? Not in Lawrence, says Jay.

Jay teaches English at a Catholic preparatory school in Reading, Massachusetts—Austin Prep, which he also attended—so he wasn't exactly prepared for politics by his professional experience—nor by his bachelor's degree in English literature from the College of the Holy Cross or his master's in secondary education from Fitchburg State College. Still, he did a commendable job helping to pass the city's complicated new zoning law—the one that designated Prospect Street R-2—and to establish an official historic district up on Prospect Hill. And he fought the good fight for Emerson, which he viewed as the opportunity of Lawrence's contemporary lifetime.

Still, I wonder if Jay has yet recovered from his disappointment at the failure of the college to move to Lawrence; he admits it deeply frustrated him, and in 1991, after serving six years, he announced that he wouldn't seek a fourth term, saying he wanted to devote more time to his two children; he was especially looking forward to coaching his daughter Libby's Little League softball team, the Flames, on the same Prospect Hill playing field where he used to be a summer park instructor during his years at Holy Cross (a coveted temporary city job for which "college boy" Jay was hired in the usual Lawrence manner, thanks to an alderman friend of the family).

Who would represent the district now? Jay had an idea. He phoned Bob one summer evening to say he thought Bob should run for the seat.

Jay knew Bob and me from our work on the Prospect Hill Neighborhood Association, a group that had been founded, with Jay's help, in the Spring of 1988 to work on local issues. That summer, the group had organized a public meeting at the Sons of Italy Hall, on Marston Street. "Will the respectful and caring residents of our area watch helplessly while decay advances, or will we at last join together to restore pride, order and beauty to the streets where we live?" Those were the words Bob wrote for the brochure our eager band of volunteers left on hundreds of Prospect Hill doorsteps in order to entice them to the meeting. Bob also acted as emcee. "What are *you* running for?" David J. Bain, then city council president (a Prospect Hill resident who had won an at-large seat), asked facetiously after Bob's rousing speech.

In January 1989, Mayor Sullivan appointed Bob to the Lawrence Planning Board; then, in the Summer of 1990, he was asked to be on the steering committee that brought the Regional/Urban Design Assistance Team of the American Institute of Architects to Lawrence to assess our problems and suggest possible solutions. (The city was number 109 for the AIA, which had been sending volunteer teams of architects and city planners to American cities since 1967.)

But had the idea of public office ever occurred to Bob before Jay suggested it? Apparently it had, though I hadn't known it—not realizing that it's almost impossible to be a congressional aide without imagining yourself as the one you're writing speeches for or advising on legislation. During the six years he worked for John Conyers, Democrat of Detroit, one of his tasks was to listen for the vote bell that called the members to the House floor, then run into the congressman's office to gesture thumbs-up or thumbs-down. "*He's* the congressman," a fellow aide would say, only half-joking, introducing Bob to visitors.

Still, Bob didn't tell Jay right away that he'd run; he said he needed time to think. But after he got off the phone, I could see there would be no thinking at all, and right away I began to imagine Jay smoothly passing the baton to Bob, who even had a plan he'd been talking about for years—in fact, ever since we came to Lawrence—to devise a way to publicize

Lawrence as a mecca for small businesses. It seemed a viable campaign platform, and I hadn't heard anybody else articulate it—not Jay, not former city council president David Bain, not even Mayor Sullivan.

Since the fifties, Lawrencian efforts to increase employment had been geared almost exclusively toward attracting big industries, and tied to the misbegotten notion that Lawrence might do well to become a one-industry town again. (The argument for Emerson contained significant traces of this line of reasoning.) Even in the 1990s, many still didn't see how unlikely this was, and they urged local government to bring new behemoths in. They particularly urged it of their city council, since they didn't seem quite sure what else the councillors were supposed to be doing. Besides, wasn't that what John Buckley had done? Hadn't he brought in AT&T and the rest? (They conveniently forgot that those plants—and jobs—ultimately went to the suburbs.) Even the "experts" backed this notion, at least until fairly recently. A 1955 Harvard University study, entitled *Lawrence: Facing the Future*, specifically advised against "a policy based on filling up old mills with small industries."

Of course, Lawrence's cheap square footage did attract some small companies, including Akko and its neighbors in the old Pacific Mills complex: a glassblower, who made colored-glass figurines sold in area malls; Nitron, a high-tech manufacturer of lightweight shoes for racehorses; and an outfit called National Hair Technologies, Ltd., whose "hair" and other ersatz body coverings have supplied a steady parade of national and international clients, including Disney Studios (woodpecker "feathers," most recently), Universal Pictures (the King Kong suit for the movie remake and the Penguin's costume for *Batman Returns*), and the late Jim Henson, creator of the Muppets. (One day, roaming around at National Hair, I bumped into a taxidermist from the Milwaukee Public Museum who had come to get a fake mane for a lion whose real one was scraggly. "It's hard to find a full-maned lion in the wild," he explained.)

One of Akko's former neighbors in the Pacific Mills was a women's clothing company, KGR, Inc. In 1986, KGR moved into larger quarters on Canal Street and, later, Island Street, where it employed 150 people full-time and another 50 or so part-time in refurbished old mill buildings along both sides of the north canal. According to owner Chester F. Sidell, the company, which started in a storefront on Essex Street in 1975, was doing close to $35 million in yearly sales in the mid-1990s to customers across the United States and Canada, as well as in Japan.

KGR was the kind of place at the core of Bob's plan—he and Chet Sidell had been acquaintances for years—and one rainy gray day, I was invited to take a tour of the KGR plant.

I felt as if I was walking into the sunshine. Meticulously renovated inside and out, every window sparkling, it was decorated with period antiques of golden oak. But it wasn't only the decor that buoyed my spirits. It was also the perkiness and professionalism of KGR's well-dressed administrative staff. For weeks, I'd been slogging around Lawrence, listening to sad tales of municipal decay and both historic and imminent business failure; now here was a Lawrence business that was obviously thriving, apparently having no trouble at all competing with garment makers overseas, whose laborers were often paid as little as a dollar a day. Sidell's workers, by contrast, were getting five to fourteen dollars per hour to cut and stitch in a brightly lit, temperature-controlled factory that appeared to be as pleasant a workplace as KGR's administrative offices.

When I asked Sidell why he had gone to such trouble and expense to renovate, the Boston native's answer wasn't exactly angry; still, it sounded like a reprimand to me: "We're not from this city. Know that real clear. The people of this city don't know what they have here."

The volunteers from the American Institute of Architects, which was comprised of residents of Nebraska, Texas, New Jersey, Arizona, and California, had written something quite similar in their final report:

> The City of Lawrence has some major strengths to offer. It is not a dead city; it is not even a dying city. There are many cities in the United States which would be envious of many of Lawrence's assets. One major problem which the city suffers from is an overly negative self-image. And that negative image is also held by Lawrence's neighbors. Conversely, if Lawrence wishes to move strongly and positively into the end of the millennium, it is important that it initiate efforts at developing pride in itself. Residents need to convince themselves, and they need to convince their neighbors in other towns, that the city is a good place to live, a good place to shop, a fun place to visit and a good place to work.

A push for city-esteem, to coin a weak phrase, was to be the other part of Bob's campaign, the flip side of the notion that Lawrence's mills were a great place for small businesses. If nothing else, Bob thought, he would force Lawrencians to listen to a positive political message for a change.

Did I say "Bob's campaign"? He admitted afterward that when he initially agreed to run, he neglected to acknowledge fully to himself that before one becomes a councillor, he is necessarily a candidate. If he thought about it at all, he concluded, as I did, that it would be a cinch. District A—which included Prospect Hill; an area just below it called Back Bay; and a part of that other once-prestigious promontory, Clover Hill—contained 10,000 souls, but only 3,800 of them were registered voters. How difficult could it be to reach them? Besides, Jay had won the seat three times; didn't he have a loyal following, a group that would be easily transferable to Bob?

Which shows you just how little either Bob or I really knew about politics then, especially Lawrence politics.

WHEN WE first moved to Lawrence, we often described it to friends back in D.C. as a city of old Italians and young Latinos. It was a reductive statement to make, but it did harbor its measure of truth, and for candidates seeking political office there, those demographics have become the principal challenge they face. In 1990, when the American Institute of Architects team visited Lawrence, it strongly recommended that the city make a much bigger effort to involve its minority population in the political process. Others have made the same suggestion (which is also a reproof). Sadly, by the mid-1990s, minority participation had not significantly improved; in 1991, when Bob decided to run, less than 10 percent (some say less than 7 percent) of the minority population in Lawrence was registered to vote.

Meanwhile, the elderly were Lawrence's most tyrannical voting block: City Clerk James McGravey estimated in 1993 that about half the city's 22,000 registered voters were sixty-five or older; and "ninety-nine percent of them vote," according to Bernard Reilly, director of the Lawrence Senior Center.

Candidates hoping to develop a coherent platform, then, have been forced to weigh the concerns of young immigrants, who would benefit directly from any new jobs that an office holder might bring (or promise to bring) to Lawrence—but who often don't vote—and those of the elderly, whose sole issue seems to be public safety. How would a long-range plan to bring employment to Lawrence cut down on pocketbook snatchings? The politician who honestly answers this question

reason for the decline of Essex Street, which, ironically, these complexes for the elderly were purposely built to be near.

Another irony of the urban-renewal era was this: many extended families who were living in tenements destined for the wrecker's ball could have afforded to move earlier but didn't. They didn't want to. A number of them had crossed an ocean to get here; they weren't budging again unless pressed. Lebanese friends of Tom Troy composed one such family of four working adults displaced by urban renewal. "None of their pays was an executive's or anything like that, but put them together and they were doing all right," and they had no intention of moving from their old neighborhood. "The thing was, that's where their friends were, and that's where they felt at home," says Troy, who concludes that urban renewal "forced them to better themselves," since, after leaving Lawrence, they bought—what else?—a single-family house in the suburbs.

IN LAWRENCE'S District A, there are no large housing units for the elderly, of course; senior citizens were still destined to be a determining factor in Bob's race, however. This would be true not because of the fifteen votes at the German Old Folks Home on Prospect Hill or the twenty or thirty at the Berkeley Retirement Home on Clover Hill, but because significant numbers of other gray-haired voters lived in each of the district's four precincts. In contrast to Tom Troy's Lebanese friends, these oldsters had had no compelling reason to "better themselves" by leaving Lawrence. As downtown became an elderly enclave because of urban renewal, other parts of Lawrence did, too, because of huddle fever.

And yet, while Bob planned his campaign strategies for the upcoming (nonpartisan) primary, he still chose to concentrate on economic development. Arguing that "the elderly may not need jobs, but they need neighbors with jobs," he set to work on the race.

LATE SUMMER, 1991. The candidates for city council register down in the smoky basement of city hall. In District A, Bob is first off the mark. It puzzles him that the man behind the desk wishes him good luck several times. Luck isn't what's going to win this election: he has already begun to comprehend the difficulties, not to mention the indignities, while asking friends, neighbors, and relatives for contributions and making small talk with strangers at a Sunday-afternoon "coffee" given by Jay Dowd and his wife, Susan, at their stylish home on Prospect Hill's Ridge Road—an event that was sparsely attended (in retrospect ominously so). Still, he is committed now. There's no backing out.

Tom Leavitt's son, Jonathan, has declared his candidacy, too. A recent dropout from the University of Massachusetts at Amherst, he has Green party interests and eagerness on his side, but no experience to speak of. In the place on the form where he has to list his occupation, he writes "painter-musician."

A twenty-nine-year-old insurance salesman named Leonard J. Degnan, Jr., is Bob's other opponent. He grew up in North Andover (as did Jon Leavitt) and ran unsuccessfully for the school committee there, but now lives with his young wife and two small daughters in a triple-decker on Prospect Hill, on the street almost directly behind us. Before getting into the insurance business through an uncle, Degnan worked on a machine that stacked cardboard shoe boxes in a Methuen factory; made semiconductors at another company; then got a white-collar job with the state auditor's office ("You know, I knew people, and I applied . . ." he tells the *Eagle-Tribune*).

Bob has already chosen a couple of campaign slogans—

"Lawrence Can Work" and "I Like Lawrence"—when he learns some sobering facts about Lenny Degnan. Not only is he the grandson of a Lawrence firefighter who served in the department for over three decades, many of those years as deputy fire chief; he is also the son-in-law of a powerful and well-connected Democratic party member, Nicholas A. Rizzo, Jr.

Nick Rizzo. Everyone in Lawrence seems instantly to recognize the name, if not to claim to know him personally, though he has been living in Andover for many years. Born in 1936, he grew up on Lawrence's Elm Street, in one of the Italian enclaves demolished during urban renewal. From Elm Street, with its tenements, its bakeries, its colored lights and laundry strung across the alleyways, he rose through local politics to become a well-known Democratic fund-raiser, notably for Carter's 1980 campaign and Mondale's in 1984; at the moment, he is the chief fund-raiser for the presidential campaign of former senator Paul E. Tsongas, who, in his 1984 book, *Heading Home*, called him a "good friend," even a surrogate older brother; he was the chief fund-raiser for all of Tsongas's other campaigns, starting with his first run for Congress in 1974.

Maybe these national connections will be too remote to be of any use in a minor race in Lawrence? Anyway, that is Bob's hope as he begins to be warned by tales about the legendary pol. Nick Rizzo smokes cigars that cost five hundred dollars a box, says a friend—he knows the person who buys the extravagant smokes for Rizzo in Montreal. He drives a $38,000 Cadillac, for which, he likes to tell people, he paid cash. And: "He acts like he's in the Mafia without being in it, you know what I mean?"

Another friend's story is perhaps the most dismaying: she says she once attended a luncheon; she doesn't remember the occasion, although she does remember that it was held at

the private club that used to be Billy Wood's son's house—
Orlando Cottage—and that Rizzo was the one who greeted
people at the door. After the food was served and eaten, Rizzo
went to the podium and introduced everyone at every table to
the whole room. My friend had met him only briefly and for
the first time that day. And neither she nor anybody else wore
a name tag. Even if everyone had been wearing one, Rizzo
wouldn't have been able to see them. Yet he never missed a
name or an affiliation, including my friend's. "He could get
Jack the Ripper elected," she concluded.

Are all the stories true? And if they are, won't it still matter to the voters what kind of candidate Lenny Degnan is?
Dull-witted. Quick-tempered. Frequently inarticulate in spite
of his big, back-slapping handshake. This is the reputation that
has followed him from North Andover. Nonetheless, he raises
over fifteen thousand dollars in campaign contributions, an absurd amount for a race so small. And the bulk of it hasn't come
from Lawrencians. Mostly it has come, instead, in one-
hundred-dollar denominations from the friends and associates
of Nick Rizzo—a list as absurd as the total: Hamilton Jordan,
former president Carter's chief of staff; Tim Kraft, Carter's appointment secretary; former Massachusetts House speaker
Thomas McGee; Timothy Finchen, deputy commissioner of
the Professional Golfers Association; John Emerson, deputy
city lawyer of Los Angeles; Dennis Kannin, chief aide to Senator Tsongas; Richard Allen, a lawyer for Warner Brothers;
even Senator Tsongas himself. What have they to do with Lawrence? What do they care? Tsongas actually unintentionally di-
minished Lawrence by making his native Lowell shine: with
his help, that other mill city on the Merrimack established the
first urban national park and, between 1975 and 1990, attracted nearly $1 billion in investments, including the former
computer giant Wang, whose demise, while it certainly slowed
Lowell's economic growth, did not dampen its rekindled city

pride. (Lawrence, during the same period, attracted only $100 million.) Or is this a sort of inferiority complex–prone Lawrencian thing to say? "They're friends of my father-in-law," Degnan tells the local paper, adding lamely, "I know them, but I've never met them." Meanwhile, Bob raises fifteen hundred dollars; Jon Leavitt amasses a little more than twice that, most of it drawn from his own savings.

Thus armed, the three go into the fray. Bob is advised to campaign in the usual low-budget Lawrence manner: by holding signs at street corners and going door-to-door at suppertime to solicit votes in person. (It is necessary to hold the signs, because a Lawrence law prohibits posting them, the city fathers imagining, I suppose, that otherwise the whole city would soon be covered in campaign detritus.) And so we get up early every morning, before Bob goes down to work at Akko and before I sit down at my desk to write, and head for a prime curbside to greet the morning commuters. We stand on the corner of Prospect and East Haverhill streets, in front of Perrotta's, the pharmacy. Or we hit the jug-handled entrance to the highway. Or the corner of East Haverhill and Ferry streets, close to the Methuen line. And we bounce our signs and wave for a full hour. Some drivers wave back; others honk. Most look right through us. We go through the same routine after work for the evening commute.

Several neighbors of ours bounce signs along with us, all of them young and middle-class, all of them wondering if they will stay in Lawrence or not (I guess they would be more inclined to if Bob won the election): Kathy, director of sales for an advertising company; Jane, a bilingual sixth-grade teacher at a Methuen school; Dave, a mechanical engineer at Raytheon; John, a computer software engineer; and Virginia, who works in the ad department of a Lowell radio station. It gets as boring as factory work must get, standing there all those hours, and we try to make the time go faster by singing the song that

Jane has written, to the tune of "The Mickey Mouse Club": "B-O-B, F-R-I, S-H-M-A-N!" It is also getting colder as summer ends and fall begins. Sometimes Jane and I walk our dogs together, carrying our FRISHMAN signs on our shoulders; we feel ridiculous, but if this is the language of Lawrence politics, we will speak it, at least for a while.

As for the other contenders: we never see Jon Leavitt on a street corner; we never see a poster in a window with his name on it—or a bumper sticker, either. Being a hippie manqué, maybe he thinks such clownish electoral antics are beneath him.

Lenny Degnan, on the other hand, has sign holders out in force. Sometimes we find ourselves on the same corner with them—on opposite sides of the street, of course. We acknowledge one another when we get to our posts, but after that we don't. All of us need to concentrate on the passing drivers, anyway. Sometimes, when city workers drive by in city pickup trucks filled with lawn mowers and shovels, they honk and wave smugly at Degnan's squad. Not a good omen. Apparently, Degnan is their man, and they no doubt have an effective network to get the word out. (Later, we learn that Degnan's uncle is Edward "Hoppy" Curran, a longtime city employee, a foreman with the Department of Public Works, who is in charge of the crew that is supposed to be taking care of the dilapidated Bellevue Cemetery on Tower Hill.)

As for going door-to-door, we are hesitant. To disturb people, unannounced, without an introduction? And at suppertime, no less? If this is the best way to get votes in Lawrence, why hasn't anyone ever knocked on *our* door? Which is not to say that we would have taken too kindly to such a visitor. Still, Jay, David Bain, and others insist this is the best strategy: to go and ask voters personally for their votes, and to do it when we will be most likely to find them at home.

And so we take their advice, going out almost every evening, starting at around five, the list of registered voters in our hands. (Yes, we; our; first person plural—because the public demands the show of respectability that a marriage can be; we joke about borrowing kids to tag along with us, to complete the family picture.) It becomes easy to pick out the places where voters live even before we look up the house number: the single-families; the well-kept duplexes; the ones with the sealed driveway, the row of marigolds, the trimmed hedges, the statue of a saint. Not the three's (or more), with the multiple mailboxes crookedly attached, names penned over names; the overflowing trashcans; the broken windows stuffed with newspaper. We walk from door to door—the pace that prevailed in the earliest days of the city. We knock, and the doors open, revealing families still in work clothes, eating; or in undershirts and shorts, or even bathrobes, watching the news on TV, already settled in for the evening. To our amazement, their faces relax when they learn what we are there for. (Are they merely relieved that we aren't missionaries of one sort or another trying to proselytize them? Or, worse, bill collectors?) Many shake our hands. A few invite us in. Most simply stop their chewing and accept the campaign literature graciously. Do they read it? Most of them are older, white; those who speak to us at any length immediately reveal the expected anger: at welfare, the "Spanish," the unswept streets, the burglaries, the vandalism. A typically one-sided conversation goes like this:

Al: "Lawrence today is not the Lawrence of yesteryear. They ruin it; the people who come in now ruin it all—"

Mary: "Watch it, Al."

Al: "I'm only speaking the truth, Mary. You can't walk the streets. Years ago, you could walk anytime day or night and be safe. All the houses were beautiful. People worked in the mills to buy those houses. They took care of their property. Now everything is gone, and the curtains are flying out the windows."

What can Bob say? He's been described by the *Eagle-Tribune* as a "liberal-turned-conservative." But that isn't accurate. If it were, he would probably agree with Al, and he doesn't. He can't have spent ten years working hard for liberal Democrats in Congress without having strong progressive attitudes, though they have been tempered by "the realities of running a small business and by the excesses of the welfare system," as he puts it. If these voters expect to hear from him despairing words that match theirs, they are disappointed; his message is a positive one, of change, of hope, of action; but he does listen to what they are trying to tell him.

While we trudge up and down every—yes, every—street in the district for weeks delivering Bob's campaign flyers by hand, Lenny Degnan mails his pamphlets from his official campaign headquarters, its windows plastered with his black-and-chartreuse DEGNAN signs, and reaches voters with phone calls placed by his phone bank. He also runs a series of professionally produced radio spots on the local station, complete with music, sound effects, and a script read by an actor. The promise: Elect Lenny Degnan and be safe from all those scary Lawrence criminals stalking you and your neighbors even as we speak (their footsteps are heard in the background).

Bob buys a few radio spots, too; his own voice delivers the message: "I'm going to say something that we don't hear very often. I *like* Lawrence. I like living on Prospect Hill; I like having my manufacturing company on Canal Street; I like the history and the mills and the old homes and the people of so many backgrounds who still live here. . . . Sure, we have problems, big problems, but we still have a lot to make us proud. I'm tired of hearing our city attacked by outsiders who don't know any better and, even worse, criticized by negative people who live here but have given up. I *haven't* given up! I *choose* to live in Lawrence and to have my business here. Please choose *me*, Bob Frishman, for city council. I'm ready to work for you."

PRIMARY DAY, a sunny, crisp one in early October. By tonight, the field will have been cut from three to the two top vote-getters. I am standing with my red BOB FRISHMAN sign alongside Tom Leavitt, who's holding a sign for Jon. His is homemade, with a daisy drawn with yellow and green Flair pens. We are off to the side of one of the four District A polling places: by law, exactly fifty feet away from its entrance. It happens to be the United Presbyterian Church, where I went with Miss Barker for the Lawrence Garden Club meeting. Voting in Lawrence is still accomplished with a pencil, so inside, retirees are sitting at tables, handing out paper ballots, then rolling them into a locked box when a voter is finished.

On the sidewalk with Tom and me are many other sign holders "doing visibility," as this picketing is called. Degnan's mother is here, along with a multitude of his other close relatives, including his wife—Nick Rizzo's daughter. There are also several young men in dark pinstriped suits, white dress shirts, and fresh haircuts, who look like undertakers, joking with the policeman on duty well inside the legal fifty feet. They work for Nick Rizzo.

Just up the street, actually within view, is another polling place—the old Prospect Street School, which Arthur Barker attended in the 1870s, when it was not quite brand-new, as did Lucille and John Piacenzo's son in the 1940s (he won second prize in a spelling bee there, Lucille once told me), and which for decades now has been the clubhouse of the local chapter of the Disabled American Veterans. On the outside, it's been renovated, the asbestos shingles removed, the clapboards painted a period-appropriate green. Inside, it's still a mess of cheap paneling and hung ceilings. Propped in one dark corner of a stairwell are crutches of all sizes, looking brittle. There are also card tables; a pool table; a menu board listing local war dead; large, full ashtrays. And stale air. Even the flag in the corner smells of smoke.

For people doing visibility, the advantage of this polling place is that you don't have to stand. There is a long stone wall bordering the front yard of the house next door, and the owners don't seem to mind if people sit on it with their signs resting on their shoulders; some have even planted them in the earth. On that wall is Bob, sunning himself alongside a Degnan supporter who, it turns out, lives not in Lawrence but in Washington, D.C. He is a professional fund-raiser. What's he doing here? Working for Nick Rizzo—not just today presumably, but for the last few weeks. He says he's been staying with his parents in nearby Reading.

Later, he will confide to Bob that the strategy has been to present Degnan to the voters he meets as "the blue-collar candidate." So the insurance salesman speaks for the blue-collar worker? But he never mentions economic development. Instead, he makes statements like these, which were printed in one of his glossy campaign pamphlets: "A lot of my neighbors are afraid. Elders concerned about walking to the store. All of us afraid of gangs, drugs addicts, and auto theft. We deserve to be protected. That's why I will make sure there are more cops on the street. . . ." And how exactly does Degnan hope to pay for these extra cops? His brochures never say.

The end-of-the-day primary tally shows Degnan: 502; Frishman: 299; Leavitt: 102. The total itself, 903 voters, is more depressing than the individual vote columns; many a large high school has more people turning out to vote in its student council election. The good news is that Jon Leavitt has immediately thrown his support to Bob. Maybe meretricious emotional appeals and money won't prevail after all.

IN THE WEEKS that remain before the general election, we continue campaigning as before, and then some. Weekdays, we hold signs and knock on doors. Only one person actually yells out his car window: "Frishman stinks!" And only one of our door-to-door contacts admits to being a Degnan supporter. ("My former boss's son-in-law is running; I think his name begins with a D. I'm supposed to vote for him.") We can't afford to have campaign buttons professionally made, so we make our own with a kit and wear these on our lapels whenever we go out.

On weekends we can be found at bean suppers—fund-raisers for other candidates (Bob can't afford his own) in big, smoky halls where Lawrencians otherwise gather to socialize and play the card game that so many Lawrencians love, Forty-fives (a cross between whist and bridge, but much more complicated than either of those games). Candidates for all the council seats as well as for the school committee are invited to attend these and circulate among the tables filled with senior citizens eating hot dogs and ham and Boston baked beans. They have been bused to the hall by the sponsoring candidate, of course, and admitted free of charge, along with children under twelve (all others pay three or four dollars). The seniors will pay later with their votes, it is understood. But for whom will they actually cast their ballot in the end? They go to everybody's bean supper, one or two a weekend for weeks, just like the candidates.

At each hall—the British Club, the Elks' headquarters, the Hibernians'—former mayor Buckley can be counted on to appear. Tall, white-haired, his eyes still bright and eager, he is nonetheless unmistakably doddering now as he waves and goes to whisper in the ear of a loyal supporter. A quiet, fallen king. Edwin O'Connor's Frank Skeffington. "Never say never," he once told me. "If you walk with me down Essex Street right now, you'd see half a dozen people would stop me and ask me,

'Are you gonna run again? Are you gonna run?' And I say, 'I don't know.' I was defeated twice and come back twice already, you know."

On other evenings, at the private social clubs—that is, the old ethnic bars grandfathered into residential blocks in certain neighborhoods—Bob throws darts and drinks a beer or two, and hears more complaints about the Spanish. "They have a lot of different names," someone tells us in earnest. "They vote three or four times. I know because I know somebody who works at the polls." I bite my tongue, preventing myself from saying, Listen, would that "they" voted *once*! (Luckily, I am not with Bob the night someone says she'll vote for him if Bob will promise to get rid of Janis Moore, who picked up her dog after he "nipped" a few people.)

"What's in it for you?" That is a question often put to Bob. He tries to tell his questioners that he already has a job; he isn't looking for one in politics. He actually wants to help the city. He is offering to be a volunteer. It seems to be an alien idea. Not to mention a foolhardy one. "Why does your husband want to buy a ticket for a ride on the *Titanic*?" Tom Troy asks me.

One afternoon, toward the end, at the well-endowed Berkeley Retirement Home—the place where Miss Barker in all likelihood will go when she must, since she's on their board (back in Lawrence, at the end of her life)—Bob actually seems to be enjoying himself on this uphill campaign trail. That is the day he plays the piano to woo the old women who assemble in their dayroom to hear all the council candidates who have come a-courting, standing in a circle around the seated ladies, licking their chops. "I knew I should have taken piano lessons," one of them mumbles.

Not too many days later, at Lydia's Hair and Nail Center of Andover, Nick Rizzo is getting a pedicure in one chair; a friend of mine is getting her hair cut in another and overhears

Rizzo tell Lydia that his son-in-law is running for Lawrence city council.

"Who's his opponent?" Lydia asks.

"Oh, he dropped out," says Rizzo.

ON ELECTION DAY—bright, frigid November in New England—I finally catch a glimpse of the man. He is dressed in a black V-necked cashmere sweater and black slacks; he would look like a priest if his hair wasn't so styled and if he wasn't also wearing up-to-the-minute green-rimmed eyeglasses. At yet another voting place, the Depression-era Storrow School, he stands beside my friend Charlene, who has a sign for Bob in her hand. They know the same people from Rizzo's Elm Street days. "Don't forget my son-in-law," Rizzo intones to his many friends and acquaintances as they pass by him on their way into the school. "You'll like him. He's young, but he's an old-timer."

After the polls close, we go to city hall, its small rotunda crowded, smoke-filled, and illuminated by the glaring lights of the local cable TV technicians. We didn't realize that one should listen to the results on local radio and wait to be summoned, the winner; that the loser wouldn't be needed—no concession speech required here; that the loser, in fact, should know enough to stay home.

Under the lights, Jay Dowd is sitting in a director's chair in his tweedy schoolteacher's jacket and being interviewed by a cable TV news reporter, none too pleased about passing his mantle on to Lenny Degnan.

AFTERMATH: A week or so after the election, I am raking leaves in my front yard, and some neighborhood kids approach.

"Hey! Is your husband Bob Fisherman?"

"Frishman. Yes."

"Did he win?"

"No."

"What was the score?"

"It was eight hundred and sixty-two to six hundred and forty-one."

"Where does the other guy live? I want to touch somebody famous."

"Why don't you stay and touch Bob when he gets home in a few minutes?"

"Are you famous if you lose?"

"Yes."

"I already touched him, anyway."

ON THE DAY of the swearing-in, we look at the photo of the new council in the newspaper. There are, in addition to young old-timer Degnan, many retirees—among them, David Clayman, a former Lawrence High School math teacher, and George Miller, who worked for many years as a supermarket meat cutter. They won't have the press of full-time jobs in addition to their council duties; but will they be effective? Both Clayman and Miller are gloom-and-doomers with little good to say about Lawrence as it is today. William X. Wall, another of the old men in the picture, is a former state representative and state senator from Lawrence; he has been reelected to the council for the fourth time; in his late eighties, he has become famous for his constituent service (which, legend has it, includes returning constituents' girdles and the like at Boston department stores). His distinctive signature appears repeatedly in the visitor book at every funeral parlor in the city—penned at the wakes he nightly attends (that is, the wakes he used to attend; he won't live out this last term). All in all, the photo looks like one that could have been taken in the fifties. And for that reason, it's frightening, at least to me. Maybe it's reassuring to the people who elected this group. At any rate, Bob doesn't belong in the picture. Perhaps he never did.

EPILOGUE: On February 22, 1993, the *Eagle-Tribune* arrives on our doorstep with a banner headline—"NICK RIZZO INDICTED FOR BANK, MAIL FRAUD—accompanied by a photo of Rizzo pulling his raincoat tightly around him. His eyes are dark, circled, dull. He'd been arrested in his bed in Andover at seven o'clock that morning. The photo was taken outside the U.S. federal courthouse in Boston. U.S. Attorney A. John Pappalardo says the forty-nine-count indictment marks the largest case of political campaign fraud in U.S. history, involving nearly $4 million. He says Rizzo defrauded the Tsongas campaign of more than $1 million, fraudulently obtained another $2.8 million, and used the money to pay gambling debts and repay private loans. Others are saying Rizzo is the reason Senator Tsongas lost the nomination. The senator, for his part, is silent. Having once called Rizzo the older brother he never had, Tsongas seems now to be cast in the role of surrogate disappointed parent. (Later, Rizzo will be tried, convicted, and given a four-year sentence. At this writing, he is incarcerated at the Federal Medical Center, in Rochester, Minnesota, due to an unspecified condition.)

Lenny Degnan has his own troubles. The North Eastern Mortgage Company, Inc., of Boston, has begun foreclosure proceedings on his Lawrence home. The mortgage on a triple-decker he owns on Tremont Street in Lawrence was foreclosed earlier in the year. Tenants did not pay their rent,

tried to rent the upstairs hall of the Hibernians for his fund-
raiser, he was informed that they were booked solid until well
into the following year.

So Martha called and rented the place in her name, then
told the duped Hibernians what she had done.

A few months after Carrero's swearing-in—on St. Patrick's
Day, in fact—there was a sign that even the Hibernians had
come around. They declared a smiling Carrero the year's Hon-
orary Irishman.

Degnan explained to the local paper. A condomii
bought with a friend in the Roslindale section of
is another soured investment: it was sold at public
in 1992.

POSTSCRIPT: In the same general election that Bob
Degnan, the first Latino was elected to a political post in
rence: Ralph Carrero, a thirty-year-old Dominican wh
lived here for twenty-seven years, now sits on the school
mittee, having received more citywide votes—4,189—thar.
of six other candidates.

Things *have* changed for the better, even in the few s.
years since 1984, when Kevin Sullivan, running on the slo
"Let's give the city back to the people who built it"—a not-
hidden message, for which nobody needed a translatior
defeated Mayor Buckley. Buckley, at least, believes tl
Sullivan's victory was directly related to his success in ta
ping voters' fearful anti-Latino sentiments, especially tho!
of the elderly. This time, however, it has to have been the e.
derly who voted Carrero in, for nobody wins in this cit
without them.

Which is not to slight the considerable efforts of Carrero
and his well-organized volunteers. Some months after the victory, a friend of mine, Joan McCarthy, told me, while I
watched her weed her potato patch and crush potato bugs and
their tiny black eggs between two handheld stones, that when
she took the candidate around her Tower Hill neighborhood to
introduce him to voters, the elderly Elspeth Kepple asked
him, "Do you speak English?"

"All she saw was this brown-skinned person standing on
her porch," said Joan.

Tom Leavitt's daughter Martha told me that when Carrero

CHAPTER 12

The River Sang and Sings On

W E ARE sitting outside in the wind, waiting for a clock to strike three. We—that is to say, Bob and I and about three hundred others—are seated in metal folding chairs on the banks of the Merrimack, where yet another old textile mill used to be. It was knocked down years ago—all those bricks so well laid, with lime not mortar, that it's said no mill building in the city has ever needed repointing. Now the space is a public park, named Pemberton, after the mill disaster of 1860. Along with the common, it is one of the few well-kept green spots in all of Lawrence (no doubt because state money helps pay for its maintenance). Den Rock Park, by contrast, in south Lawrence—forty-seven and a half acres designated in 1878 as a cemetery (but never used as such), then redesigned as a park in 1894—is in shocking shape. The day I visited, I was disconcerted by the surreal landscape. At every turn of the supposedly pastoral pathways, I encountered piles of illegally dumped construction debris, ragged easy chairs and other household junk, appliances shot full of bullet holes. I never returned. Here, on Pemberton's lawn, the setting is downright genteel.

The reason for the gathering is a long-anticipated celebration. It is fall 1991, and the restoration of the huge clock tower of the old Ayer Mill—in splendid view across the river—is finally completed. In the fifties, when the textile companies pulled out, the clock stopped, all four of its faces frozen at 2:30. Its striking bell disappeared shortly afterward. Sold for scrap? No one remembers. The clock's restorers bought a new one, nearly five thousand pounds, cast in bronze by a foundry in Holland. For the last few days, the clock's hands have been traveling around the faces again, keeping perfect time, but the bell has not yet struck the hours. Today the silence will end, and there are lots of people who hope this means the start of a new day for Lawrence. Plenty of others, however, don't think the historically correct restoration of a single architectural artifact—even if it does dominate the city's skyline—will change one iota the dire conditions on the streets below.

The Ayer Mill is now owned by New Balance, one of the few companies that managed to survive Lawrence's short-lived foray into the footwear industry; in fact, it has thrived, making expensive sports shoes with high-powered stitching machines operated by as few employees as possible, nonunionized, of course. But New Balance, though it officially owns the clock, was not the force behind the restoration. New Balance "keeps America running," but it can't keep its own clock running, went the local joke, told by the project's supporters.

In the end, New Balance did contribute to the cause; several other corporate sponsors did, too. The Greater Lawrence Community Foundation (now known as the Merrimack Valley Community Foundation), a group made up of local foundation trustees and business people, led the fund-raising effort. Money, lots of it, also came from former textile mill workers, their children, and their grandchildren. And it's funny, isn't it, that these families would want to venerate the clock, considering that bell-time ruled their lives for all those years? No, not very funny. They're obviously proud of the hours and hours of hard work the clock represents. Who knows? Their support for the project may even be an unconscious attempt to buy back the time they or their family members spent tending those tyrannical textile-mill machines. In 1918, after Billy Wood got rich, he bought the old Wamsutta Cotton Mills building in New Bedford, Massachusetts, where, forty-eight years earlier, he had worked as an office boy for four dollars a week. To own it, instead of being owned by it, was to him, perhaps, a sweet reversal—a kind of revenge—though he claimed to a reporter that his intentions were merely to make a museum out of it (he died before he could).

Three-quarters of a million dollars was the foundation's ambitious goal, and they reached it. The money paid for all the materials and supplies plus the services of the restoration architect; the team of clock restorers; the dial makers; the hand makers; the cutters of the new frosted glass for the faces; the steeplejacks who repaired the tower's copper roof and gargoyle weather vane; the crane operators who hauled everything up; the carpenters who refurbished the weather-damaged interior; and the electricians who rewired the clock to restore its nighttime illumination. But I suppose it isn't surprising to learn that some who did not support the project thought it was a ridiculous price to pay for "roses," especially since Lawrence needs so much else.

Another novel aspect of the fund-raising effort was the way the foundation "sold" to its donors the four clock faces, the eight hands, and all the individual hours of the week. (In other words, there was a chance to buy time literally as well as figuratively.) Appropriately, the descendants of Frederick C. Ayer, the mill building's namesake, bought a face—for five thousand dollars. So, however, did Joseph Powierza, a retired refrigerator and air-conditioning mechanic on a fixed income "who lived through the era that saw the city of Lawrence rise and fall as the greatest textile city in the world." Thomas A.

Delaney, an Essex County jail guard who retired after he won millions in the state lottery, bought a hand—for $2,500—in memory of the mill workers in his family. And an hour, Monday 4:00 a.m., "the start of the work week," was bought—for six hundred dollars—by the Nardozzas, in memory of "Giuseppe, Felicia, and John."

Six-hundred-dollar hours were also bought for a wool sorter, a mender, and a night watchman who had worked in the mills; for a loom fixer; for a boiler-room worker; for a grandmother "who emigrated from Poland to Lawrence at age twelve and immediately went to work in the mills"; for "two hard-working immigrants from Lithuania"; and for a mother who once read the clock from her kitchen window and used it to get her children to school on time. Alice Henning, of Lawrence, bought an hour for her husband Carl's seventy-fifth birthday: "He called the Ayer Mill his alma mater," Mrs. Henning reported. A local bank bought an hour to honor the river.

The complete list of donors and their dedications runs five tabloid-size newspaper pages in length, and even includes Bob, who bought an hour to honor his grandfather's arrival in the United States on Labor Day 1909. Alexander Bolker came from Russia, disembarked at Baltimore, and went straight on to relatives in Omaha, Nebraska (or Oo-MA-hoo-NEE-brrrra-ska, as his family pronounced it to bewildered railway-station employees who tried to help them find their train). Al actually did live in Lawrence for a while. When he and Bob's grandmother retired in the early 1960s, they took an apartment there while the Frishmans built an addition to their Andover house for them. There weren't many inexpensive apartments to rent in Andover at the time (no more than there are today), and so it was the Immigrant City that accommodated them.

A NUMBER of people were invited to speak at the celebration of the clock. One of them was Father Lamond, formerly of the Spanish Center, who slowly climbed the steps of the temporary stage to give the invocation against the backdrop of clock and the river, and a green-and-orange billboard advertising Newport cigarettes.

Father Lamond told the crowd that the year he was born, 1909, was the same year the Ayer Mill was built, and he referred to today's occasion as a "born-again event," since the clock was having a rebirth. Expressing the hope that Lawrence would rise again, too, he then read a poem by Frost, "A Lone Striker," which is about a mill worker who, late to work one morning and knowing his pay will be docked, goes instead to the forest, and never does return to his mill job: "The factory was very fine; / He wished it all the modern speed. / Yet, after all, 'twas not divine, / That is to say, 'twas not a church. . . ."

Listening to him, I found it easy to believe that things really would turn out all right for Lawrence, that if the Greater Lawrence community could successfully act in concert on the clock project, then maybe we could collaborate on some others. But then the director of the foundation approached the podium to give his speech, and I didn't feel all that hopeful anymore. Bill Dalton, an Andoverite, flubbed his opening lines by saying, "Here in Andover. . . ." He wore a bow tie, navy blue blazer, and gray flannel pants, and the preppy uniform, in its way, was a gaffe, too, I thought. Or was I being overly sensitive? After all, I could be accused of dressing preppily myself. (Certainly I wasn't nearly as sensitive as the Lawrencian father of a friend who remains convinced that the south-pointing clock dial was fixed first because it faces Andover.)

Still, I took Dalton's attire and his misstatement (not to mention my friend's father's remarks) as reminders that differences—and long-standing resentments—among Lawrence and its surrounding communities prevail.

Oh, well, the striking of the clock will be inspiring even if Bill Dalton wasn't, I thought to myself as the minute hand moved to twelve. We all listened for the bell. Waited and listened; straining—in vain.

The hand passed its mark, and still we heard nothing. A few more minutes passed, and we were informed that, apparently, the bell had struck but that we were too far away to hear it, or the wind had carried the sound away, or something.

The orchestra began to play, and cake for three hundred was being served under a canopy, but I didn't want to stay. I had expected to feel the bell resounding in my chest. I had been prepared to be teary-eyed, inspired once again to boost Lawrence. Instead, I felt sharp pangs of disappointment, and foreboding. Was Lawrence simply fated to fail at everything it tried?

That evening, on our way to the movies, Bob and I passed by the tower just as the hands reached seven o'clock. We stuck our heads out the car windows and heard the bell at last, but only faintly.

Later still, the bell was adjusted, and I, for one, heard it striking hourly, richly, especially in foggy weather, when the air was thick and moist and the sound traveled through it better than on drier days. Lying in bed with the windows open, I could hear it so clearly, it sounded as if the entire Ayer Mill had been moved to the middle of my front lawn.

TO MY *former* front lawn, I should say. I must quickly add, however, that at the time of the clock celebration, I thought we would live in Lawrence for another good long while; that whatever we hoped to accomplish either in our personal lives or in our work, we could accomplish there. Then, a few months after the ceremony—in January 1992—Bob turned forty and began to make plans to do what he had always in-

tended: turn his longtime hobby—collecting and repairing antique clocks and watches—into a business. He had never
planned to stay at Akko forever; he had only hoped to see his
parents through some difficult times—times that lasted nearly
ten years. Now he would slowly—over the next eighteen
months—cut back his hours to no hours at all. He would also
give up his shares in the company, and the plant manager,
Lawrence-born Richard Messina (he moved to Methuen years
ago), who was once an hourly employee punching the time
clock, would become president of Akko (Dan Frishman remains chairman of the board).

But why did the change mean we had to leave Lawrence?
The name Bob chose for his new business—Bell-Time Clocks,
after the Winslow Homer print depicting bell-time in Lawrence—confirms that we didn't have any immediate plans to
leave the city. One thing Bob did propose to do, however, was
to conduct the business out of our house. And this was the
reason that, before long, we started to doubt that Prospect
Street was the best place for us to be.

In Washington, we had seen gentrification. In Lawrence,
we had watched the film roll in reverse. Windows that had
been whole for a century were broken. Houses were abandoned and small stores boarded up. Trash accumulated along
fences and in gutters, got caught in the branches of trees.
Hostess Chocodiles; Ruffles Cheddar & Sour Cream; Soft 'N
Chewy Tangy Taffy—the junk-food wrappers of the world,
from St. Louis, from New Orleans, from Dallas—all found
their way to the streets of Lawrence.

More serious a problem than ugliness was the persistent
threat of arson. What started to worry me even more than the
fires themselves, however, was our attitude toward them: we'd
become so accustomed to sirens and smoke in the middle of
the night that we'd stopped wondering whose house it was this
time. Even when we could tell by the intensity of the sounds

and the noxious fumes that the property was nearby, all we did was get up and shut all the windows, so we could go back to sleep.

And lately, beyond these old familiar signs of blight, I'd begun to notice some new ones. I've mentioned my observation that working-class people don't walk their dogs as a rule, but gradually I did start to see dogs on leashes on Prospect Street: muzzled pit bulls. They were the "pets" of gang members and drug dealers, of the lowest rank, of course: the higher-ups don't walk; they ride, and rarely show their faces, though I once saw three men with expensive-looking haircuts stop their fancy car in front of my house to count the money in their laps. The driver sped away, quick as a cockroach, when he saw me watching from the upstairs window.

When my old German shepherd died, I acquired a new one, who turned out to be much less friendly than Heidi, and I'm afraid I wasn't sorry. Except for having our car vandalized more than once, we had not been the victims of a "real" crime. But how long could our luck last? We also worried that customers might hesitate to leave their valuable timepieces or family heirlooms in Bob's care because of where we lived.

Still, we resisted the idea of uprooting ourselves and focused instead on some other recent changes in the neighborhood—positive ones. Lawrence was not about to be gentrified, not by a long shot, and I doubt that it ever will be; but something like gentrification was happening to the house next door, where my disgruntled former neighbor, Rejean, used to live. Bruno and Jane Zwecki, the Polish-American owners of the three-family house, had both died, one not long after the other. In 1990, their grandson took over the place, but he was young and overwhelmed. In one season, the shrubs were overgrown, the tulips choked. The picket fence was rammed by a car and never fixed. Trash began to pile up and blow into our yard. Houses—neighbors—so close to one another can't help but impinge. When the estate was settled, the house was put on the market, and we dreaded the worst: an absentee-landlord villain.

But the worst didn't happen; after all, real estate speculators aren't buying much in Lawrence these days, as we've seen. Instead, the house was sold to a family. Owner-occupants. Latino. Two parents who arrived from Puerto Rico in 1985; three children, two of them born here; two well-behaved dogs; two cars; one job. The mother is the bread winner—a social worker. The father, less fluent in English than his wife, stays home and tends the yard, the kids, and the upstairs apartments, one of which is rented out to an elderly woman and her daughter (the other, at this writing, remains empty).

To say Mr. Fajardo "tends the yard" is a serious understatement. Immediately upon arrival, he began to transform the place. He fixed the picket fence, painted it; painted everything else in sight, too—porch, window woodwork, cement steps leading up to the porch, rocks, front pathway; he even applied a coat of white, to a height of four feet, to the trunks of the old pine trees standing in the front yard, a decorative flourish common in the Caribbean, I'm told. He also edged the walkway with bricks; wired architectural columns for outdoor lighting along the front path; fixed the barn's slate roof and removed the plywood that had covered its windows; planted a vegetable garden; fenced it in; built a swing set for his children; and put out a proud shingle showing the house number.

Snowblower, lawn mower, rake, hammer, shovel. "What's he doing now?" Bob and I would ask each other whenever one of us was drawn to the window by the sound of his labors. Mr. Fajardo seemed, to us, as obsessed as a suburbanite. He actually made our property look bad, and we couldn't have been happier.

Are such new neighbors as these unusual for Lawrence? For the time being, sadly, they are, though Jorge Santiago, of the local Latino social-service agency, Centro Panamericano, refuses to believe they will remain so. "For quite some time," he told me, "I've been talking to Hispanics in Boston about finding a mecca for our middle class. Boston was difficult because the banks were reluctant to lend money. Then they were talking about Gloucester, but Gloucester already has the Portuguese. They were talking about Provincetown, but Provincetown has mostly gays. So the place that looks like it has the greatest potential is Lawrence.

"You see a lot of Hispanics investing in property here, grocery stores, restaurants, cab companies, et cetera. You see Hispanics buying up what is available," he said, adding that he jokingly told the chamber of commerce that what they needed to do was cut down all the oak trees on Essex Street and put in palm trees, and light up pink flamingos instead of Christmas lights. "And they looked at me like, 'This son of a bitch is crazy,' and it's only a joke, but . . ." He paused, smiled, because it really wasn't a joke at all. " 'Buy yourself three trucks, man, and I'll show you the way to get rich!' " he said, speaking now to an imaginary Latino on his way up.

Before I left Centro Panamericano that day, I told Santiago that I wished all those hard workers good luck. But could anyone assure me that the middle-class Latinos wouldn't eventually move up and *out*, like all the other ethnic groups before them? Not even Santiago, who lives in Methuen, could.

AND SO we left not only Prospect Street but Lawrence, having bought this business-zoned property here in Andover—in Shawsheen Village, to be exact. An anomaly, a white clapboard Colonial Revival on the brick side of the village, it's not far from Arden and Orlando Cottage and Miss Barker's condominium; in fact, it's quite close to the house where Bob grew up. Have we arrived at last where we belong? The first person we met in our new neighborhood was a guy resembling Bill Clinton; he was walking his dog (pedigreed, of course) on a leash.

Our new house, at 53 Poor Street, is on an old (Colonial-era) road to the river, though the interstate prevents access these days.

And yes, *Poor* Street it is—a venerable Andover family name; blacksmith Joseph Poor's farmhouse (c. 1830) is just up the block. Though Billy Wood had several other old manses torn down to make way for his dream village, that particular dwelling, for some reason, was allowed to stand. Still, I'm surprised Wood didn't rechristen the street with a new, loftier appellation; I guess such a flourish would have been too obvious, even for him.

Am I being unkind to Wood? Perhaps I shouldn't be. It's unlucky to speak ill of the dead. Both he and John, my former neighbor—one rich, one "poor"—both suicides. There's a lesson in that, too, somewhere.

The Lawrence house is for sale, but from the beginning, the real-estate agent has not been encouraging. When she came for the appraisal, she shook her head solemnly as she surveyed the polished maple floors, the Italian ceramic tile around the fireplace hearth, the original light fixtures, the old wooden icebox—a pristine relic—in the pantry by the back door. When we sat down at the dining room table, she said, "Do you want the bad news now?"

We said yes.

We would be lucky to get sixty thousand for it, she said.

That's about what we paid for it, we replied, and if we could get that, it would be enough.

Now months have passed, and she wants us to cut a driveway into the wide front lawn. The lack of off-street parking is a problem, she says. She also tells us that people to whom she shows the property "fall in love with the house" but don't like the neighborhood. And: "If you could move this place, I could sell it for four hundred thousand."

If I could move the place, I wouldn't want you to sell it; I would live there. I think this but do not say it.

I USED TO have a T-shirt that said LAWRENCE: THE SPIRIT IS WORKING. I bought it at the annual Bread and Roses Festival on the common. It shows a bird, probably an eagle, soaring against a blue background. Or was it meant to be a phoenix, emblem of Lawrence rising up out of the ash heap? Whatever it was, the shirt is a dust rag now; but, as I use it to polish a table or a piece of glass, I think about the layers of the slogan's meaning.

I wore that shirt proudly in the days when I believed that the spirit *was* working, when I thought that Lawrence had a good chance of resurrection. Now, on days when the headlines in the *Eagle-Tribune* are particularly bleak, I tend to see the slogan as a taunt.

But I shouldn't let a newspaper determine my opinions, my mood. Maybe I should stop reading it altogether. I need to remember what I have seen with my own eyes in Lawrence. From this distance, though physically nothing—less than half a mile—it's frightfully easy to forget, especially since I don't visit the city much anymore. There is little reason for me to go there, except to get our car serviced, or buy fresh pita bread at the Lebanese grocery, or go see our friends the Dowds. (Perhaps here is the place to mention that every one of the other regulars among the volunteers in Bob's campaign for city council—the two engineers, the teacher, and so on—have, like us, left Lawrence.)

Jay and Susan remain city boosters, but with their jaws set more firmly than I remember having seen them before. But perhaps they only look that way when Bob and I drop by. I'll admit I feel guilty when I see them. We've literally left them behind. And I miss the laughs we used to have around their dining room table as we compared the reactions of people at parties who were surprised at our address. Now Bob and I joke between ourselves that we no longer have the cachet we used to have in the days when we were "the couple who lives in Lawrence."

RELIEF IS, I suppose, what I feel more than anything else now that I am living on the other side of the river. That came as a surprise. I haven't lived in a "safe" neighborhood since I left Greenwich for college in Washington, D.C., over twenty-five years ago, and I'd forgotten that there is a lot to be said for the luxury of not having to wonder who is watching me leave the house; not having to look over my shoulder when I come home at night. Many people comment that even my dog is less nervous, perhaps sensing my calm.

Amazement is something I also often feel: I am amazed at the efficiency of the Andover town government, for example. We pay twice as much property tax here, it's true (though half as much car insurance), and get about twenty times as much service for it. The *day after* I wrote a note to the Department of Public Works telling them that the sidewalk in front of my house needed fixing, they were out there working on it. The *day after* I called to request a blue plastic recycling tub, one appeared on my front doorstep, with my name typed on an envelope containing the recycling schedule. And when Bob went to get a letter of compliance from the inspector of buildings so he could apply for his business license, he came home to report that Kaija Gilmore was "no-nonsense, very efficient," giving him the impression that "she followed the rules."

"He's a Lawrence type," I heard myself say to Bob after meeting an Andover town employee who did *not* impress me.

WHEN Bob and I moved to Lawrence, we thought it had a chance of becoming a middle-class city. Does that sound naïve? Well, I guess we were. Now I would be thrilled to see it become a working-class city again. We actually need a working-class city. We don't need another Andover; we need another Lawrence—the way Lawrence used to be. Its other sobriquet—other than Immigrant City, that is—was once the City of Workers. I like the sound of that. I'd like it to deserve that name again—to be the kind of place it was in the days of Jay Dowd's ancestors, when people got their photo taken in their work clothes. And if those same people started to move up and out, the way they used to, I'd consider that a plus, not a minus—a victory—especially if the movers were making room for yet another group of newcomers. Sound familiar? That's the way things used to work. Will they work that way again? I wish I knew.

FALL 1994. Along with the coming of the cool weather, my part-time teaching obligations at the private boarding school have resumed, and so has my commute to and from a decidedly elite world. Sometimes I feel like an intruder there. An imposter. A colleague makes the following comment of a day student who is in some academic trouble: "Well, I don't know how much help she's getting at home—her father is a carpenter."

I wager that her remark was not meant to be heard by another carpenter's daughter. But my feelings weren't hurt; I didn't hide my head in shame and self-loathing; and I know it is because I have lived in Lawrence that I think less of her for saying such a thing, not less of myself. For I've come to see my experience, and my family's, and those of all the working class, in context—as an integral and necessary part of the American culture—and for the first time in my life, I'm honestly proud of it.

I think that my years of living in Lawrence also have enabled me to see the city itself in context. If I had never been even the temporary Lawrencian I was—if I had moved straight to Andover from Washington—I know exactly what I would be like, what my opinions would be, and I cringe at the imagined portrait. "I hate people who 'love Lawrence' from a distance," says Susan Dowd. Yes, I think to myself, if I had never lived in Lawrence, I can just hear myself making that very same patronizing declaration that Susan so abhors.

Living there also made me realize that its most serious problems cannot be solved from within. Yes, I know I said at the outset that I would propose no solutions, but I will offer this much: Lawrence's difficulties were created by state and federal policies, and by national social and economic trends, and only changes at those levels will correct them. A blurring of borders between towns rather than an ever-sharper definition of them would be a start. *Regionalism* is the word, though in some circles it's anathema. An Episcopal priest who was for a time associate rector at a church in Lawrence but who lives in Andover told me Andoverites who talk about regionalizing the schools "are shot at." Tom Troy admitted that trying to get Andover to cooperate with the Merrimack Valley Project's regional fire department idea seems to him "an impossible situation."

Yet, as long ago as 1911, the authors of the Lawrence housing exposé were insisting that the regional approach was the way to solve the city's most intractable problems. "The people who are generally interested in the city's welfare," they wrote, "will welcome the day that wipes out the fictitious lines of the present political unit and establishes the unit more nearly according to the economic facts by including it in the towns, Methuen and the Andovers." The Harvard study from the fifties says much the same thing: "Lawrence's problem is also a problem of its major suburbs, even though these may presently refuse to recognize it."

"Americans don't seem to come together," my young Cambodian acquaintance, Heng Meas, once observed. He had been telling me about a picnic—"a summer gathering"—he had attended in Fall River, Massachusetts. On this annual occasion, he and other Cambodians from cities and towns all over the state meet to "share what we used to share in the old days," said this nineteen-year-old, as if he were an ancient.

Before he left for his freshman year at Amherst College, he sounded more his age. "I am sort of nervous about going," he told me, "about what the expectations will be. I will be looked at very closely because I am from Lawrence. So I'm nervous and scared."

More recently, he has written to ask me: "Did you know that Robert Frost taught at Amherst for a while? He received his third Pulitzer Prize while a professor here." Also: "How is Lawrence? Is there any hope? Please tell me, what do you see?"

What can I say? I wouldn't dare reveal to him the depressing news that I told an Andoverite I was writing a book about Lawrence and the person responded, "Oh? D.H.?" Lawrence, Massachusetts, and other cities like it are out of sight, out of mind for so many here and in other privileged pockets of the country.

I wonder if I should describe the new people in the Zweckis' house. But Heng's family fits roughly the same de-

scription: such a success story wouldn't be news to him. Besides, I think what he really wants to know is if I have seen evidence of advancement that is larger than family-size—
investments by the wider world in Lawrence.

And the answer to that is no. At least not yet.

Maybe I should simply describe for him the boat ride I
took on the Merrimack in the late summer of 1994, as I was
completing the manuscript for this book.

A few years ago, *The New York Times* reported that so
many cars have been driven into the Lawrence portion of the
Merrimack by people hoping to make false insurance claims
that some of the hulks, piled one on top of the other, were actually visible above the waterline. It was not a story the local
paper carried, and, in fact, seemed somewhat far-fetched: the
river, just a few yards from shore, drops off to a depth of sixty
feet. Admittedly, though, I wasn't expecting my boating trip to
be particularly pastoral, so the shock of the river's rustic beauty
was all the greater.

I was a guest of the Greater Lawrence Community Boating Program, a regional nonprofit recreation facility whose
boathouse is in south Lawrence, just above the dam, but
whose participants come from all over the Merrimack Valley.
Shortly after his campaign for city council, Bob was asked to
be a trustee of the White Fund, the Lawrence charitable organization, and since the boating program regularly receives local foundation grants, trustees and spouses were invited by its
executive director, R. Peter Koehler, for a tool up and down
the river.

We would be going in a motorized launch, but boaters
who sign up for the program—adults and children alike—
canoe and sail in rented vessels, taking lessons if they like, all
for modest, subsidized fees. On the afternoon of our trip, I
saw kids of every color, solo or in pairs, handling sailboats like
old salts.

Koehler himself piloted our launch, taking the southerly route, away from the mills, because, of course, boats can't get past the Great Stone Dam. We went all the way to Lowell, fourteen miles upriver and back. And no, we didn't bump into any submerged cars. In fact, once we got past Methuen, the scenery was a wilderness so unspoiled, I could imagine it looked just as it did when Native Americans lived there. Cruising past the steep leafy banks rising on both sides, for the first time I could see the shape of the river valley in which I've been living all these years. There wasn't even any other traffic out there except, at one point, a group of water skiers, and at another, two graceful seaplanes in a cove.

Along the way, Koehler pointed out to us some surprising sights: a great blue heron; a hermit's shack on an island, with a sign declaring it THE RIVIERA. He also mentioned that the purple loosestrife, growing in profusion along the river's edge—not to mention clogging every stream, creek, and ditch in the Northeast—is a plant indigenous to Australia. Its seeds got transported to America in the raw wool used by the mills; in the processing, they were spit out into the river as waste.

Although the mills sullied the Merrimack for decades, it is clean now, Koehler told us; in fact, it's swimmable. (Luckily: though they're not supposed to, kids from north Lawrence sometimes swim across the river to the boathouse in order to participate in the Community Boating Program; we also saw numerous rope swings tied to trees high above the river and kids using them to push off from the cliffs and cannonball into the deep waters below.) When Koehler was a boy growing up German-American on Prospect Hill and regularly playing near the river's edge, he once tripped and slid into the water, and his leg was purple for a week. But because the river bottom is sandy, it has acted as a filter and allowed the swiftly moving current to sift through the pollutants, lift them up, and carry them out to sea. A muddy bottom would have trapped them, and the river would have needed dredging, like the Hudson in New York. The Merrimack has cleaned itself.

What I liked best about my ride on the river wasn't the clean, silky water, however; it was the way I couldn't ever tell exactly where I was. Lawrence? Andover? Methuen? Lowell? Where did one municipality begin and another end? It was Koehler who had to read the map of the river, the landmarks he knew so well, and situate us. Only one thing was quite clear to me: the river that divided these communities, one from another, all those years ago, still connects them, us, all.

WHEN I VISITED Terri Kelley at Lawrence High School a couple of years ago, her students had already left for the day, but during class time she had asked each of them to write me a letter saying all the things they wanted me to tell my readers. I have read these letters many times. They were written by immigrants and the children of immigrants from Hungary, Korea, Lebanon, Vietnam, Cambodia, Puerto Rico, and the Dominican Republic, as well as by a few descendants of the first immigrant wave. Sometimes they fill me with hope, sometimes with despair. I'm hopeful because the students themselves sound that way; on the other hand, I want to see these young people get every opportunity, and I'm afraid not all of them will.

The letters also make me proud, however—of Lawrence. It's doing a job the whole country takes credit for, but Lawrence is doing most of the work. All of America's Lawrences are. Here is one letter that is fairly typical:

> Dear Ms. Schinto: I came to Lawrence in March 1990 [from Fitchburg, Massachusetts, having been born in Puerto Rico in 1977], scared to death about the rumors I heard about this beautiful city, but when I started school I loved

it. I had never seen such a quiet school. I made friends quicker than I did in any other school outside the city. None of the garbage I heard was true. I was prejudiced of Lawrence just like many people are now. In fact, all *most* people see is drugs, violence, and all the negativity of the city. What most people fail to see is the talent hidden inside this beautiful city. Many don't see the talent of the Lawrence High School Girls Ensemble, the Honor Students who work hard every day to make it in this competitive world, or the greatness of having many races in a school where everyone is treated equally. We are privileged to be able to live in a place where we don't have to travel to another country in order to learn its customs because it's right next door. . . .

This one is typical, too, though it was obviously written by someone who is newer to the country:

Dear Ms. Schinto: I've been a L.H.S. student for 3 years and I like it. Lawrence High isn't that bad as they say it's only rumors and it's like they say you can't judge a book by it's cover. I attended Lawrence High since I come to the U.S. 3½ years ago [from Lebanon] and I lived in Lawrence. I like Lawrence because this is the place where I learned to speak English and I like L.H.S. because their the one who taught me how to speak English and because of the cultural difusion and there's some people that speak your own language too. I like L.H.S. because it's the one that gives you all the information about this country when I came here I didn't know nothing so the teacher and the students helped me. I don't know what would be happen if I didn't come to Lawrence or attended L.H.S.

And here's another letter, eloquent in its way. It wasn't addressed to me specifically, so perhaps it is addressed to us all:

A lot of people feel that Lawrence is a hard place to live. They feel that Lawrence High School is for hoodlums and criminals. They couldn't be more mistaken! I like this city, and I love this school. Of course there are a few bad people who have nothing better to do than cause trouble. But if you try to ignore those people and don't let them bring you down with them, then you can make it. At Lawrence High, everybody has the opportunity for a wonderful education, but some people don't seize that opportunity. Although the school system has practically no money, they are working their hardest for us, Lawrence's future.

Permissions
Acknowledgments

1983–1984"; excerpts from unpublished memoirs of Cornelius A. Wood in unrestricted papers of Edward Roddy. Reprinted by permission of Museum of American Textile History.

Jeanne Schinto was born in Greenwich, Connecticut, in 1951. A graduate of George Washington University, with a master's degree from Johns Hopkins University, she has published a novel, *Children of Men*, and a collection of stories, *Shadow Bands*. Her essays and articles have appeared in the Washington *Post*, the Boston *Globe*, the *Yale Review*, and many other places; her fiction has been included in *The Best American Short Stories*. She is also the editor of *The Literary Dog: Great Contemporary Dog Stories* and *Show Me a Hero: Great Contemporary Stories about Sports*. She lives in Andover, Massachusetts, with her husband.

A NOTE ON THE TYPE

This book was set in Caledonia, a face designed by William Addison Dwiggins (1880–1956) for the Mergenthaler Linotype Company in 1939. It belongs to the family of types referred to by printers as "modern," a term used to mark the change in type styles that occurred around 1800. Caledonia was inspired by the Scotch types cast by the Glasgow typefounders Alexander Wilson & Sons circa 1833. However, there is a calligraphic quality about Caledonia that is completely lacking in the Wilson types.

Dwiggins referred to an even earlier typeface for this "liveliness of action"—one cut around 1790 by William Martin for the printer William Bulmer. Caledonia has more weight than the Martin letters, and the bottom finishing strokes of the letters are cut straight across, without brackets, to make sharp angles with the upright stems, thus giving a modernface appearance.

W. A. Dwiggins began his association with the Mergenthaler Linotype Company in 1929, and over the next twenty-seven years he designed a number of book types, the most interesting of which are Metro, Electra, Caledonia, Eldorado, and Falcon.

Composed by Creative Graphics,
Allentown, Pennsylvania

Printed and bound by Quebecor Printing Martinsburg,
Martinsburg, West Virginia

Designed by Cassandra J. Pappas

This book was set in Caledonia, a face designed by William Addison Dwiggins (1880–1956) for the Mergenthaler Linotype Company in 1939. It belongs to the family of types referred to by printers as "modern," a term used to mark the change in type styles that occurred around 1800. Caledonia was inspired by the Scotch types cast by the Glasgow typefounders Alexander Wilson & Sons circa 1833. However, there is a calligraphic quality about Caledonia that is completely lacking in the Wilson types.

Dwiggins referred to an even earlier typeface for this "liveliness of action"—one cut around 1790 by William Martin for the printer William Bulmer. Caledonia has more weight than the Martin letters, and the bottom finishing strokes of the letters are cut straight across, without brackets, to make sharp angles with the upright stems, thus giving a modernface appearance.

W. A. Dwiggins began his association with the Mergenthaler Linotype Company in 1929, and over the next twenty-seven years he designed a number of book types, the most interesting of which are Metro, Electra, Caledonia, Eldorado, and Falcon.

Composed by Creative Graphics,
Allentown, Pennsylvania

Printed and bound by Quebecor Printing Martinsburg,
Martinsburg, West Virginia

Designed by Cassandra J. Pappas